Models of category counts

Models of category counts

B. FINGLETON

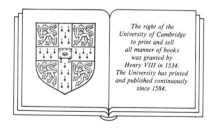

The right of the
University of Cambridge
to print and sell
all manner of books
was granted by
Henry VIII in 1534.
The University has printed
and published continuously
since 1584.

CAMBRIDGE UNIVERSITY PRESS

Cambridge

London   New York   New Rochelle

Melbourne   Sydney

Published by the Press Syndicate of the University of Cambridge
The Pitt Building, Trumpington Street, Cambridge CB2 1RP
32 East 57th Street, New York, NY 10022, USA
296 Beaconsfield Parade, Middle Park, Melbourne 3206, Australia

© Cambridge University Press 1984

First published 1984

Printed in Great Britain at the University Press, Cambridge

Library of Congress catalogue card number: 83–26250

British Library cataloguing in publication data
Fingleton, Bernard
Models of category counts.
1. Social sciences – Statistical methods
I. Title
519.5   HA29

ISBN 0 521 25297 0 hard cover
ISBN 0 521 27283 1 paperback

DJ

For my Father

Contents

Preface

This book describes models of category counts from the perspective of the social, environmental and behavioural scientist. The literature on the analysis of category counts, also variously referred to as contingency table, categorical or cross-tabulated data analysis, has developed apace since the heady era of previous decades, and the aim has been to capture the flavour of recent developments. Naturally, in a diverse subject area of growing importance and application, it is necessary to be selective, and the book draws in particular on a fairly coherent body of literature judged to be relevant to the non-statistician or applied statistician primarily interested in data analysis, without, it is hoped, disparaging the contribution made by writers on more-general or theoretical topics.

Since the focus of the book is application, particular attention is given to the analysis of real data sets. Chapter 1 contains an introduction to basic concepts and notation in the context of the two-way table and in Chapter 2 the notion of the multiway table is developed. Chapter 3 investigates the fitting of alternative models to the multiway table, with consideration given to the important topic of multiple-hypothesis tests. Chapter 4 contains a discussion of issues related to the sample design, and outlines some straightforward methods of handling data obtained by means other than simple random sampling. Chapter 5 features methods of analysing large, unwieldy tables and tables where quantitative values or scores are assigned to variable levels, and Chapter 6 integrates various themes pursued in earlier chapters in the special context of observations over time.

The book has its origins in courses I was invited to teach at summer schools of the European Consortium for Political Research at Essex University in the early 1980s. I am grateful to the staff and students of the ECPR for that stimulating experience, which provided the groundwork for much of the material in this book. I am especially grateful to Graham Upton who has, over a number of years, played an important role in shaping my ideas as to what data analysis is all about, and to Pat Altham and Professor Murray Aitkin for considerable help on various topics. May I also thank Nick Galway for helping me to understand some finer points of **GENSTAT**, the Mathematics Editor and his staff at Cambridge University Press for their help and guidance, and Christine Sansom for converting my illegible handwriting into a readable manuscript with veritable accuracy, patience and good humour. Finally I wish to thank my family, colleagues and friends. Needless to say, none of the above can be held responsible for any errors or opinions.

Bernard Fingleton
Cambridge, 1984

1 Independence and association in the two-dimensional table

Introduction

This book describes models of category counts where each count is the observed frequency with which a unique combination of the levels of categorical variables occurs in a sample. This observed frequency provides an estimate of the probability of the variable-level combination in the population. The variable-level combinations are jointly displayed as a contingency table. Consider, for example, the simple two-way table formed by observing two categorical (as opposed to continuous) variables. Table 1.2 is a typical example with rows representing the categories of the variable residential area (A) and columns representing the categories of the variable preferred political party (B). For convenience, both A and B are treated as dichotomies, that is, each has two levels. More-complex data sets involving polytomies and more than two variables (and hence multiway tables) are investigated at length later; we remain with the two-way table in this first chapter to introduce some basic notation and concepts.

It is important at the outset to make explicit any assumptions that are implied by a methodology and, therefore, upon which the results of any analysis are conditional. The mere act of drawing up a contingency table represents a conscious structuring of a multifarious reality prior to analysis in which the variation present is subdivided according to distinct categorical variables. Although this may enable one to obtain plausible models, it is, it seems, an imposed world-view that may not be universally shared. Nonetheless, it is argued that, like the visual display unit, economic time series and scattergram, each of which is a device for data display, analogous to the contingency table, proffering its own salient information, the table of counts is an organising framework through which to view reality which is eminently suited to many practical situations.

Initially, raw data usually comprise a list, as in Table 1.1, which is only subsequently organised as a table. Of course, the advantage a contingency table like Table 1.2 has over a list is that it is a convenient and succinct summary of the data. It contains less information than the list from which it is derived since it does not tell us the order in which respondents were interviewed (assuming the list to be sequential), but in many studies this is redundant information and nothing is lost by ignoring it. Table 1.2 not only takes up less space than the complete list but also allows one to make a cursory examination of how frequently the various combinations of A and B occur, and to compare this set of numbers $\{f_{ij}\}$ with other sets $\{e_{ij}\}$ that would, on average, occur if various prespecified circumstances prevailed. In other words, the $\{e_{ij}\}$ are the expected frequencies generated according to some model. One of the most important models, or pre-suppositions about the mechanism generating the observed data, is that A and B are mutually independent. This will be discussed in some detail subsequently with respect to real data, and in later chapters we will consider other sets of expected data, and their allied models, which correspond to more-intricate propositions than simple independence.

It can be seen from Table 1.2 that the imaginary sample listed in Table 1.1 includes f_{21} rural Labour party 'affiliates' and that f_{ij} is the frequency in cell

Table 1.1. *Observations from which to construct a 2 × 2 contingency table*

Person number	Residential area (A)	Political party (B)
1	A_1	B_1
2	A_2	B_1
3	A_2	B_2
4	A_1	B_1
:	:	:
:	:	:
f_{00}	A_2	B_2

key: f_{00} = total sample size.
    A_1 = urban area.
    A_2 = rural area.
    B_1 = Labour party.
    B_2 = not Labour.

Table 1.2. *Basic notation in a 2 × 2 contingency table*

	B_1	B_2	Total
A_1	f_{11}	f_{12}	f_{10}
A_2	f_{21}	f_{22}	f_{20}
Total	f_{01}	f_{02}	f_{00}

(i,j). Altogether there are f_{10} urban residents and f_{20} rural residents, whilst f_{01} are 'affiliated' to the Labour party and f_{02} are not.

Another presupposition prior to an analysis is that the variable levels employed in any table pertain to the true categories of a categorical variable and not some amalgamation of them. The effects of category amalgamation are discussed in a later chapter. The fact is that in many analyses the categories defining the table cells are only surrogates for true variable levels, and may be the result of coalescing some more finely divided categorisation or even a continuum. For example, residential areas may be perceived to assume positions on a graduated scale ranging from totally rural to totally urban and it is a considerable simplification to dichotomise this 'continuum', as in Table 1.2. However, this kind of simplification need not necessarily involve an information loss of the magnitude implied by the nominal-level representation of a continuous variable. There are important recent developments in contingency table analysis related to the logit model mentioned later (Goodman 1979*a*; Clogg 1982*b*; Duncan 1979) which take account of scores or quantitative values assigned to the levels of categorical variables. These are outlined in more detail in Chapter 5. Assigning a quantity to a category implies that the value is representative of all the individuals allotted to that category, though this may sometimes be too gross a generalisation with non-experimental data involving the uncontrolled variation of a continuous variable. It is true that in many cases the information loss incurred may be immaterial to the understanding of the system of interest, though, ultimately, the decision to opt for categorisation must be based on the costs and benefits involved, as perceived by the individual analyst.

A range of different models is available for data that cannot justifiably be reduced to tables of counts. Those models are not really separate from each other or from the models considered here, for links exist at the theoretical level to draw them together under the umbrella title of generalised linear models (Nelder & Wedderburn 1972; Nelder 1974; Dickinson 1977). It is generally acceptable to consider contingency table counts as Poisson (or, equivalently, multinomial (Birch 1963)) distributions, as described in Chapter 4. However, in the more general context, normal, gamma or other distributions may be appropriate. These comprise other types of generalised linear model, probably the most familiar of which is the classical linear regression model with normal errors.

A common algorithm exists for fitting many variants of generalised linear model, namely the method of iterative weighted least squares (see Chapter 5), and this provides the unifying framework with which to integrate otherwise disparate models. This algorithm forms the core of the interlinked GLIM and GENSTAT programs and gives immense scope in the selection of models that can be fitted (Baker & Nelder 1978). GENSTAT is used extensively in Chapters

5 and 6 for its capacity to easily provide the maximum likelihood estimates of the more specialised models encountered there. However, other forms of generalised linear model within the capacity of this package are not fitted. These comprise a vast field with an extensive literature which lies beyond the scope of this book.

While information loss may be a justifiable reason to reject the contingency table approach and opt for other types of generalised linear model, it is no longer true, as it was in the past, that contingency table analysis is an under-developed science from which only naive conclusions can be drawn, in contrast to the sophisticated multivariate analysis of continuous data. As a result of the considerable advances in the techniques of categorical data analysis, allied to the developing methodology outlined above (see Fienberg 1980), equally sophisti-cated analyses of either categorical or continuous variables, or both together, are now possible. The analyst of relations between categorical variables can now isolate the interactions between variables after allowing for other variables in the same way that the exponent of multiple regression can estimate partial regres-sion coefficients. This is in stark contrast to the era when social, environmental and behavioural scientists were of necessity confined to the analysis of two-way tables, a restriction inviting fallacious inferences in the presence of multi-variable associations.

Given that tables of counts are the focus of interest, there are a number of different approaches that could be adopted. This book does not attempt to cover all methods but a selection is made of what are judged to be of most practical value to the data analyst. Thus the emphasis is very much on the log-linear model, with some consideration also being given to the logit model. These interrelated approaches are by far the most versatile, comprehensive, and commonly used modelling procedures, though they in no way exhaust the available options. Hildebrand *et al.* (1977) and Bishop *et al.* (1975) describe some alternatives, and Fienberg (1980) traces various strands in the literature. Although estimation throughout is by maximum likelihood, alternatives exist which are described briefly in Chapter 5.

Independence in 2 × 2 tables
To establish more fully what is meant by this important proposition of independence, let us restrict ourselves initially to the simplest possible situation of two dichotomous variables such as those mentioned above. As will be seen, the discussion extends naturally to the $I \times J$ table.

It is illuminating to consider the quantity p_{ij}, the probability that an individual chosen at random from a population belongs to cell (i, j), even though in reality we would be presented with a set of numbers $\{f_{ij}\}$ and the set $\{p_{ij}\}$

could never be known exactly, given sample data. Nevertheless, the definition of independence is with respect to the $\{p_{ij}\}$ of Table 1.3 where strict equalities apply and where there is no need to consider the perturbing effects of random sampling variation.

Independence can be defined as the particular circumstance where knowing a person's A category is not going to help us guess his or her B category. Consequently,

$$p_{11}/p_{01} = p_{12}/p_{02} = p_{10}/p_{00} = p_{10}$$

and

$$p_{11} = p_{01}p_{10}$$

Likewise,

$$p_{11}/p_{10} = p_{21}/p_{20} = p_{01}$$

and

$$p_{11} = p_{10}p_{01}$$

If A and B are independent, then, generally, $p_{ij} = p_{i0}p_{0j}$; $i,j = 1, 2$. Furthermore, since $p_{11}/p_{12} =$ the odds on a B_1 response given that individuals are A_1, and $p_{21}/p_{22} =$ the odds on a B_1 response given that individuals are A_2, the independence condition requires that $p_{11}/p_{12} = p_{21}/p_{22}$.

In other words, independence means that the category proportions for B are unaltered by which A category is considered. Two equivalent ratios take a value of exactly 1.0 when there is independence. These are the odds ratio $(p_{11}/p_{12})/(p_{21}/p_{22}) = 1.0$, and the cross-product ratio, $p_{11}p_{22}/p_{21}p_{12} = 1.0$ (Mosteller 1968).

Table 1.3. *Theoretical probabilities in a 2 × 2 table*

	B_1	B_2	Total
A_1	p_{11}	p_{12}	p_{10}
A_2	p_{21}	p_{22}	p_{20}
Total	p_{01}	p_{02}	p_{00}

$$\sum_i p_{ij} = p_{0j}$$

$$\sum_j p_{ij} = p_{i0}$$

$$\sum_i \sum_j p_{ij} = p_{00} = 1.0$$

It has already been stated that the $\{p_{ij}\}$ are theoretical probabilities and are unknown, though they can be estimated from sample data since $\hat{p}_{ij} = f_{ij}/f_{00}$, where $\hat{p}_{ij}$ signifies the maximum likelihood estimate of p_{ij}.

If A and B are independent, then we know that $p_{ij} = p_i p_j$; since $\hat{p}_{i0} = f_{i0}/f_{00}$ and $\hat{p}_{0j} = f_{0j}/f_{00}$, $\hat{p}_{ij} = f_{i0}f_{0j}/f_{00}^2$ and hence $e_{ij} = f_{00}\hat{p}_{ij} = f_{i0}f_{0j}/f_{00}$.

Given a total of f_{00} observations in the table, the expected frequency in the (i, j) cell is e_{ij}, given independence. A comparison of the set of expected frequencies $\{e_{ij}\}$ with the set observed $\{f_{ij}\}$ provides the basis of a test of the independence assumption. Table 1.4 contains these frequencies.

We note that the set of observed frequencies in Table 1.4 differs somewhat from that to be expected were the variables independent, though we cannot be sure at this point whether the difference between $\{f_{ij}\}$ and $\{e_{ij}\}$ should be assigned to sampling variation or whether it represents a consistent deviation that would be repeated in other samples. In order to choose between these optional interpretations we utilise the familiar chi-squared test of independence. In fact, we adopt two asymptotically equivalent formulae for our test statistic, since the less familiar of the two allows us to discuss in simple terms one very important issue that is relevant to all the tests performed throughout this book.

The two formulae are:

$$X^2 = \sum_i \sum_j (f_{ij} - e_{ij})^2/e_{ij}$$

$$X^2 = [\log (f_{11}f_{22}/f_{12}f_{21})]^2/(f_{11}^{-1} + f_{12}^{-1} + f_{21}^{-1} + f_{22}^{-1})$$

Using the first formula, $X^2 = [(21 - 8.76)^2/8.76] + [(25 - 37.24)^2/37.24] + [(3 - 15.24)^2/15.24] + [(77 - 64.76)^2/64.76] = 33.3$, a highly unlikely observation from the χ^2 distribution to which X^2 would approximate were noise perception and pressure-group support independent. Conventionally, we would accept

Table 1.4. *Observed frequencies and corresponding expected frequencies assuming independence*

	Observed			Expected		
	B_1	B_2	Total	B_1	B_2	Total
A_1	21	25	46	8.76	37.24	46
A_2	3	77	80	15.24	64.76	80
Total	24	102	126	24	102	126

key: A_1 = respondent supports anti-Stansted airport pressure group.
$\quad$ A_2 = respondent does not support pressure group.
$\quad$ B_1 = respondent considers the local area noisy.
$\quad$ B_2 = respondent does not consider the local area noisy.

any value of $X^2 \geqslant \chi^2_{1,\,0.05} = 3.84$ as being sufficiently unlikely, thus suggesting that the variables are related, though of course such high values could occasionally occur by chance (with probability $\alpha = 0.05$) since 'freak' samples can occur spuriously suggesting association when none in fact exists in the population as a whole. Such a mistaken inference is referred to as a type I error. We could reduce this probability α (the probability of a type I error or level of risk) to, say, 0.01, in which case the critical value would then be $\chi^2_{1,\,0.01} = 6.64$, though this would be at the cost of increasing the probability of a type II error, which occurs when the sample deceptively suggests independence.

The alternative and less familiar formula for X^2 will usually produce similar values to those generated by the above formula in large samples since both statistics are distributed asymptotically as χ^2. We now find that

$$X^2 = \{\log\,[(21 \times 77)/(25 \times 3)]\}^2/$$
$$[(1/21) + (1/25) + (1/3) + (1/77)] = 9.43/0.43 = 21.73,$$

which, although somewhat less than 33.3, also has a very small probability of occurring in the χ^2_1 distribution.

Note that the numerator of this equation is a function of the cross-product ratio $(f_{11}f_{22}/f_{12}f_{21})$ defined above with probabilities, where we established that it will assume a value 1.0 with independent variables. Thus $\log\,(f_{11}f_{22}/f_{12}f_{21})$ has a mean of 0, assuming independence, and since it has an approximately normal distribution it will lie within 1.96 standard deviations of this mean in 95% of random samples. The standard deviation is the square root of the denominator in the above X^2 equation. In fact, the relation between the normal and chi-squared distributions is illuminated by this equation since it shows that χ^2 is simply the square of a normally distributed variable with mean 0 and variance 1.0.

The denominator is a function of the observed cell frequencies and it will increase in value as they diminish. What this in effect means is that, given two samples of different size, ostensibly displaying the same degree of association as measured by the sample cross-product ratio $f_{11}f_{22}/f_{12}f_{21}$, one could very easily conclude that there is evidence of association in the population on the basis of the larger sample and its resulting X^2 value, whereas perhaps X^2 would not be deemed an unusual observation from a χ^2_1 distribution in the smaller sample due to the inflation of the denominator, which consequently deflates X^2.

This is illustrated in a concrete way by Table 1.5 which describes a smaller sample drawn from the same Stansted population as the data in Table 1.4. Both tables display an equivalent degree of association between pressure-group support and noise perception, on the basis of direct comparison of respective cross-product ratios, but Table 1.5 provides less-convincing (though still highly significant) statistical evidence of non-independence.

From Table 1.5 we find that $X^2 = \{\log [(5 \times 20)/(2 \times 2)]\}^2/$
$[(1/5) + (1/2) + (1/2) + (1/20)] = 10.36/1.25 = 8.29$ and that
$P(\chi_1^2 > 8.29) = 0.004$, as opposed to $P(\chi_1^2 > 21.73) = 0.000\,003$, for the
larger sample in Table 1.4. The small observed frequencies of Table 1.5 raise
questions about the validity of the assumption that X^2 approximates to χ^2,
given independence, since they produce one distinctly small expected value.
The question of the validity of the X^2 approximation to χ^2 for the 2 × 2 table
has been considered by a number of authors, commencing with Yates (1934)
who introduced a continuity correction giving $X^2 = \Sigma_i \Sigma_j (|f_{ij} - e_{ij}| - \frac{1}{2})^2/e_{ij}$.
This is an often-used formula, though Fienberg (1980) reports that it may
increase the probability of a type II error when referred to the χ_2^1 distribution.
We refrain from using it here. Fisher's exact test (see Upton 1978) is an
alternative approach, though difficult to generalise to the multiway table. Small
samples are discussed in the context of the multiway table in Chapter 5. The
converse problem, inference from large samples, is considered in Chapter 6.

The main point of the current discussion is the possibility that our conclusions about the presence or absence of association depend on the size of the
sample. Although the chosen measure, the (log) cross-product ratio, will still, on
average, take a value one (zero) in the absence of association whatever the
sample size, the normal range of its variation around this expected value will not
be stable. This is illustrated by comparing the square roots of the denominators
used to calculate X^2 for Tables 1.4 and 1.5, $\sqrt{(0.43)}$ and $\sqrt{(1.25)}$ respectively.
Thus, although the cross-product ratio is marginally larger for Table 1.5, it could
more easily have been generated by sampling from a population in which the
variables are independent.

The above illustrates that a large sample provides more evidence, or information, on which to base conclusions about a population, and this generalisation
is true for the variety of hypotheses tested throughout this book. This is why,
formally, we can never accept a null hypothesis, which, in the present context,
is the statement that there is no association between the variables. The most we
can do is fail to reject it on the grounds of insufficient evidence of the existence

Table 1.5. *A small sample
from the Stansted population*

	B_1	B_2
A_1	5	2
A_2	2	20

key: as in Table 1.4.

of association in the population from which the sample is drawn. One can never prove conclusively that no association exists in the population simply because another analyst may take a larger, more revealing, sample which provides the evidence we failed to detect.

The above comments are made with reference to the simple two-way table and data generated by the independence model, though they are equally applicable to the larger tables and more-complex models to be encountered in later chapters. A further comment on these and related issues is to be found later in the book after some of the details of these complexities have been made more explicit.

The $I \times J$ table

The notation and concepts applicable to the 2×2 table are easily extended to the $I \times J$ table which summarises data such as that in Table 1.6. The essential difference between Table 1.6 and Table 1.1 is that the former describes the variation of two polytomous variables rather than two dichotomies. The essence of this variation would be discernible from a two-way contingency table such as Table 1.7.

If A and B were independent, we would find that $f_{ij}/f_{i0} \approx f_{0j}/f_{00}$, where f_{ij} is the observed frequency in typical cell (i, j). Although exact equalities are unlikely because of random sampling variation, this approximate equality would hold for all i, j. In terms of theoretical cell probabilities, independence can again be defined as $p_{ij} = p_{i0}p_{0j}$, $i = 1, 2, \ldots, I; j = 1, 2, \ldots, J$.

Table 1.6. *Observations from which to construct an I × J contingency table*

Person number	Residential area (A)	Political affiliation (B)
1	A_3	B_6
2	A_1	B_2
3	A_1	B_2
:	:	:
:	:	:
f_{00}	A_2	B_4

key: A_1 = inner city. B_1 = Labour party.
        A_2 = suburbs. B_2 = Liberal party.
        A_3 = rural. B_3 = Social Democrats.
                        B_4 = Conservative party.
                        B_5 = other parties.
                        B_6 = unaffiliated.

Table 1.8 is an $I \times J$ contingency involving two polytomous variables, car availability and fatigue, compiled from data originally analysed by Bowlby & Silk (1982). We find that $X^2 = \Sigma_i \Sigma_j (f_{ij} - e_{ij})^2 / e_{ij} = 23.42 > \chi^2_{8, 0.05} = 15.51$, indicating significant association between car availability and fatigue. This is a rather general statement in which no attempt is made to identify the source of the interaction between the two variables. These data are discussed from another viewpoint in relation to the saturated log–linear model later in this chapter, and in Chapter 5 we attempt to make more-precise statements about the way in which pairs of polytomous variables interact. Note that the enlarged critical value $\chi^2_{8, 0.05}$ reflects the fact that the independence model is here fitted

Table 1.7. *Basic notation in an $I \times J$ contingency table*

	B_1	B_2	B_3		B_4	B_5	...	B_J	Total
A_1	f_{11}	f_{12}	f_{13}	...				f_{1J}	f_{10}
A_2	f_{21}	f_{22}	f_{23}	...				f_{2J}	f_{20}
A_3	f_{31}	f_{32}	f_{33}	...				f_{3J}	f_{30}
.								.	.
.								.	.
A_I	f_{I1}	...						f_{IJ}	f_{I0}
Total	f_{01}	f_{02}	f_{03}	...				f_{0J}	f_{00}

Table 1.8. *An $I \times J$ contingency table from a shopping survey in Oxford*

	B_1	B_2	B_3	B_4	B_5	Total
A_1	55	11	16	17	100	199
A_2	101	7	18	23	103	252
A_3	91	20	25	16	77	229
Total	247	38	59	56	280	680

key: A_1 = no car availability.
    A_2 = some car availability.
    A_3 = full car availability.
The level assigned to respondents on the fatigue variable B is determined by the extent of their agreement with the assertion: 'I find getting to grocery shops very tiring.'
    B_1 = disagree.
    B_2 = tend to disagree.
    B_3 = in between.
    B_4 = tend to agree.
    B_5 = agree.

to a table involving polytomies. More generally, one chooses the χ^2_{df} distribution, where $df = (I - 1)(J - 1)$. The rationale for this is discussed in Chapter 3.

Multiplicative models
Independence
The set of theoretical probabilities consistent with the independence condition $\{p_{ij}\}$ is not constant. There is variation from table to table in the likely value of p_{ij} to be encountered in typical cell (i, j). There is also (usually) regulated variation in p_{ij} from cell to cell in any given table. Therefore, another way to express independence is to make the p_{ij} depend on controlling factors that set their general level for the table (η), and establish their pattern of internal variation (τ_i^A, τ_j^B). It is convenient to relate p_{ij} to these controls in a multiplicative equation so that $p_{ij} = \eta \tau_i^A \tau_j^B$. Thus in the 2×2 table, $p_{11} = \eta \tau_1^A \tau_1^B$ and $p_{12} = \eta \tau_1^A \tau_2^B$, and so on. Independence is therefore defined as a model with a number of parameters. In fact, it is possible to visualise η as the 'average' cell probability (though it is actually a geometric mean) and the appropriate cell probabilities under conditions of independence are this 'average' adjusted by multiplying by τ_i^A and τ_j^B.

That this adjustment is necessary, even under conditions of independence, is illustrated by reconsidering the marginal totals of Table 1.4 since it is probably true on the evidence in the sample that most people in the population do not support the anti-Stansted pressure group and most people do not consider the local area noisy. These factors alone will increase the probability of encountering people who are not dissatisfied with the noise level and at the same time not pressure-group supporters, even in the absence of any association between noise-pollution perception and pressure-group support. Likewise, the probability of encountering noise-sensitivity pressure-group supporters (p_{11}) will be below average.

The τ parameters therefore represent the necessary adjustments to the 'average' η to account for the fact that the various categories of the variables are not equally likely, and this fact alone changes the probability of each cell being occupied by an individual chosen at random from the population.

If we consider the following table (Table 1.9), which conforms to the independence condition, conditional on the marginal probabilities of the

Table 1.9. *A table of probabilities* $\hat{p}_{ij}$ *displaying independence*

0.069	0.296
0.121	0.514

Stansted survey, the role of the τ and η is highlighted. Note that, allowing for rounding, $p_{ij} = p_{i0}p_{0j}$; $i, j = 1, 2$. It has also been stated that $p_{ij} = \eta \tau_i^A \tau_j^B$, where $\hat{\eta} = (0.069 \times 0.296 \times 0.121 \times 0.514)^{1/4} = 0.189$. Table 1.9 possesses cell probabilities that deviate considerably from 0.189 and to achieve, say, $\hat{p}_{11}$ of the table, one needs to multiply $\hat{\eta}$ by $\hat{\tau}_1^A = 0.485$ and by $\hat{\tau}_1^B = 0.758$. The role of τ_1^A is to act as a control to take account of the relative sparsity of pressure-group supporters. The other parameter τ_1^B performs a similar function for the noise-perception variable. Notice also that $\tau_2^A = 1/\tau_1^A$; $\tau_2^B = 1/\tau_1^B$; so that $\Pi_i \tau_i^A = 1.0$ and $\Pi_j \tau_j^B = 1.0$. Thus $\hat{p}_{22} = \hat{\eta} \hat{\tau}_2^A \hat{\tau}_2^B = 0.189 \times (1/0.485) \times (1/0.758) = 0.514$.

The extension to the $I \times J$ table is illustrated by Table 1.10 which contains probability estimates assuming that the variables fatigue and car availability of Table 1.8 are independent.

The probabilities of Table 1.10 are consistent with the following parameter estimates.

$$\hat{\eta} = \left(\prod_{ij} \hat{p}_{ij} \right)^{1/15} = 0.0473$$

$$\hat{\tau}_1^A = 0.882 \qquad \hat{\tau}_2^A = 1.117 \qquad \hat{\tau}_3^A = 1.015$$
$$\hat{\tau}_1^B = 2.541 \qquad \hat{\tau}_2^B = 0.391 \qquad \hat{\tau}_3^B = 0.607 \qquad \hat{\tau}_4^B = 0.576 \qquad \hat{\tau}_5^B = 2.880$$

Thus, any cell probability of Table 1.10 can be reproduced (not quite exactly, but this is due to rounding) by multiplying together the appropriate parameters. Note also that the above-mentioned constraints, $\Pi_i \tau_i^A = 1.0$ and $\Pi_j \tau_j^B = 1.0$, apply equally to the $I \times J$ table.

Other models

The role of the τ is also illustrated by Table 1.11 which also displays independence but in which the two categories of variable A are equally likely to occur. The parameter estimates of this model are $\hat{\eta} = (\Pi_{ij} \hat{p}_{ij})^{1/4} = 0.245$, $\hat{\tau}_1^A = 1.0$, $\hat{\tau}_2^A = 1.0$, $\hat{\tau}_1^B = 1.22$, $\hat{\tau}_2^B = 0.817$. The fact that $\hat{\tau}_i^A = 1.0$ ($i = 1, 2$) is a reflection of the equiprobable A categories. Since both are equally likely to be

Table 1.10. *Cell probabilities assuming independence*

	B_1	B_2	B_3	B_4	B_5	Total
A_1	0.106	0.016	0.025	0.024	0.121	0.292
A_2	0.135	0.021	0.032	0.030	0.153	0.371
A_3	0.122	0.019	0.029	0.028	0.139	0.337
Total	0.363	0.056	0.086	0.082	0.413	1.000

occupied no adjustment is necessary and we multiply by 1.0, which of course has no effect. Alternatively, one could omit the parameter so that the model becomes $p_{ij} = \eta \tau_j^B$. Equally, we could have a model where $p_{ij} = \eta \tau_i^A$.

Equiprobable rows and columns and independence results in Table 1.12 with parameters $\hat{\eta} = 0.25$, $\hat{\tau}_1^A = 1.0$, $\hat{\tau}_2^A = 1.0$, $\hat{\tau}_1^B = 1.0$, and $\hat{\tau}_2^B = 1.0$. Thus the model could be succinctly described as $p_{ij} = \eta$.

The saturated model

Parameters were also omitted from the independence model since they were assumed in that model to take the value 1.0 and hence were superfluous. One could have written the independence model more fully as $p_{ij} = \eta \tau_i^A \tau_j^B \tau_{ij}^{AB}$, where $\tau_{ij}^{AB} = 1.0$ for $i = 1, \ldots, I$ and $j = 1, \ldots, J$. If the set of parameters $\{\tau_{ij}^{AB}\}$ were allocated other values, then we would no longer have the independence model but, rather, the so-called saturated model. One would then have exhausted the full set of parameters (effects) available for the control of cell probabilities in the $I \times J$ table.

The set of probabilities in Table 1.13 does not display independence since it is derived directly from Table 1.4 which has already been used to show a high degree of association between noise perception and pressure-group support in Stansted. Although the probabilities generated by the independence model in no way conform therefore to Table 1.13, it can be reproduced, exactly, in fact, by assigning appropriate values to the parameters of the saturated model.

Table 1.11. *A table displaying independence and equally probable A categories*

	B_1	B_2	Total
A_1	0.3	0.2	0.5
A_2	0.3	0.2	0.5
Total	0.6	0.4	1.0

Table 1.12. *A table with equiprobable cells*

	B_1	B_2	Total
A_1	0.25	0.25	0.5
A_2	0.25	0.25	0.5
Total	0.5	0.5	1.0

Utilising appropriate methods of parameter estimation, which will become evident as we proceed, it turns out that $\hat{\eta} = 0.148$, $\hat{\tau}_1^A = 1.228$, $\hat{\tau}_2^A = 0.814$, $\hat{\tau}_1^B = 0.425$, $\hat{\tau}_2^B = 2.353$, $\hat{\tau}_{11}^{AB} = 2.155$, $\hat{\tau}_{12}^{AB} = 0.464$, $\hat{\tau}_{21}^{AB} = 0.464$, $\hat{\tau}_{22}^{AB} = 2.155$. Thus the $\{\hat{\tau}_{ij}^{AB}\}$ parameters are the extra adjustments required to reproduce the $\{\hat{p}_{ij}\}$ after allowance has already been made for the variprobable margins, and they relate directly to the previously mentioned cross-product ratio since $(f_{11}f_{22}/f_{12}f_{21})^{1/4} = (21 \times 77/25 \times 3)^{1/4} = 2.155$. The $\{\tau_{ij}^{AB}\}$ are thus interaction terms representing the influence of the association between A and B on $\{p_{ij}\}$. Note that, because of the constraints $\Pi_i \tau_{ij}^{AB} = 1.0$ and $\Pi_j \tau_{ij}^{AB} = 1.0$, only one of the parameters is independent: the rest can be deduced.

In fact *any* table of probabilities can be reproduced by the saturated model and we illustrate the role of the τ parameters for the $I \times J$ table by reproducing in Table 1.14 the cell probabilities of the Oxford shopping survey (see Table 1.8).

From our earlier chi-squared analysis of Table 1.8 we know that variables A and B of Table 1.14 are not independent, hence the parameters $\{\tau_{ij}^{AB}\}$ must be allocated values other than 1.0 to approximate the observed probabilities: the values assigned to these parameters in the lower part of Table 1.14 ensure that

Table 1.13. *Estimated probabilities of various Stansted responses*

	B_1	B_2
A_1	0.167	0.198
A_2	0.024	0.610

Table 1.14. *Observed cell probabilities in the Oxford shopping survey*

	B_1	B_2	B_3	B_4	B_5
A_1	0.081	0.016	0.024	0.025	0.147
A_2	0.149	0.010	0.026	0.034	0.151
A_3	0.134	0.029	0.037	0.024	0.113

$$\hat{\eta} = \left(\prod_{ij} \hat{p}_{ij}\right)^{1/15} = 0.046$$

$\hat{\tau}_1^A = 0.885$	$\hat{\tau}_2^A = 0.999$	$\hat{\tau}_3^A = 1.131$		
$\hat{\tau}_1^B = 2.541$	$\hat{\tau}_2^B = 0.368$	$\hat{\tau}_3^B = 0.616$	$\hat{\tau}_4^B = 0.588$	$\hat{\tau}_5^B = 2.952$
$\hat{\tau}_{11}^{AB} = 0.780$	$\hat{\tau}_{12}^{AB} = 1.076$	$\hat{\tau}_{13}^{AB} = 0.936$	$\hat{\tau}_{14}^{AB} = 1.042$	$\hat{\tau}_{15}^{AB} = 1.221$
$\hat{\tau}_{21}^{AB} = 1.269$	$\hat{\tau}_{22}^{AB} = 0.607$	$\hat{\tau}_{23}^{AB} = 0.933$	$\hat{\tau}_{24}^{AB} = 1.249$	$\hat{\tau}_{25}^{AB} = 1.114$
$\hat{\tau}_{31}^{AB} = 1.010$	$\hat{\tau}_{32}^{AB} = 1.531$	$\hat{\tau}_{33}^{AB} = 1.145$	$\hat{\tau}_{34}^{AB} = 0.768$	$\hat{\tau}_{35}^{AB} = 0.736$

the probabilities generated by the ensuing (saturated) model reproduce the observed probabilities 'exactly'.

The estimated probability that a person will have no car available and yet disagree most vehemently that grocery shopping is tiring, $\hat{p}_{11}$, is obtained by multiplying by, among other things, the interaction parameter $\hat{\tau}_{11}^{AB}$. Alternatively, the probability in cell $(1, 5)$ requires one to multiply by 1.221. What this means is that, after accounting for the effect of differential marginal probabilities, there is less chance of cell $(1, 1)$ being occupied than cell $(1, 5)$, which accords with what one would reasonably expect. Note again that these individual parameter values are not all independent due to the need to satisfy the constraints that their products across rows and down columns equal 1.0, though other constraints on their values are absent, unlike other unsaturated models.

What we have is a perfect model, but also a complex one due to the large number of independent parameters. One can attempt to simplify such a model by imposing lesser constraints than $\{\tau_{ij}^{AB}\} = 1.0$ for all i, j, which was required by the, albeit simple, independence model. One approach is to identify trends in the parameters so that our model contains a few parameters which make these trends explicit. We explore this approach in Chapter 5.

The log–linear model

The preceding multiplicative models are very often represented in the literature by analogous log–linear models. Thus the saturated multiplicative model $p_{ij} = \eta \tau_i^A \tau_j^B \tau_{ij}^{AB}$ with constraints $\Pi_i \tau_i^A = \Pi_j \tau_j^B = \Pi_i \tau_{ij}^{AB} = \Pi_j \tau_{ij}^{AB} = 1.0$ is equivalent to the saturated log–linear model $\log (p_{ij}) = \mu + \lambda_i^A + \lambda_j^B + \lambda_{ij}^{AB}$ with constraints $\Sigma_i \lambda_i^A = \Sigma_j \lambda_j^B = \Sigma_i \lambda_{ij}^{AB} = \Sigma_j \lambda_{ij}^{AB} = 0$. The functional relationship between the model parameters is thus: $\mu = \log (\eta)$, $\lambda_i^A = \log (\tau_i^A)$, $\lambda_j^B = \log (\tau_j^B)$, $\lambda_{ij}^{AB} = \log (\tau_{ij}^{AB})$. Naturally, the other multiplicative models that have been mentioned also possess equivalent log–linear versions. Thus $p_{ij} = \eta \tau_i^A \tau_j^B$ becomes $\log (p_{ij}) = \mu + \lambda_i^A + \lambda_j^B$; $p_{ij} = \eta \tau_i^A$ becomes $\log (p_{ij}) = \mu + \lambda_i^A$; $p_{ij} = \eta$ becomes $\log (p_{ij}) = \mu$. One mustn't forget of course that they also have equivalent constraints.

Thus we have alternative models in which the logs of the cell probabilities are obtained by addition of a number of parameters, each subject to additive constraints analogous to the constraints of the multiplicative model. The question may be asked: 'Why bother to complicate matters by taking logs, even though many social scientists have a familiarity and feel for linear models arising from a grounding in the linear regression model and the analysis of variance?'

It is precisely this relation to the family of generalised linear models outlined earlier in this chapter which makes the transformation such a good idea, for in this form the model can more easily be assimilated and placed in an overall context. For example, it is easy to see the broad similarities between the log-linear model and the ANOVA model $E(y_{ij}) = \mu + \alpha_i + \beta_j + (\alpha\beta)_{ij}$ with constraints $\Sigma_i \alpha_i = 0$, $\Sigma_j \beta_j = 0$, $\Sigma_i (\alpha\beta)_{ij} = 0$, $\Sigma_j (\alpha\beta)_{ij} = 0$. An essential difference between the two is, of course, that the ANOVA model deals with categorical factors and a continuous response, whereas the log-linear model is appropriate when all variables are categorical and this has important theoretical ramifications concerning the applicability of the Poisson distribution which was alluded to earlier. These differences need not concern us too much at this juncture however, and it is the unified framework within which we can set the log-linear model that we wish to emphasise.

A further important advantage of the log-linear model is the approximate normality of the sampling distribution of the model parameters, and we make extensive use of this property in subsequent chapters. In practice, one is not presented with theoretical probabilities but with observed cell frequencies $\{f_{ij}\}$ obtained as a consequence of random sampling. The parameters of, say, the saturated log-linear model fitted to such data are, therefore, likewise subject to sampling error and our knowledge of a log-linear model parameter's standard error and approximately normal sampling distribution can be used to assess the significance of any parameter estimate's departure from zero (see Chapter 2). We say zero because a λ parameter of zero is, of course, equivalent to a τ parameter of one: both mean that no effect is present.

Whereas the presence or absence of λ parameters in a log-linear model determines the effects we wish to incorporate, the λ estimates are independent of the size of the sample, for it is the role of μ to represent the 'average' cell frequency. This dimensionless quality of the λ is illustrated by reference to the observed frequencies in the Oxford shopping survey (Table 1.8) and the equivalent probabilities (Table 1.14). The λ parameters of the saturated log-linear model, fitted to both tables, are equal and can be obtained by taking logs of the τ parameter estimates of Table 1.14. This equality reflects the identical data structure that underlies both the probabilities and frequencies. The fact that the numbers in Table 1.8 are 680 times larger than those in Table 1.14 is accounted for solely by the $\mu = \log(\eta)$ estimates, 3.445 and 0.046 respectively.

The parameter estimates and expected frequencies described thus far can be obtained using the computer program ECTA (Fay & Goodman 1975). This is consistent with Goodman's approach to log-linear modelling, and derives maximum likelihood estimates of the cell frequencies on the basis of the Deming-Stephan (1940) algorithm, also referred to as 'iterative proportional fitting'. Another well-known program that utilises this algorithm is BMDP (Brown & Benedetti 1977).

Alternative log–linear models

Alternative versions of the log–linear model exist which differ from the family outlined above in that different constraints are imposed on the parameters. Some constraints are necessary, as pointed out by Upton (1980), since a model without constraints would be rather imprecise, as illustrated by the two sets of estimates of the parameters of the saturated log–linear model fitted to Table 1.15.

Without constraints, there is a lack of a unique solution to the problem of estimating the parameters that, allowing for round-off error, reproduce the $\{\hat{p}_{ij}\}$, for we find the following estimates are equally consistent with the data:
$\hat{\eta} = 0.22, \hat{\tau}_1^A = 1.57, \hat{\tau}_2^A = 0.63, \hat{\tau}_1^B = 1.1, \hat{\tau}_2^B = 0.91, \hat{\tau}_{11}^{AB} = 0.79, \hat{\tau}_{12}^{AB} = 1.27,$
$\hat{\tau}_{21}^{AB} = 1.27, \hat{\tau}_{22}^{AB} = 0.79; \hat{\eta} = 0.22, \hat{\tau}_1^A = 1.57, \hat{\tau}_2^A = 0.63, \hat{\tau}_1^B = 2.0, \hat{\tau}_2^B = 0.91,$
$\hat{\tau}_{11}^{AB} = 0.43, \hat{\tau}_{12}^{AB} = 1.27, \hat{\tau}_{21}^{AB} = 0.72, \hat{\tau}_{22}^{AB} = 0.79.$

Without constraints we have, in fact, nine independent parameters to determine four cell values; our model is not very succinct and possesses negative degrees of freedom! In the constrained situation, knowing just four parameter values allows one to deduce the remaining five of the saturated model. We thus have four independent parameters and four cells, giving zero degrees of freedom.

One alternative system of constraints that has been adopted by, for example, Plackett (1981), and which is utilised in the computer packages GENSTAT and GLIM, is to constrain certain parameters to zero. For example, $\lambda_1^{'A} = \lambda_J^{'B} = \lambda_{Ij}^{'AB} = \lambda_{iJ}^{'AB} = 0; i = 1, \ldots, I; j = 1, \ldots, J;$ these apply of course to the saturated log–linear model. Since these constraints are different from those adhered to up to now, the parameter estimates are also necessarily different. This is demonstrated by the estimates in Table 1.16 of the saturated model parameters, using both GENSTAT and ECTA. Holt (1979) produces equivalent estimates via GLIM.

Listing 1 (Appendix) gives details of the GENSTAT commands required for Table 1.16. Note the order of the factor levels required to emplace zeros as in this table, a response to the fact that zero is always attached to level 1 wherever it is located. Putting the levels in their more natural order, as is done in later chapters, produces yet another set of parameters based on the same constraint principle (but differing in detail) which generates exactly the same expected

Table 1.15. *A table of probabilities*

	B_1	B_2
A_1	0.3	0.4
A_2	0.2	0.1

frequencies. Still other parameter sets consistent with these same expected frequencies can be produced by differently organised factor levels.

The constraints imposed on the GENSTAT estimates mean that μ' has a different meaning to μ, even though in this example they do, somewhat fortuitously, have identical estimated values. This can be shown if we realize that $\log(e_{44}) = \hat{\mu}' + \hat{\lambda}'^A_4 + \hat{\lambda}'^B_4 + \hat{\lambda}'^{AB}_{44} = \hat{\mu}'$ since $\lambda'^A_I = \lambda'^B_J = \lambda'^{AB}_{IJ} = 0$. Thus $\hat{\mu}'$ cannot be interpreted as an 'average' frequency since it is simply the log of one cell frequency, unlike $\hat{\mu}$ which is the log of the geometric mean of the $\{e_{ij}\}$. The pattern of imposed constraints ensures that the GENSTAT parameters differ in other respects. For example, $\log(e_{34}) = \hat{\mu}' + \hat{\lambda}'^A_3 + \hat{\lambda}'^B_4 + \hat{\lambda}'^{AB}_{34}$. Thus it can be deduced that $\hat{\lambda}'^A_3$ is necessarily -1.0, a somewhat different value from $\hat{\lambda}^A_3 = 0$ obtained via the alternative constraints.

The $\{\lambda'^{AB}_{ij}\}$ parameters which evidently represent the interaction between A and B, give us one particular definition of interaction in the $I \times J$ table. We present the alternative definition that is consistent with the adopted Goodman-like constraint system later in the chapter. Interaction in typical cell (i, j) is defined as $\hat{\lambda}'^{AB}_{ij} = \log(e_{ij}e_{IJ}/e_{iJ}e_{Ij}) = \log[(e_{ij}/e_{iJ})/(e_{Ij}/e_{IJ})]$. Thus the interaction between A and B for cell $(2, 2)$, λ'^{AB}_{22}, is obtained by taking the odds

Table 1.16. *Parameter estimates using GENSTAT and ECTA*

	Observed (expected) frequencies $\{f_{ij}\} = \{e_{ij}\}$			
	B_1	B_2	B_3	B_4
A_1	60	49	134	22
A_2	25	122	60	49
A_3	25	122	148	20
A_4	74	40	55	55

Parameter estimates (GENSTAT)

$$\hat{\lambda}'^{AB}_{ij} = \begin{Bmatrix} 0.7 & 1.1 & 1.8 & 0 \\ -1.0 & 1.2 & 0.2 & 0 \\ -0.1 & 2.1 & 2.0 & 0 \\ 0 & 0 & 0 & 0 \end{Bmatrix} \quad \begin{Bmatrix} -0.9 \\ -0.1 \\ -1.0 \\ 0 \end{Bmatrix} = \hat{\lambda}'^A_i$$

$$\hat{\lambda}'^B_j = \{0.3 \quad\quad -0.3 \quad\quad 0 \quad\quad 0\} \quad\quad \hat{\mu}' = 4.0$$

Parameter estimates (ECTA)

$$\hat{\lambda}^{AB}_{ij} = \begin{Bmatrix} 0.4 & -0.4 & 0.4 & -0.4 \\ -0.5 & 0.5 & -0.4 & 0.4 \\ -0.5 & 0.5 & 0.5 & -0.5 \\ 0.6 & -0.6 & -0.5 & 0.5 \end{Bmatrix} \quad \begin{Bmatrix} 0 \\ 0 \\ 0 \\ 0 \end{Bmatrix} = \hat{\lambda}^A_i$$

$$\hat{\lambda}^B_j = \{-0.3 \quad\quad 0.3 \quad\quad 0.5 \quad\quad -0.5\} \quad\quad \hat{\mu} = 4.0$$

of a randomly chosen individual occupying the second row, second column (as opposed to the second row, last column) of the $I \times J$ table. If there is no interaction these odds will be the same if we take the last row rather than the second row, and hence so will the log odds. Thus, in this system, the last row and column act as norms.

Similar arguments apply in the case of $\{\lambda_i'^A\}$ and $\{\lambda_j'^B\}$, which we define as $\hat{\lambda}_i'^A = \log (e_{iJ}/e_{IJ})$ *and* $\hat{\lambda}_j'^B = \log (e_{Ij}/e_{IJ})$, thus giving, for example, $\lambda_1'^A = \log (22/55) = -0.9$.

Given that at least two sets of parameter estimates exist, even though the expected cell frequencies on which they are both based are identical, there is good reason to interpret parameter estimates with care. Some analysts go even further. Holt (1979), for example, advocates that, 'individual parameter estimates should not be interpreted directly' and notes that, 'odds ratios (calculated on the expected cell frequencies) have important invariance properties not possessed by the individual parameter estimates' and that, 'direct interpretation of the individual parameter estimates is potentially misleading and may result in different interpretations of the same data set depending on the computer program used'. This is illustrated by the λ estimates derived above, where the Goodman-type system indicates no row effects for Table 1.16, whereas the Plackett system does not. It must, however, be realised that the $\{\lambda_i'^A\}$ parameters, for example, are the log of the odds of occupying cell (i, J) to cell (I, J), whereas the $\{\lambda_i^A\}$ parameters are the differences between the average log frequency in row i and the overall average log frequency, as encapsulated by the formula

$$\hat{\lambda}_i^A = \sum_j \log e_{ij}/J - \sum_i \sum_j \log e_{ij}/IJ = \log \left[\left(\prod_j e_{ij}\right)^{1/J}/\eta\right].$$

There are similar ambiguities concerning the interaction parameters, though, again, both sets are internally consistent: as Holt (1979) states, both sets of results are correct. Identical (saturated) models are fitted to Table 1.16 in the sense of including the same effects and interactions, and, 'it must be stressed that the computer programs are not in error'. The difference lies in which is actually meant by interaction. In the case of GLIM or GENSTAT estimates, the last row and column comprise the norms against which odds of occupying particular rows or columns are 'compared'. With the Goodman system (which we adopt generally in the first part of this book), one examines the odds of typical cell (i, j) to the row 'average' as a ratio to an equivalent comparison for column j of the 'average' row frequency to the overall geometric mean. This is illustrated by the formula $\hat{\lambda}_{ij}^{AB} = \log [e_{ij}/(\prod_j e_{ij})^{1/J}/(\prod_i e_{ij})^{1/I}/(\prod_{ij} e_{ij})^{1/IJ}]$ which contrasts somewhat with the earlier definition.

Finally, in Table 1.17 we analyse some real data to further illustrate that different parameter estimates are provided using the two alternative systems, though in this case both are equally significant. The observed data are presented in full in Table 2.5.

The interaction parameter estimates are $\hat{\lambda}_{11}^{'CD} = 0.6342$ with standard error = 0.2366 and $\hat{\lambda}_{11}^{CD} = 0.1586$ with standard error = 0.0592. Note that, since we are dealing with a 2 × 2 table, $\lambda_{11}^{'CD} = 4\lambda_{11}^{CD}$ and the standard error is also four times larger. Thus, in both cases, the ratio of the parameter to its standard error is 2.68 and $P(|z| > 2.68) = 0.007$, where z is $N(0, 1)$. Also, since $\hat{\lambda}_{11}^{'CD} = \log(f_{11}f_{22}/f_{12}f_{21}) = 0.6342$, the log cross-product ratio, with standard error $(f_{11}^{-1} + f_{12}^{-1} + f_{21}^{-1} + f_{22}^{-1})^{1/2} = 0.2366$, the independence chi-squared $X^2 = 0.6342^2/0.2366^2 = 7.18 > \chi_{1,\,0.05}^2 = 3.84$ and $P(\chi_1^2 > 7.18) = 0.007$. This reaffirms the likelihood of association between car ownership and shopping behaviour in the population. Note that, generally, the increment in X^2 (or Y^2, see Chapter 3) incurred in setting an interaction to zero is a less ambiguous method of determining an interaction's significance since it is unaffected by the constraint system adopted.

We have by no means reached the final stage of the analysis, for Table 1.17 is produced by collapsing over or, equivalently, ignoring other variables. This process is discussed in some detail in later chapters, for it is evident that the above measures of association are not totally reliable when the two-way table has been created by collapsing over a multiway cross-classification.

Table 1.17. *A two-way table produced by collapsing Table 2.5 over variables A and B*

	D_1	D_2
C_1	71	156
C_2	35	145

key: C_1 = not car owner.
C_2 = car owner.
D_1 = usually visit nearest shops.
D_2 = do not usually visit nearest shops.

2 The multidimensional table

In order to facilitate our understanding of the multiway table we make use of
a real data set gathered by the author and comprising a sample taken at random
from the population of the town of Dukinfield, Greater Manchester, England.
These data have already been partially analysed in the last chapter (see Table
1.17). Although Table 1.17 does not make this obvious, more than two charac-
teristics of each person were recorded, a fact that would become evident were
the complete data set listed as in Table 2.1, though this form of data display
would be most cumbersome and totally unrevealing.

   A more succinct way of summarizing the data is as in Table 2.2. Thus f_{1211}
is the number of people in the sample with attribute combination $A_1 B_2 C_1 D_1$, in
our example the number of young high-income, non-car owners who use their
nearest shops. We could quickly scan down Table 2.2 to identify the most
commonly occurring attribute combination, though such a list might not be very
useful for many other purposes. To highlight other salient aspects of the data
set, other forms of data display are necessary. Thus in Table 1.17 we wished to
show how car ownership and shopping behaviour were related by constructing
a two-way table involving, for the sake of clarity, only those variables.

Table 2.1. *Multidimensional raw data*

Person number	Age	Income	Mobility	Behaviour
1	A_2	B_1	C_1	D_1
2	A_1	B_2	C_1	D_2
3	A_1	B_1	C_1	D_2
⋮	⋮	⋮	⋮	⋮
f_{0000}	A_2	B_1	C_2	D_2

key: A_1 = young. A_2 = old.
B_1 = low income. B_2 = high income.
C_1 = not car owner. C_2 = car owner.
D_1 = use nearest shops. D_2 = use other shops.

The notation of Table 2.3 appropriate to a collapsed multiway table like Table 1.17 is similar to that used previously for the basic 2×2 table (Table 1.2), with the distinction that we are reminded of the other variables for which we have data but which are not explicit.

In Table 1.17, $f_{0011} = 71$, the number of non-car owners visiting their nearest shopping centre. This number is the result of pooling together the number of young, low-income non-car owners, old, low-income non-car owners, etc, since we are not interested in the age (A) or income (B) variables at this juncture. Similarly, $f_{0022} = 145$ is the number of car owners who bypass their nearest shops: we ignore the existence of age (A) and income (B) variations within this subgroup.

The table margins show that further collapsing can take place. Thus $f_{0020} = 180$ is the number of car owners in the sample and f_{0000} is the total sample size, having collapsed over all four variables.

$$\sum_i \sum_j \sum_k \sum_l f_{ijkl} = f_{0000} = 407$$

Table 2.2. *A way of summarising multidimensional data*

A_1	B_1	C_1	D_1	f_{1111}	A_1	B_1	C_1	D_2	f_{1112}
A_2	B_1	C_1	D_1	f_{2111}	A_2	B_1	C_1	D_2	f_{2112}
A_1	B_2	C_1	D_1	f_{1211}	A_1	B_2	C_1	D_2	
A_2	B_2	C_1	D_1	.	A_2	B_2	C_1	D_2	.
A_1	B_1	C_2	D_1	.	A_1	B_1	C_2	D_2	.
A_2	B_1	C_2	D_1	.	A_2	B_1	C_2	D_2	
A_1	B_2	C_2	D_1		A_1	B_2	C_2	D_2	
A_2	B_2	C_2	D_1		A_2	B_2	C_2	D_2	f_{2222}

Table 2.3. *Notation for observed frequencies in a collapsed table*

	D_1	D_2	Total
C_1	f_{0011}	f_{0012}	f_{0010}
C_2	f_{0021}	f_{0022}	f_{0020}
Total	f_{0001}	f_{0002}	f_{0000}

key: $\sum_i \sum_j f_{ijkl} = f_{00kl}$

$\sum_i \sum_j \sum_l f_{ijkl} = f_{00k0}$

$\sum_i \sum_j \sum_k f_{ijkl} = f_{000l}$

We have justified the information loss incurred by collapsing a 2^4 table down to a 2^2 table by claiming that this avoids obscuring the relationship between pairs of variables. However, this is a practice that can produce fallacious results, in that, for example, an apparent relation between a pair of variables, such as C and D, may in fact be induced by more-complex relations between all four variables. When examined at just one level of a subsequently collapsed variable, C and D may be independent of each other, or the strength of the relation may differ from, or indeed be the reverse of, that displayed by the collapsed table.

If, for example, we reconsider the shopping data presented in Table 1.17, but disaggregate it according to whether respondents are young or old, as in Table 2.4, we see that the association between variables C and D varies between the two subtables thus produced. For the young subgroup, we find the following values for the measures of association we have adopted.

$$f_{11}f_{22}/f_{12}f_{21} = 2.01$$
$$\hat{\lambda}_{11}^{CD} = 0.175 \text{ with standard error, } \sqrt{[\text{Var}(\hat{\lambda}^{CD})]} = 0.097$$
$$X^2 = 0.49/0.151 = 3.25$$
$$P(|z| \geq \hat{\lambda}^{CD}/\sqrt{\text{Var}(\hat{\lambda}^{CD})} = 1.8) = P(\chi^2 \geq X^2 = 3.25) = 0.07$$

For the older group,

$$f_{11}f_{22}/f_{12}f_{21} = 1.59$$
$$\hat{\lambda}_{11}^{CD} = 0.115, \sqrt{[\text{Var}(\hat{\lambda}^{CD})]} = 0.077$$
$$X^2 = 0.212/0.095 = 2.23$$
$$P(|z| \geq \hat{\lambda}^{CD}/\sqrt{[\text{Var}(\hat{\lambda}^{CD})]} = 1.49) = P(\chi^2 \geq X^2 = 2.23) = 0.136$$

Thus we find that there is more evidence of association between car ownership and shopping behaviour if we examine the young rather than the old respondents. In fact, the cross-product ratio for the young exceeds the value obtained for the sample as a whole (see Table 1.17), though, because of the smaller sample, it is more likely to be generated at random assuming the null hypothesis of no association holds, and would only be significant if we accepted

Table 2.4. *Table 1.17 disaggregated according to whether respondents are old or young*

	A_1 (young)			A_2 (old)	
	D_1	D_2		D_1	D_2
C_1	19	51	C_1	52	105
C_2	15	81	C_2	20	64

a 10% level of risk ($\alpha = 0.10$). Also, since we have not allowed for other influences (for example, income) this conclusion is itself provisional as we subsequently observe when the saturated model is fitted to the full table (Table 2.5).

There even exist collapsed tables displaying pairwise association between variables that are independent at each of the levels of a third variable (Blyth 1972; Simpson 1951). The possibility of such paradoxical occurrences makes it imperative to avoid drawing conclusions solely considering variables one pair at a time, when the existence of complex interrelations between several variables can potentially distort our inferences.

The saturated model for multidimensional tables

Since it is not advisable to estimate the relations between pairs of variables by ignoring other interacting variables and collapsing with respect to them, it is necessary to resort to methods that allow all the interrelationships between the variables to be considered simultaneously.

Just as it is possible to reproduce cell frequencies or probabilities $\{\hat{p}_{ij}\}$ exactly in a two-dimensional table using the saturated log–linear model,

$$\log(p_{ij}) = \mu + \lambda_i^A + \lambda_j^B + \lambda_{ij}^{AB}$$

$$\sum_i \lambda_i^A = \sum_j \lambda_j^B = \sum_i \lambda_{ij}^{AB} = \sum_j \lambda_{ij}^{AB} = 0$$

the cell frequencies in a multidimensional table can likewise be reproduced exactly by a saturated log–linear model with extra parameters to handle the fact that more-complex associations are possible. These parameter estimates can then indicate the size and direction of these associations. Thus, with three variables, A, B and C, not only can A and B be related, but also A and C and B and C. Parameters, equivalent to $\{\lambda_{ij}^{AB}\}$ in the two-dimensional table, are needed to represent such associations.

The saturated log–linear model in such a situation would be

$$\log(p_{ijk}) = \mu + \lambda_i^A + \lambda_j^B + \lambda_k^C + \lambda_{ij}^{AB} + \lambda_{ik}^{AC} + \lambda_{jk}^{BC} + \lambda_{ijk}^{ABC}$$

with equivalent constraints to those outlined for the two-dimensional model to remove redundancies and ensure that the number of independent parameters equals the number of cells in the table.

The model shows that not only are parameters necessary to represent the pairwise association of A, B and C, but also the parameter set $\{\lambda_{ijk}^{ABC}\}$ is necessary to reproduce the $\log(\hat{p}_{ijk})$ exactly. These latter parameters are required to account for the possibility that the nature of the association between, for example, variable A and B may vary according to the category of C. Likewise, the association between B and C may vary according to the category of A. Of course, in reality there may be no such association and we may be justified in dropping the $\{\lambda_{ijk}^{ABC}\}$ from the model, in other words setting them all exactly equal to zero, in which case we would have an unsaturated model. The latter may perform almost equally as well as the saturated model in generating a set of expected frequencies $\{e_{ijk}\}$ that accord with those observed $\{f_{ijk}\}$.

The data in Table 2.5 and the parameters of the fitted saturated log–linear model serve to illustrate the above points, demonstrate the natural extension to higher-dimensional tables, provide a link between log–linear and multiplicative versions and lead us onto further aspects of the interpretation of log–linear parameter estimates.

Prior to fitting the saturated model to these data, it is worth noting the existence of a zero in the multidimensional table. This occurs not because of the logical impossibility of old, high-income people who are not car owners and who use a centre other than their nearest $(A_2B_2C_1D_2)$ (which in fact would be called a structural zero (see Bishop *et al.* 1975, p. 177)), but because the size of the sample, 407, was not sufficiently large to provide an estimate other than zero of the unknown, but small, positive theoretical probability of this particular cell being occupied by a randomly chosen member of the population.

Sampling zeros present a major challenge to the analyst, since they are all too common and certainly tend to complicate matters. In this particular case, the presence of 0 makes it impossible to estimate the parameters of the saturated log–linear model since these are functions of log (f_{ijkl}), and log $(0) = \infty$. Suffice

Table 2.5. *Observed frequencies as a result of cross-classifying individuals by four dichotomous variables*

	C_1			C_2		
	A_1	A_2		A_1	A_2	
B_1	17	51	B_1	12	18	D_1
B_2	2	1	B_2	3	2	
	C_1			C_2		
	A_1	A_2		A_1	A_2	
B_1	48	105	B_1	57	53	D_2
B_2	3	0	B_2	24	11	

key: A_1 = young. C_1 = not car owner.
A_2 = old. C_2 = car owner.
B_1 = low income. D_1 = use nearest centre.
B_2 = high income. D_2 = use other centre.

it to say at this juncture that the recommended solution adopted here is the addition of 0.5 to the observed cell frequencies. This is not a totally arbitrary strategy, since it is even recommended 'irrespective of whether there are zero cell frequencies' (Upton 1978a, p. 65) when fitting the saturated model, for theoretical reasons (Plackett 1981).

The parameter estimates of the fitted saturated log–linear model are as follows:

$$\hat{\mu} = 2.407 \; (\hat{\eta} = 11.1) \qquad\qquad \hat{\lambda}_{11}^{BC} = 0.487 \; (\hat{\tau}_{11}^{BC} = 1.628)$$
$$\hat{\lambda}_1^A = 0.085 \; (\hat{\tau}_1^A = 1.09) \qquad\qquad \hat{\lambda}_{11}^{BD} = -0.101 \; (\hat{\tau}_{11}^{BD} = 0.904)$$
$$\hat{\lambda}_1^B = 1.195 \; (\hat{\tau}_1^B = 3.305) \qquad\qquad \hat{\lambda}_{11}^{CD} = 0.318 \; (\hat{\tau}_{11}^{CD} = 1.374)$$
$$\hat{\lambda}_1^C = -0.254 \; (\hat{\tau}_1^C = 0.776) \qquad\qquad \hat{\lambda}_{111}^{ABC} = -0.181 \; (\hat{\tau}_{111}^{ABC} = 0.834)$$
$$\hat{\lambda}_1^D = -0.440 \; (\hat{\tau}_1^D = 0.644) \qquad\qquad \hat{\lambda}_{111}^{ABD} = 0.068 \; (\hat{\tau}_{111}^{ABD} = 1.070)$$
$$\hat{\lambda}_{11}^{AB} = -0.385 \; (\hat{\tau}_{11}^{AB} = 0.699) \qquad\qquad \hat{\lambda}_{111}^{ACD} = -0.053 \; (\hat{\tau}_{111}^{ACD} = 0.948)$$
$$\hat{\lambda}_{11}^{AC} = -0.011 \; (\hat{\tau}_{11}^{AC} = 0.989) \qquad\qquad \hat{\lambda}_{111}^{BCD} = -0.211 \; (\hat{\tau}_{111}^{BCD} = 0.809)$$
$$\hat{\lambda}_{11}^{AD} = -0.164 \; (\hat{\tau}_{11}^{AD} = 0.849) \qquad\qquad \hat{\lambda}_{1111}^{ABCD} = 0.073 \; (\hat{\tau}_{1111}^{ABCD} = 1.076)$$

Although the saturated model has in fact more than the 16 parameters listed above, it is overparameterised and the remaining parameters can be deduced from the constraints imposed. For example, since

$$\sum_i \hat{\lambda}_i^A = 0, \quad \text{then} \quad \hat{\lambda}_2^A = -0.085$$

Similarly, since $\Sigma_i \hat{\lambda}_{ijkl}^{ABCD} = 0$, $\hat{\lambda}_{2111}^{ABCD} = -0.073$.

To deduce other parameter estimates it is worthwhile tabulating them as follows for dichotomies:

	D_1			D_2	
	C_1	C_2		C_1	C_2
B_1	−	+	B_1	+	−
B_2	+	−	B_2	−	+

Thus, $\hat{\lambda}_{111}^{BCD}$ is negative as indicated. Given this, the remaining members of the set $\{\hat{\lambda}_{jkl}^{BCD}\}$ have signs so that the marginal totals are zero. All members of this set have identical absolute values since we have dichotomous variables.

The values in brackets are the estimated parameters of the equivalent saturated multiplicative model. Hence $\exp(\mu) = \eta$, $\exp(\lambda_{ijk}^{ABC}) = \tau_{ijk}^{ABC}$. Since we have four variables A, B, C, D, there are $n!/(r!(n-r)!)$ sets of parameters denoting pairwise association ($r = 2$).

$$\frac{n!}{r!(n-r)!} = \frac{4!}{2!2!} = 6;$$

$$(\{\lambda_{ij}^{AB}\}, \{\lambda_{ik}^{AC}\}, \{\lambda_{il}^{AD}\}, \{\lambda_{jk}^{BC}\}, \{\lambda_{jl}^{BD}\}, \{\lambda_{kl}^{CD}\})$$

Likewise, there are $4!/3!1! =$ four sets of parameters denoting three-way ($r = 3$) association ($\{\lambda_{ijk}^{ABC}\}, \{\lambda_{ijl}^{ABD}\}, \{\lambda_{ikl}^{ACD}\}, \{\lambda_{jkl}^{BCD}\}$); and just one set $\{\lambda_{ijkl}^{ABCD}\}$ for four-way association.

The saturated model is, in fact, more of a tautology than a model in the sense that it is in actuality merely another way of writing down the observed frequencies $\{f_{ijkl}\}$ since they exactly correspond to the set of expected frequencies $\{e_{ijkl}\}$ produced by the model. Thus,

$$
\begin{aligned}
\log\,(e_{1221}) = \log\,(f_{1221}) = {} & \hat{\mu} + \hat{\lambda}_1^A + \hat{\lambda}_2^B + \hat{\lambda}_2^C + \hat{\lambda}_1^D + \hat{\lambda}_{12}^{AB} + \hat{\lambda}_{12}^{AC} \\
& + \hat{\lambda}_{11}^{AD} + \hat{\lambda}_{22}^{BC} + \hat{\lambda}_{21}^{BD} + \hat{\lambda}_{21}^{CD} + \hat{\lambda}_{122}^{ABC} + \hat{\lambda}_{121}^{ABD} + \hat{\lambda}_{121}^{ACD} \\
& + \hat{\lambda}_{221}^{BCD} + \hat{\lambda}_{1221}^{ABCD}
\end{aligned}
$$

Although no generalization is involved, the saturated model does provide useful evidence of which associations are negligible, and thus can guide us to a model of fewer parameters. From the above parameter estimates it can be seen that the average (log) frequency μ is subject to a number of adjustments of varying magnitude representing a variety of influences which operate to produce the frequency in any cell.

Taking as an example the subgroup of young, high-income car owners using the nearest centre ($A_1 B_2 C_2 D_1, f_{1221} = 3$), the salient influences are as follows. The initial consideration is the size of the sample. The effect of this is represented by the geometric mean η (log $(\eta) = \mu$). Next, the varying probabilities of the variable categories, prior to subsequent effects that also influence the observed totals, must be represented. This is accomplished by multiplying by (adding on) the estimates of $\tau_i^A (\lambda_i^B), \tau_j^B (\lambda_j^B)$ and so on. We see that most important of these is $\tau_2^B (\lambda_2^B)$ which represents the relative scarcity of high-income people.

Such influences do not exactly reproduce the observed frequencies, and the other factors need to be included. Consider the following example: the observed number of high-income car owners ($A_1 B_2 C_2 D_1$ are part of this group) is not simply a response to the probability of having a high income (λ_j^B) and the probability of owning a car (λ_k^C). Not only do these influences act independently, but they also interact. Having a high income increases one's chance of owning a car. Thus we include a parameter (λ_{jk}^{BC}) representing the association between variables B and C which also affects the cell frequencies over and above the λ_j^B and λ_k^C effects. The other pairwise associations also influence the cell frequency and are represented by the equivalent parameters, the most important of which for cell (1, 2, 2, 1) are $\lambda_{12}^{AB} (\hat{\tau}_{12}^{AB} = 1/0.699), \lambda_{22}^{BC} (\hat{\tau}_{22}^{BC} = 1.628)$ and $\lambda_{21}^{CD} (\hat{\tau}_{21}^{CD} = 1/1.374)$.

These pairwise associations themselves vary in magnitude according to the level of a third variable. For example, we have noted earlier that the above-mentioned interaction between car ownership and choice of shopping centre

(λ^{CD}) will vary according to the age of the respondent. This influence is represented in the model by the parameter λ_{121}^{ACD} which serves to marginally increase the (log) expected frequency for cell $(1, 2, 2, 1)$ of Table 2.5. Note that this represents a 'damping' of the relation between variables C and D for the young respondents and contrasts with our earlier conclusion, based on Table 2.4, which did not simultaneously allow for the other possible effects represented in the saturated model. The $\{\lambda_{ikl}^{ACD}\}$ parameters are relatively minor but we must necessarily include all effects, no matter how insignificant, into a saturated model to be able to reproduce the observed frequencies exactly.

Thus we even have to include the $\{\lambda_{ijkl}^{ABCD}\}$ parameter set, even though it is obviously of minor importance and a somewhat difficult influence to describe. This is why unsaturated models that assume complex interactions are zero are to be advocated.

The standard errors of parameter estimates

The point must be emphasised that, since the saturated model is fitted to sample data, the parameters under discussion are merely estimates of true unknown values and have sampling distributions. In fact, some parameters with small estimated values like $\hat{\lambda}_{1111}^{ABCD}$ could possibly be zero in actuality. It turns out, most fortunately, that, as with the closely related log cross-product ratio, these sampling distributions are approximately normal (Goodman 1970) and the standard errors are quite easily calculated.

Although they are all identical for the parameters of the saturated model fitted to Table 2.5, since it involves dichotomous variables only, the standard errors of the various parameters do in fact vary according to which parameters are estimated in models comprising polytomous variables. Thus direct comparison of parameter estimates, as above, is not always legitimate. Generally, comparisons of the magnitude of deviations of the λ estimates from zero need to be on a standardised basis so that relative probabilities under the null hypothesis that $\lambda = 0$ can be evaluated using the standard normal distribution since $\hat{\lambda}/\sqrt{[\text{Var}(\hat{\lambda})]}$ is distributed (approximately) as $N(0, 1)$. If we accept a risk of five in 100 of making a type I error, then a value exceeding 1.96 will be deemed to indicate that the true value of λ does indeed differ from 0 since such a large value will only occur in five in 100 samples when $\lambda = 0$.

Note that, in general, $\hat{\lambda} = \Sigma_i \Sigma_j \Sigma_k \Sigma_l a_{ijkl} \log(f_{ijkl})$, where each parameter is a linear combination of the log cell frequencies and where $\{a_{ijkl}\}$ are appropriately defined according to the parameter we wish to estimate (Goodman 1978, p. 149; Upton 1978a, p. 63). Thus, in the simple 2^4 table, Table 2.5, the saturated model parameter estimate for the interaction between car ownership and behaviour is $\hat{\lambda}_{11}^{CD} = (1/16) \log(f_{1111}) - (1/16) \log(f_{1121}) +$

$(1/16) \log (f_{1211}) - (1/16) \log (f_{1212}) + \cdots + (1/16) \log (f_{2222}) - (1/16) \log (f_{2212}) = 0.318.$

Since Var $[\log (f_{ijkl})] \approx 1/f_{ijkl}$, where f_{ijkl} is a typical cell frequency generated by a Poisson probability process (see Plackett 1962 and Chapter 4), and since Var $(aX) = a^2$ Var (X), where a is a constant, then

$$\text{Var } [\hat{\lambda} = \Sigma_i \Sigma_j \Sigma_k \Sigma_l a_{ijkl} \log (f_{ijkl})] = \Sigma_i \Sigma_j \Sigma_k \Sigma_l (a_{ijkl})^2/f_{ijkl}$$
$$= (a_{ijkl})^2 \Sigma_i \Sigma_j \Sigma_k \Sigma_l (1/f_{ijkl}).$$

Thus, for the data in Table 2.5, $\sqrt{[\text{Var } (\hat{\lambda})]} = [(1/16)^2 \Sigma_i \Sigma_j \Sigma_k \Sigma_l (1/f_{ijkl})]^{1/2} = 0.132$, and in this case this holds for all parameters.

In tables involving variables with differing numbers of levels the $\{a_{ijkl}\}$ vary with the result that the parameter standard errors vary accordingly. This can be illustrated if we reexamine the λ_{11}^{AB} estimate of the saturated log–linear model fitted to our 3 × 5 table of fatigue perception against car availability (Tables 1.8 and 1.14).

We have already established that $\hat{\tau}_{11}^{AB} = 0.78$; thus $\hat{\lambda}_{11}^{AB} = \log (0.78) = -0.248$. This is obtained from the following equations.

$$\hat{\lambda}_{11}^{AB} = \log (\hat{\tau}_{11}^{AB}) = \log \left[\left(f_{11}/\prod_j f_{ij}^{1/J} \right) \Big/ \left(\prod_i f_{i1}^{1/I} / \prod_{ij} f_{ij}^{1/IJ} \right) \right]$$

thus

$$\hat{\lambda}_{11}^{AB} = \log (f_{11}) - (1/J) \log (f_{10}) - (1/I) \log (f_{01}) + (1/IJ) \log (f_{00})$$
$$= \log (f_{11}) - (1/J) \log (f_{11}) - (1/J) \log (f_{12}) - \cdots - (1/J) \log (f_{15})$$
$$- (1/I) \log (f_{11}) - (1/I) \log (f_{21}) - (1/I) \log (f_{31})$$
$$+ (1/IJ) \log (f_{11}) + (1/IJ) \log (f_{12}) + \cdots + (1/IJ) \log (f_{35})$$

thus, a_{11}, associated with f_{11}, is $(15 - 3 - 5 + 1)/15 = 8/15$, and $a_{21} = (0 - 0 - 5 + 1)/15 = -4/15$ using the formula (Goodman 1973c; 1978, p. 454) $a_{ij} = (IJ\delta_{io}^i \delta_{jo}^j - I\delta_{io}^i - J\delta_{jo}^j + 1)/IJ$ in which the Kronecker delta $\delta_{io}^i = 1$ if $i = io$ and $\delta_{io}^i = 0$ otherwise. In this case $io, jo = 1$ since we are estimating λ_{11}^{AB}. The whole set $\{a_{ij}\}$ for the 3 × 5 table is given below. It enables us to estimate manually the standard errors of parameters like λ_{11}^{AB} and thus have confidence in the standard error estimates that are automatically, and otherwise somewhat mysteriously, produced by conventional computer programs.

$$\{a_{ij}\} = \begin{pmatrix} 8/15 & -2/15 & -2/15 & -2/15 & -2/15 \\ -4/15 & 1/15 & 1/15 & 1/15 & 1/15 \\ -4/15 & 1/15 & 1/15 & 1/15 & 1/15 \end{pmatrix}$$

Using these quantities we find that Var $(\hat{\lambda}_{11}^{AB}) = [(8/15)^2/55] + [(-2/15)^2/11] + [(-2/15)^2/16] + \cdots + [(1/15)^2/77] = 0.0125.$

Generalisations of these equations for n-way tables with polytomous variables are given by Goodman (1978). Note that, generally, standard error estimates are usually conservative (that is, marginally too large) for the unsaturated models considered later.

If we return to our 2^4 shopping data (Table 2.5) it can be argued that, since $\hat{\lambda}_{11}^{CD}/\sqrt{[\text{Var}(\hat{\lambda}_{11}^{CD})]} = 0.318/0.132 = 2.41$, we can fairly safely assume that λ_{11}^{CD} does not equal zero. Note that for the 2 × 2 table (Table 1.17) produced by collapsing Table 2.5 over variables A and B,

$$\sqrt{[\text{Var}(\hat{\lambda}^{CD})]} = \sqrt{\left[(\tfrac{1}{4})^2 \sum_i \sum_j (1/f_{ij})\right]}$$

$$= \tfrac{1}{4}\sqrt{[(f_{11}^{-1} + f_{12}^{-1} + f_{21}^{-1} + f_{22}^{-1})]} = 0.059$$

that is, $\tfrac{1}{4}$ of the standard deviation of the log cross-product ratio. This reaffirms the link between the log–linear model parameters and the cross-product ratio. Note also that Var $(\hat{\lambda}^{CD})$ is much less for the 2 × 2 table than for the 2^4 table on which it is based. As will be noted in Chapter 5, despite our warning earlier of the danger of fallacious inferences from collapsed tables, there is much to be said for collapsing complex tables when it is legitimate to do so, since there will be a commensurate reduction in standard errors.

Having given some thought to how parameter standard errors are obtained we are now in a position to test whether a particular parameter of the saturated log–linear model differs significantly from zero, though we must bear in mind the dependence of parameter values on imposed constraints (see Chapter 1) and take note of the existence of non-zero parameter covariances in which inordinately large parameters may render others inordinately large in order to satisfy the constraints. Furthermore, our interpretation of ostensibly significant parameters must make allowance for the fact that such improbable occurrences (assuming $\lambda = 0$) are usually discovered as a result of simultaneous scrutiny of a large number of parameters.

Thus we must acknowledge that, though values of $\hat{\lambda}/\sqrt{[\text{Var}(\hat{\lambda})]} > 1.96$ are only occasionally possible (five in 100 samples) on an individual basis, simply because of sampling fluctuation, when a large number of parameters are considered at the same time, the presence of such values becomes inevitable. Table 2.6 quantifies this on the assumption of zero parameter covariance.

Thus, although standardised values between -1.96 and 1.96 provide a guide as to which effects are operative, they are by no means infallible.

If we were required to analyse data cross-classified according to eight dichotomous variables, then the number of saturated log-linear model parameter estimates simultaneously compared would be immense. The number would in fact be

$$\sum_{r=1}^{n} \frac{n!}{r!(n-r)!} = 8 + 28 + 56 + 70 + 56 + 28 + 8 + 1$$

$$= 255$$

and, assuming that the true parameter values were all zero, the probability that the standardised values all lay within the range -1.96–1.96 is $(0.95)^{255} \approx 0.000\,002$, a highly unlikely occurrence. Of course, if some or all of the variables are polytomous, the number of simultaneous saturated model parameter estimate comparisons escalates even more tremendously, and assigning significance to standardised values exceeding the critical values should be done with even more trepidation.

Thus, accepting or rejecting effects cannot be done solely with reference to the standardised values obtained via the saturated model. A further consideration is that, using the hierarchy of models to be discussed subsequently, it is seen that the inclusion or exclusion of particular parameters logically requires other related parameters to be included or excluded also, irrespective of their standardised values.

Table 2.6. *The varying probabilities of correctly interpreting independent parameter estimates*

No. of parameters simultaneously compared	Probability that their standardised values *all* lie between -1.96 and 1.96
10	0.599
50	0.077
100	0.006

3 Unsaturated models

Marginal equalisation and corresponding parameters

It has already been intimated that unsaturated models, resulting from setting some of the saturated model parameters to zero, may perform adequately in that a set of expected frequencies $\{e_{ijkl}\}$ may be produced that does not deviate too drastically from $\{f_{ijkl}\}$. In fact, there is a wide variety of unsaturated models that can be fitted to any multidimensional table, each differing according to the parameters included.

One particular model, the independence model, has already been discussed with respect to two-dimensional tables. It is again discussed here because it illustrated some fundamental properties of hierarchical log–linear models. The expected frequencies $\{e_{ij}\}$ were previously estimated in two ways. First, $e_{ij} = f_{i0}f_{0j}/f_{00}$ since $p_{ij} = p_{i0}p_{0j}; f_{i0}$ = observed total, row i; f_{0j} = observed total, column j. The second method of obtaining estimates of the expected frequencies is to solve the familiar log–linear equation,

$$\log(e_{ij}) = \hat{\mu} + \hat{\lambda}_i^A + \hat{\lambda}_j^B; \quad \sum_i \hat{\lambda}_i^A = \sum_j \hat{\lambda}_j^B = 0.$$

The λ_i^B and λ_j^B estimates are adjustments to the 'average' cell frequency to account for the fact that particular variable categories may be more frequently occupied than average, and this itself will tend to increase or decrease particular cell frequencies, even though the model assumes zero association between the variables A, B.

In three dimensions, the definition of complete mutual independence between three variables is:

$$p_{ijk} = p_{i00}p_{0j0}p_{00k}$$

These unknown probabilities must be estimated by the following equation.

$$\hat{p}_{ijk} = \frac{f_{i00}f_{0j0}f_{00k}}{f_{000}f_{000}f_{000}}$$

Hence,

$$e_{ijk} = \frac{f_{i00}f_{0j0}f_{00k}}{f_{000}^2}$$

These probabilities, or equivalent expected frequencies, can also be obtained by the unsaturated log–linear model $\log (p_{ijk}) = \mu + \lambda_i^A + \lambda_j^B + \lambda_k^C$.

Birch (1963) has shown how the maximum likelihood estimates $\{e_{ijk}\}$ satisfy other equations and that the equations satisfied match the λ included in the model precisely. Furthermore, this correspondence is not restricted to the mutual independence model under discussion, but it extends to any hierarchical model and any number of (polytomous) variables.

To illustrate this, let us return to the above independence model and sum the $\{e_{ijk}\}$ over sundry variables, as outlined by Upton (1980). Summing over variables B and C produces the equation

$$e_{i00} = \frac{f_{i00} f_{000} f_{000}}{f_{000}^2}$$

$$e_{i00} = f_{i00} \qquad (i = 1, \ldots, I)$$

In other words, the initial definition of mutual independence implies an equalisation of the observed and expected frequencies in the categories of variable A. It is easy to show that this also applies to the other two variables of the three-way table.

$$e_{0j0} = f_{0j0} \qquad (j = 1, \ldots, J)$$

$$e_{00k} = f_{00k} \qquad (k = 1, \ldots, K)$$

The equalisation of observed and expected marginal frequencies is demonstrated numerically by Table 3.1, a $2 \times 2 \times 2$ table of hypothetical frequencies.

It is noteworthy that these estimates $\{e_{ijk}\}$ could equally well have been obtained by the corresponding unsaturated log–linear model of mutual independence, $\log (p_{ijk}) = \mu + \lambda_i^A + \lambda_j^B + \lambda_k^C: \Sigma_i \lambda_i^B = \Sigma_j \lambda_j^B = \Sigma_k \lambda_k^C = 0$. The

Table 3.1. *Equalised observed and expected marginal frequencies*

	C_1			C_2			
	B_1	B_2	Total	B_1	B_2	Total	
A_1	8	22	30	12	8	20	Observed frequencies
A_2	2	28	30	8	22	30	$\{f_{ijk}\}$
Total	10	50	60	20	30	50	
A_1	7.44	19.83		6.20	16.53		Expected frequencies
A_2	8.93	23.80		7.44	19.83		$\{e_{ijk}\}$

$f_{100} = e_{100} = 50$ $f_{010} = e_{010} = 30$ $f_{001} = e_{001} = 50$
$f_{200} = e_{200} = 60$ $f_{020} = e_{020} = 80$ $f_{002} = e_{002} = 50$

inclusion of the parameter set $\{\lambda_i^A\}$ goes hand in hand with the equalisation of the sets of observed and expected frequencies $\{f_{i00}\}$ and $\{e_{i00}\}$. Likewise, including $\{\lambda_j^B\}$ means that $\{f_{0j0}\}$ and $\{e_{0j0}\}$ are equal, and $\{\lambda_k^C\}$ in the model means that $\{e_{00k}\}$ and $\{f_{00k}\}$ are equivalent.

To demonstrate the above identity of parameters included in the model and equalised marginal totals, let us consider the observed frequencies in Table 3.2 (initially discussed in Upton & Fingleton 1979). In this table the variables A, B and C are identical to those in Table 2.5, while variable D is a dichotomous response variable. Individuals are allotted to level 1 of variable D if they behave

Table 3.2. *Frequencies demonstrating the correspondence of parameters and equalised margins*

			Observed frequencies $\{f_{ijkl}\}$		Expected frequencies $\{e_{ijkl}\}$	
			A_1	A_2	A_1	A_2
D_1	C_1	B_1	18	65	24.63	59.10
		B_2	2	1	1.89	0.38
	C_2	B_1	15	25	18.02	18.54
		B_2	3	4	7.05	3.39
D_2	C_1	B_1	47	91	40.37	96.90
		B_2	3	0	3.11	0.62
	C_2	B_1	54	46	50.98	52.46
		B_2	24	9	19.95	9.61

Parameters included	Corresponding equalised marginal totals
μ	$f_{0000} = e_{0000}$
λ_i^A	$f_{i000} = e_{i000}$
λ_j^B	$f_{0j00} = e_{0j00}$
λ_k^C	$f_{00k0} = e_{00k0}$
λ_l^D	$f_{000l} = e_{000l}$
λ_{ij}^{AB}	$f_{ij00} = e_{ij00}$
λ_{ik}^{AC}	$f_{i0k0} = e_{i0k0}$
λ_{jk}^{BC}	$f_{0jk0} = e_{0jk0}$
λ_{kl}^{CD}	$f_{00kl} = e_{00kl}$
λ_{ijk}^{ABC}	$f_{ijk0} = e_{ijk0}$

as though they were conforming to a particular 'law' governing the way in which extra travel effort is compensated by more attractive destinations. They are assigned to level 2 if they choose destinations such that their behaviour apparently violates the prescribed rule. The following unsaturated model is used to generate the expected frequencies of Table 3.2:

$$\log (P_{ijkl}) = \mu + \lambda_i^A + \lambda_j^B + \lambda_k^C + \lambda_l^D + \lambda_{ij}^{AB} + \lambda_{ik}^{AC} + \lambda_{jk}^{BC}$$
$$+ \lambda_{kl}^{CD} + \lambda_{ijk}^{ABC}.$$

This model generates expected frequencies on the basis of parameters that allow for relations between age, income and car ownership by including parameters such as $\{\lambda_{ijk}^{ABC}\}$, and for the fact that there are varying marginal frequencies, so that, for example, $\{\lambda_j^B\}$ is included to adjust the expected frequencies for the relatively low probability of high-income respondents. The expected frequencies are also generated on the assumption of a direct interaction between car ownership and behaviour (λ^{CD}), whilst direct relations between age and behaviour and income and behaviour are assumed to be non-existent. As can be seen from Table 3.2, this model in fact provides expected frequencies that only roughly approximate to those observed, and we would be justified in considering it inadequate if we accepted a 5% risk of being wrong. However, we are not concerned at this juncture with the technicalities and arguments involved in the search for acceptable models, but merely with the fact that sets of observed and expected frequencies are equalised and that the sets involved depend upon the model utilised to generate the expected frequencies. These equalised table margins and their associated parameters are given in Table 3.2.

These correspondences extend to any (hierarchical) model, including those with polytomous variables. It is also evident that the existence of certain equalities implies the existence of others, as exemplified by Table 3.3. According to the model fitted, since $\{\lambda_{ij}^{AB}\}$ is included, then $f_{1100} = e_{1100}$ and $f_{1200} = e_{1200}$. Hence, $f_{1100} + f_{1200} = e_{1100} + e_{1200}$ and, therefore, $f_{1000} = e_{1000}$. The inclusion of $\{\lambda_{ij}^{AB}\}$ implies the inclusion of $\{\lambda_i^A\}$ and $\{\lambda_j^B\}$. In general, if $f_{ij00} = e_{ij00}$, then this implies $f_{0j00} = e_{0j00}$ and $f_{i000} = e_{i000}$.

It is easy to demonstrate a whole series of other equalisations of observed and expected marginal frequencies that arise merely as a consequence of other

Table 3.3. *Observed and expected frequencies, collapsing over C and D*

	B_1	B_2		B_1	B_2
A_1	f_{1100}	f_{1200}	A_1	e_{1100}	e_{1200}
A_2	f_{2100}	f_{2200}	A_2	e_{2100}	e_{2200}

margins being set equal. For the model fitted in Table 3.2, these implications are as follows.

Parameter set	Implied parameter set
$\{\lambda_{ijk}^{ABC}\}$	$\mu, \{\lambda_i^A\}, \{\lambda_j^B\}, \{\lambda_k^C\}, \{\lambda_{ij}^{AB}\}, \{\lambda_{ik}^{AC}\}, \{\lambda_{jk}^{BC}\}$
$\{\lambda_{kl}^{CD}\}$	$\mu, \{\lambda_k^C\}, \{\lambda_l^D\},$
$\{\lambda_{jk}^{BC}\}$	$\mu, \{\lambda_j^B\}, \{\lambda_k^C\},$
$\{\lambda_{ik}^{AC}\}$	$\mu, \{\lambda_i^A\}, \{\lambda_k^C\},$
$\{\lambda_{ij}^{AB}\}$	$\mu, \{\lambda_i^A\}, \{\lambda_j^B\}$, all other parameter sets imply μ

The existence of these implications indicates that the above model is one of a hierarchical series, differentiated according to the parameters present. Some model parameters cannot be independently removed from a model in this series because their existence is implied by more-complex parameters (see Bishop *et al.* 1975, p. 69 for a detailed technical discussion of Birch's 1963 results).

It can be argued that these constraints on which parameters can and cannot be removed from a model limits ones choice somewhat, since models such as $\log(p_{ijk}) = \mu + \lambda_{ijk}^{ABC}$ are not feasible under the maximum likelihood estimation scheme. In fact, one must resort to an alternative estimation procedure to acquire this degree of flexibility, as discussed also in Chapter 5. Models estimated by maximum likelihood in which parameters not equivalent to equalised marginal totals are fitted via GENSTAT in later chapters. However, there are a variety of reasons for remaining, initially at least, within the hierarchical family. One good reason is that, even with the above constraints on model choice, there is still a very large number of potential models, and thus we are quite likely to find a satisfactory model from among this large set without needing to consider non-hierarchical formulations that are somewhat difficult to interpret. This is true whether we consider log–linear or ANOVA models (Smith 1976, p. 492; Fienberg 1980, p. 43). We should set against this lack of interpretability the loss of efficiency, reflected in inflated standard errors, brought about by including parameters representing minor effects that would be set to zero in non-hierarchical models.

Some standard algorithms (such as ECTA) presuppose the comparison of members of the hierarchy, and the goodness-of-fit statistic normally adopted, Y^2, has consistent properties in the hierarchical scheme. Unlike Pearson's X^2, which is similar in value and also asymptotically distributed as χ^2, the removal of parameters from hierarchical log–linear models automatically increases Y^2. This consistency facilitates the testing of the conditional significance of parameters and thus allows one to choose an adequate model unequivocally.

Shorthand notation

One excellent feature of working with the set of hierarchical log–linear models is the shorthand notation that it facilitates. This can be adopted to represent the cumbersome log–linear equations in a neat and succinct fashion. The shorthand is based on the above-mentioned implication of one parameter set by another, and is very useful when a large number of competing models are being compared. For example, the model

$$\log (p_{ijkl}) = \mu + \lambda_i^A + \lambda_j^B + \lambda_k^C + \lambda_l^D + \lambda_{ij}^{AB} + \lambda_{ik}^{AC} + \lambda_{jk}^{BC}$$
$$+ \lambda_{kl}^{CD} + \lambda_{ijk}^{ABC}$$

can be written much more succinctly as ABC/CD since the parameters implied by $\{\lambda_{ijk}^{ABC}\}$ and $\{\lambda_{kl}^{CD}\}$ exhaust all parameters included in the model. An alternative but equivalent notation favoured by, for example, Aitkin (1980), is to write the model as $A * B * C + C * D$. If one considers the model

$$(p_{ijkl}) = \mu + \lambda_i^A + \lambda_j^B + \lambda_k^C + \lambda_l^D + \lambda_{ij}^{AB} + \lambda_{ik}^{AC} + \lambda_{jk}^{BC} + \lambda_{il}^{AD}$$
$$+ \lambda_{kl}^{CD} + \lambda_{ijk}^{ABC}$$

with, of course, the usual constraints imposed on the parameters, the inclusion of the extra parameter (set) AD distinguishes this model from that above, and the notation changes to $ABC/AD/CD$ or, equivalently, $A * B * C + A * D + C * D$.

Paradoxically, fewer parameters in the longhand version of the model can result in less-succinct shorthand, due to the removal of parameter sets that implied several others which must now as, a consequence, be made explicit. Thus the saturated model

$$\log (p_{ijk}) = \mu + \lambda_i^A + \lambda_j^B + \lambda_k^C + \lambda_{ij}^{AB} + \lambda_{ik}^{AC} + \lambda_{jk}^{BC} + \lambda_{ijk}^{ABC},$$

$$\sum_i \lambda_i^A = \cdots \sum_k \lambda_{ijk}^{ABC} = 0,$$

is represented by ABC since this implies all other parameters, whereas the model

$$\log (p_{ijk}) = \mu + \lambda_i^A + \lambda_j^B + \lambda_k^C + \lambda_{ij}^{AB} + \lambda_{ik}^{AC} + \lambda_{jk}^{BC},$$

$$\sum_i \lambda_i^A = \cdots \sum_k \lambda_{jk}^{BC} = 0,$$

is written as $AB/AC/BC$.

In fact, Aitkin's (1980) notational system is only one of several alternatives to the one adopted, which each exploit the fact that compact versions of hierarchical models estimated via maximum likelihood can be written by simply specifying the most complex of the model parameters, since they automatically imply the inclusion of subordinates. We list below several popular alternative forms of the model fitted to Table 3.2. The differences between them are purely ones of symbolism. They each mean the same thing.

Author	Shorthand	Longhand
Upton (1978*a*)	*ABC/CD*	$\log(p_{ijkl}) = \mu + \lambda_i^A + \lambda_j^B + \lambda_k^C + \lambda_l^D + \lambda_{ij}^{AB} + \lambda_{ik}^{AC} + \lambda_{jk}^{BC} + \lambda_{ijk}^{ABC} + \lambda_{kl}^{CD}$
Fienberg (1980)	[123] [34]	$\log(M_{ijkl}) = \mu + \mu_{1(i)} + \mu_{2(j)} + \mu_{3(k)} + \mu_{4(l)} + \mu_{12(ij)} + \mu_{13(ik)} + \mu_{23(jk)} + \mu_{123(ijk)} + \mu_{34(kl)}$
Goodman (1978)	$\{ABC\}\{CD\}$	$\log(F_{ijkl}) = \theta + \lambda_i^A + \lambda_j^B + \lambda_k^C + \lambda_l^D + \lambda_{ij}^{AB} + \lambda_{ik}^{AC} + \lambda_{jk}^{BC} + \lambda_{ijk}^{ABC} + \lambda_{kl}^{CD}$

This list is by no means exhaustive, and Goodman (1978) himself switches between an almost bewildering set of alternative notational forms for both the log-linear and multiplicative versions of the models. These differences provide no real difficulty for the initiated but, clearly, a standard and simple notational system should be adopted in a pedagogic book. Rather than attempt to introduce yet another set of hieroglyphics to standardise previous systems, the clear, concise and comprehensive notation of Upton (1978*a*) has been largely adopted throughout as a vehicle for understanding the concepts represented by the notation. Once these have been established, it becomes much easier to switch between the variety of systems adopted elsewhere in the literature with relatively little bemusement.

One source of puzzlement may be the precise meaning of our expected frequencies $\{e_{ij}\}$ for the two-way table. Some of the literature (for example, Fienberg 1980) adopts the term 'estimated expected', whereas elsewhere the words 'expected' and 'estimated expected' are used interchangeably (see Bishop *et al.* 1975; Goodman 1978). Strictly speaking, the expected frequency is an unknown quantity that can only be estimated and this is why Altham (1979) qualifies the term by referring to 'expected' values obtained from a maximum likelihood estimate $\hat{p}$ of unknown probability p. In this book we likewise adhere to this simplifying convention, adopted also by Upton (1978*a*), Plackett (1981) and others, of using the words 'expected frequency' to mean the maximum likelihood estimate, especially as it relieves us of the constant necessity to distinguish between F_{ijk} or M_{ijk} (the expected frequency) and $\hat{M}_{ijk}$ or $\hat{F}_{ijk}$ (the estimated expected frequency) in our discussion. Such nuances probably add little to the understanding of what models mean at this stage, and can usually be dropped from general discussion – indeed, we have reached this far without any reference to these niceties. However, they cannot be totally ignored if we wish to consult some of the other texts and delve into the advanced statistical literature.

Goodness of fit

Unlike saturated models, unsaturated log–linear models generate a set of expected frequencies $\{e_{ijk}\}$ which may or may not approximate to the observed frequencies $\{f_{ijk}\}$. Since the observed frequencies are the consequence of random sampling, a degree of disharmony between $\{e_{ijk}\}$ and $\{f_{ijk}\}$ can be tolerated since it may be nothing more than random variation, and the chosen model may actually be a true representation of the associations present in the population.

So far we have been largely concerned with one particular unsaturated model, the independence model, and one particular measure of the closeness of the expected frequencies generated by this model to the observed frequencies, namely the 'independence' chi-squared, X^2 and the related cross-product ratio. Not only is this measure appropriate to the whole range of other unsaturated models that might also be fitted to any given data set, but there is also another commonly utilised goodness-of-fit statistic which possesses certain advantages over the more familiar X^2 and should at least be used in conjunction with it. This is the likelihood-ratio statistic Y^2. Both X^2 and Y^2 possess different formulae, but they produce similar values, especially for large samples. The formulae in the three-variable context are

$$X^2 = \sum_i \sum_j \sum_k \frac{(f_{ijk} - e_{ijk})^2}{e_{ijk}}$$

and

$$Y^2 = 2 \sum_i \sum_j \sum_k f_{ijk} \log (f_{ijk}/e_{ijk})$$

Since the $\{f_{ijk}\}$ will vary from sample to sample, even when a particular model such as $A/B/C$ holds, both X^2 and Y^2 have χ^2 sampling distributions varying around an average. This average or expected X^2 or Y^2 value will depend on the size of the table and will vary according to the number of constraints imposed so that certain observed and expected marginal totals are equalised. The more constraints imposed, in other words the more parameters in the fitted model, the greater the tendency for the observed and expected frequencies to conform. Furthermore, since the X^2 goodness-of-fit statistic is the sum of a number of positive contributions, one per cell, it will tend to be large for tables with many cells and small for small tables irrespective of the veracity of the model generating the expected frequencies and the associated marginal constraints.

The mean of the χ^2 distribution to which X^2 and Y^2 approximate when the fitted model holds reflects these influences. It is, in fact, the number of degrees of freedom.

df = (number of cells in the table)

— (number of independent parameters in the fitted model)

In fact, this formula applies to the whole family of hierarchical log–linear models including those fitted to multidimensional tables and polytomous variables, though, as will be discovered later, it does require some adaptation in certain more-complex circumstances than those so far considered. Suffice it to say at this juncture that the mean (df), together with the critical value of the appropriate distribution which will only be infrequently exceeded when the correct model has been chosen, form the yardsticks for comparing observed X^2 and Y^2 statistics with their likely values. This is illustrated by returning to the data in Table 3.2 in which the expected frequencies are generated by the model ABC/CD. It has already been noted that the observed frequencies only roughly approximate to these estimates, and this is substantiated by the fact $Y^2 = 13.34 > \chi^2_{6,\,0.05} = 12.59$. Such a large value of Y^2 is unlikely to be generated given that ABC/CD is true, and we must formally reject this model as inadequate. Note that we have 6 df for this test, reflecting the fact that though the model contained ten parameters and thus ten 'constraints' imposed by the observed frequencies on the expected, there are still six remaining sets of constraints that were not imposed. In other words, the unsaturated model ABC/CD sets six parameters to zero, which, if they were otherwise included, would produce a saturated model fitting the observed data exactly but with $0\ df$.

Model selection strategies

It is by now apparent that a large number of models can be fitted to a set of observed data, and that one suitable criterion for choosing a model is the associated Y^2 value. However, minimising this statistic cannot be the sole criterion since we would inevitably choose the saturated model from among the many candidates in view of its perfect fit and Y^2 of zero. We are also interested in parsimonious models, in other words in choosing the simplest model that is not inconsistent with the observed data. Such a model is easier to interpret than complex models (such as the saturated model) and identifies the essential relations between the variables without attributing undue weight to apparent relations that could quite easily be due to sampling variation. Bishop *et al.* (1975, p. 313) discuss how the use of a simpler model may actually give greater precision to the estimates $\{e_{ijk}\}$ than a more complex model from the same hierarchical family that is also consistent with the observed frequencies.

Various strategies have been adopted to determine which parameters of the saturated model can legitimately be set to zero. These are designed to obviate the necessity to compare all possible combinations of parameters, since the number of such model comparisons can easily get out of hand.

Saturated model estimates

One course of action which could be to simply include in an unsaturated model those parameters with large standardised values when the saturated log–linear model is fitted. Although this method can provide an initial guide to potentially suitable models (see Goodman 1970; 1971; Bishop *et al.* 1975), there are a number of reasons why such models should be treated with scepticism. These have been pointed out by Aitkin (1979; 1980), who notes that, when the saturated model is fitted, the standard errors, and hence the standardised values of particular effects, are adjusted for all others, and hence 'a substantial loss of power may result' (Aitkin 1979, p. 240). In other words, by this method the analyst will be less likely·to detect associations that actually exist. This is reiterated in Aitkin (1980) where it is argued that, 'if many terms in the saturated model are unnecessary, the standard errors of the estimated parameters may be considerably inflated, leading to small z scores for terms which are in fact necessary'. Relating this to the parameter estimates of the saturated model fitted in Table 2.5, it is note-worthy that of those parameters involving the interaction of factors A, B and C with response D, only one, λ_{11}^{CD}, has a significantly large z score (standardised value) with $z = \hat{\lambda}^{CD}/\sqrt{[\text{Var}\,(\hat{\lambda}^{CD})]} = 0.318/0.132 = 2.41$.

Another reason to avoid undue weight being given to standardised values obtained from the saturated model is that, 'the z scores for each parameter in the saturated model depend on the parameterisation of the model, that is, on the constraints imposed on the usual overparameterised model' (Aitkin 1980). This is exemplified by the widely differing parameter estimates produced by Holt (1979) using two alternative systems of constraints and discussed at the end of Chapter 1.

Stepwise methods

Using these methods, parameters are added or subtracted to arrive at models more parsimonious than the saturated model, using the backward selection or forward elimination procedures familiar to exponents of multiple regression (Draper & Smith 1981).

The basic difference between forward selection and backward elimination is that one is, essentially, the reverse of the other, although 'it cannot be expected that a backward selection technique will lead to the same result as a forward selection technique' (Wermuth 1976, p. 256). Both methods require the analyst to commence from an initial model and in the version described by Goodman

(1971) and outlined in Fienberg (1980) the initial model for a four-way table is one of the following set.

Model	Parameters set to zero
$A/B/C/D$	all two-way and higher interactions
$AB/AC/AD/BC/BD/CD$	all three-way and higher interactions
$ABC/ABD/BCD/ACD$	all four-way interactions
$ABCD$	none

The first three of these models are fitted (or more if the table is of higher dimension) to determine a starting point. If, say, $A/B/C/D$ does not fit the data using the Y^2 approximation to χ^2, but $AB/AC/AD/BC/BD/CD$ and $ABC/ABD/BCD/ACD$ do ($ABCD$ will always fit perfectly), then one searches for a model between $A/B/C/D$ and $AB/AC/AD/BC/BD/CD$.

Using backward elimination, the procedure is to set to zero the least significant parameter of two-way association. Thus we arrive at a more parsimonious model, but the removal of one parameter has the consequence of automatically increasing Y^2. We are justified in removing the parameter if it is found that the consequent increase in Y^2 is minimal, and this is assessed by a conditional test of the parameter.

Parameter (set) removed	Increase in Y^2	Increase in df
AB or $\{\lambda_{ij}^{AB}\}$	3.3	1

In the above hypothetical example, the increase in Y^2 does not exceed the critical value of 3.84 ($\chi^2_{1,\,0.05} = 3.84$) and thus the AB effect need not be retained. Note that the increase in df need not necessarily be 1, but depends on the number of independent parameters in the omitted set. The model $AC/AD/BC/BD/CD$ is thus adopted. The next least significant parameter set is then removed and the consequent increase in Y^2 examined to see if it is inordinately large. If this is AC, then the two models being compared are $AC/AD/BC/BD/CD$ and $AD/BC/BD/CD$. As above, the conditional test of the AC parameter is the difference between the Y^2 of the two models that are identical except for AC. This difference is compared with $\chi^2_{d,\,0.05}$, where d is the difference in the degrees of freedom.

The possibility of adding back previously excluded terms should be investigated. Thus, it may be that the reintroduction of AB will produce a significant reduction in Y^2, even though its removal did not formerly create a significant increase. This is because the Y^2 associated with any particular parameter set is conditional on the other parameters present. This process of eliminating successive parameters and attempting to re-introduce previously excluded ones continues until we are unable to delete or add any terms, in which case we have arrived at a satisfactory model. An example of stepwise selection applied in this way to the spatial behaviour data of Table 2.5 is given later in this chapter (see Tables 3.16–3.20) where comparisons are made with the outcome of other methods.

As mentioned previously, another strategy for selecting an initial model, from which parameters are subsequently successively eliminated, is to incorporate those parameters that have large standardised values (exceeding ±1.96) in the saturated model into an unsaturated one. This is adopted by Upton (1978*a*, p. 74). In this exercise, the previously mentioned sceptical stance should be adopted, and the comments made by Upton (1981*a*) are worth repeating, since he notes that, 'Fitting the saturated model usually provides an immediate initial guide as to which interactions are of importance. I have said usually, but, in fact, prior to the present data, I do not recall a failure. What is unique, so far as my experience is concerned, is the number of variables here present, and I presume that it is this large number coupled with an average cell frequency of less than four which is the source of the present trouble, since on this occasion only one or two of the required interactions are clearly indicated by the saturated model.' What we have here then is a case where the sheer complexity of the fitted saturated model results in a reduction in the power of the model to detect significant interactions. The data in question are discussed in Chapter 4.

Since by using this strategy we are not restricted to searching within a particular hierarchical level, the exclusion of a particular parameter set may imply the exclusion of others. Thus the conditional test of a parameter set may require more-careful model parameterisation, with the explicit introduction of the implied parameter sets. For example, in order to test *ABCD*, one needs to compare *ABCD/AE/BE/CE/DE* and *ABC/ABD/ACD/BCD/AE/BE/CE/DE* which differ only by the exclusion of *ABCD* from the latter.

Screening

It has already been mentioned that scrutiny of the standardised values of the saturated model should be done with care, since the parameter standard errors are overestimated. Also, it is apparent from the above comments that the parameter estimates and their contribution to the overall Y^2 can vary depending on which other parameters they are conditional on.

Useful information about the need to incorporate a particular parameter into an initial unsaturated model can be obtained by screening (Brown 1976) the data. This involves making a number of estimates of the Y^2 contribution of each parameter as opposed to single point estimates as above. The purpose of the estimates is to provide approximate bounds to the range of the Y^2 contribution which we have already acknowledged as a conditional quantity.

In order to estimate these bounds, two extreme situations are compared. As Upton (1978a, p. 88) points out, the 'marginal' test tests an effect, say ABC, by comparing a simple model, in which the effect is the most complex parameter, with an even simpler model from which ABC is absent. Thus ABC and $AB/AC/BC$ are compared. The Y^2 contribution of ABC is obtained from a test 'adjusted for all effects marginal to it' (Aitkin 1979, p. 240).

The 'partial' test compares two relatively complex models, both of which are identical except for the parameter set under test, which is now a simple effect. In our example, $ABC/ABD/BCD/ACD$ is compared with $ABD/BCD/ACD$. The models thus adjust the effect 'for all main effects and two-way interactions, and all three-way interactions' (Aitkin 1979, p. 210).

Each parameter tested therefore has two associated statistics indicating the bounds of its Y^2 contribution after adjusting for the presence or absence of various other effects. If both Y^2 contributions are large, using the critical value of the appropriate χ^2 distribution as a guide, then there is evidence that the parameter sets are required in an initial unsaturated model. If both marginal and partial Y^2 contributions are small, then one's initial model may exclude the parameter. If one contribution is large and the other small, then models both with and without the parameter in question should be considered in a subsequent stepwise selection procedure.

Screening is not without its critics, for, as pointed out by Aitkin (1979), the evidence presented by the marginal association test, since it is based on simple models, is not adjusted for excluded effects represented by parameters such as D, AD, BD and so on. If there are substantial interactions involving variable D, 'this may lead to substantial confounding of effects' (Aitkin 1980), where the interactions involving variable D are attributed to the parameter being screened. The partial association tests may suffer from a loss of power due to the fact that they involve fairly complex models.

A further, but really rather minor, disadvantage of both screening and stepwise selection procedures is the large number of models that must be fitted. Using screening to identify an initial unsaturated model from which to commence stepwise searches, one is required to fit not a single model as in the case of the saturated model, but four models per parameter. Even with rapidly converging programs, such as ECTA and GLIM, which are designed to facilitate the fitting of a large number of alternative models in quick succession without recourse to complex design matrices, a lot of computer time can be used.

One way in which the number of parameters to be screened can be reduced is to decide *a priori* on a number of parameters to be included in the final model. This subset need not therefore be screened as we are in no doubt that it should be included. A rule which will become familiar later is that if we make the distinction between factor and response variables, then we must of necessity include all the factor interactions in any final hierarchical model. We provide the rationale for this rule in Chapter 4 but, basically, it is necessary so that our estimation of factor–response interactions is not distorted by interactions between factors that exist but are unrepresented in fitted models. This inclusion of all factor interactions greatly reduces the number of parameters that are optional to the model and hence require screening. Thus in the four-way Table 2.5 of Chapter 2, we may consider variables A, B and C as factors and D as the response, in which case the ABC interaction, and all those implied by it, are included in the final model and all models leading to the final model. The results of screening the optional factor–response interactions from Table 2.5 are given in Table 3.4. These may be obtained 'manually', though screening is an easily automated procedure which may be added to standard programs, as has been done at the University of Essex. Screening is also now an integral part of the BMDP package.

The screening of AD involves fitting ABC/AD and ABC/D to obtain the marginal contribution, and $ABC/AD/BD/CD$ and $ABC/BD/CD$ to obtain the partial contribution. We note at this stage that the only obviously significant parameter is CD, with both contributions exceeding the critical value of $3.84 = \chi^2_{1,\,0.05}$. This supports our earlier conclusion based on saturated model parameters. Further discussion of this result is deferred to a later section of this chapter where alternative model selection strategies are discussed.

Table 3.4. *The results of screening Table 2.5 treating A, B and C as factors and D as a response*

Parameter	df	Marginal contribution	Partial contribution
AD	1	4.6	2.2
BD	1	2.2	0.2
CD	1	7.4	4.4
ABD	1	0.0	0.1
ACD	1	0.2	0.0
BCD	1	2.2	2.5
$ABCD$	1	1.2	1.2

Simultaneous test procedures

Aitkin (1978; 1979; 1980) has introduced what are referred to as simultaneous test procedures (STP) to compensate for the enhanced probability of encountering, merely as a result of chance, interactions that are 'significant' using conventional criteria when a set of interactions is scrutinised. The STP accomplish this by providing adjusted significance levels in order to detect truly significant interactions, that is, those that are more than the unavoidable outcome of chance. The initial step is to convert the usual type I error rate into adjusted type I error rates as follows.

If, for example, we first determine a type I error rate α, conventionally set at 5%, then a model with k effects to be tested will have an overall type I error rate of $\gamma = 1 - (1 - \alpha)^k$ for the null hypothesis that all these k effects are null. Therefore, if a model has 11 effects to be tested, then $\gamma = 1 - (0.95)^{11} = 0.431$. Such a situation would arise if we were testing the significance of simultaneously setting to zero all parameters representing two-way, three-way and four-way interactions in a 2^4-way table.

We know that there is a 5% chance of a type I error on each parameter, and hence a 43.1% chance of at least one incorrect rejection of a true null hypothesis. If one is prepared to accept the per effect risk of 5% for a type I error, as is usual, then this implies acceptance of the overall risk of 43.1%. Table 3.5 illustrates the relative propensity of the individual and family errors, since it gives an idea of the standardised values (approximately normally distributed with zero mean and unit variance) that would on average occur were the null hypothesis that all 11 parameters are zero actually true. Note that, though 'significant' standardised values exceeding 1.96 only occurred on five of the 110 occasions that numbers

Table 3.5. *Simulated parameter estimates*

Para-meter set	1	2	3	4	5	6	7	8	9	10
λ^{AB}	0.75	0.44	1.28	−0.92	−0.49	−1.02	−0.36	<u>2.50</u>	1.20	0.26
λ^{AC}	0.49	−0.81	−1.64	−0.13	0.43	0.51	−0.33	1.23	0.83	0.69
λ^{AD}	−0.90	0.08	1.29	−1.61	0.80	−0.84	0.58	−0.45	−1;31	−0.14
λ^{BC}	−0.09	−1.08	0.04	−0.53	−0.13	0.03	<u>2.07</u>	−1.81	−0.40	−0.56
λ^{BD}	0.48	−0.59	0.45	−0.47	−0.43	1.87	−<u>1.12</u>	−0.64	1.24	−0.34
λ^{CD}	−0.48	1.79	<u>2.80</u>	−0.77	−0.38	−0.81	−1.18	−0.29	−0.07	−1.07
λ^{ABC}	0.45	0.08	−<u>0.36</u>	−0.31	0.13	0.43	0.67	−1.20	0.30	0.30
λ^{ABD}	0.58	−0.51	1.84	−1.16	−<u>2.17</u>	0.97	0.94	1.37	1.76	1.09
λ^{BCD}	−1.40	0.45	0.81	0.70	−<u>0.76</u>	0.80	−0.75	0.06	0.34	−0.51
λ^{ACD}	0.47	1.54	1.32	0.58	0.32	0.52	−0.15	−0.77	−0.04	0.28
λ^{ABCD}	1.61	−0.46	1..64	0.58	<u>2.01</u>	0.92	−0.22	0.56	0.31	0.66

were generated from the N $(0, 1)$ distribution, roughly in accordance with the known propensity of type I errors, the null hypothesis that all 11 parameters are simultaneously zero would be rejected (wrongly) on four of the ten simultaneous tests represented by the ten columns of Table 3.5. To put it another way, since each of the columns of Table 3.5 is an equally likely set of standardised values when all 11 parameters are actually zero, there is approximately a 40% chance of coming across a set of 11 standardised values that forces one to conclude that at least one of the parameters is not zero. This is roughly in accordance with $\gamma = 0.431$.

Given a 43% level of risk overall, we therefore reject the null hypothesis if, as a result of fitting the model with all 11 parameters set to zero, $Y^2 \geqslant \chi^2_{11, 0.431}$. If $\chi^2_{11, 0.05}$ is taken as the critical value, there is a ridiculously small level of risk per parameter and the null hypothesis is accepted far too often. If $\chi^2_{1, 0.05}$ is chosen as the critical value, one is advocating an overall type I error rate of 97.4% since $\chi^2_{11, 0.974} = \chi^2_{1, 0.05} = 3.84$ and one's final model would comprise many parameters – exactly the opposite result to that which Aitkin's rules are designed to achieve.

If the overall type I error rate exceeds 0.5, then the analysis tends to be liberal rather than conservative and adoption of such a value would reflect the importance of not overlooking possibly interesting effects. As Aitkin (1978, p. 205) notes in the analogous context of ANOVA models, 'the choice of α and γ is determined to some extent by the purpose of the study' and 'in a confirmatory study, a more conservative choice of $\alpha = 0.025$ or $\alpha = 0.01$ (corresponding to $\gamma = 0.316$ or 0.14) would be appropriate'.

The desire to avoid overfitting characterises the STP. Aitkin (1980, p. 177) describes how stepwise procedures tend to exacerbate this phenomenon and this leads to extra computer usage, since what were initially considered to be significant effects may be subsequently rejected as models entering the effects in different orders are compared. For example, the test (using STP) that all three-way interactions are zero may indicate that there is insufficient evidence to believe otherwise, whereas stepwise fitting of the individual three-way effects may find one significant. However, it must be remembered that the 4 three-way effects in a four-way table can be fitted in 24 different stepwise sequences of which one, say ABC, ABD, then BCD, and finally ACD, is actually used. Undue significance should not therefore be assigned to the fact that one of the four parameters of one of the 24 possible orders in which they could have been considered produces a Y^2 value beyond the conventional critical value of, say, $\chi^2_{d, 0.05}$. What STP does is allow for the fact that different sequences will produce different results and that, occasionally, we are going to hit on one that appears significant merely by chance.

Applications of simultaneous test procedures

Illustrations of STP are given by applying it to data sets to which unsaturated models were previously fitted using stepwise procedures (Upton & Fingleton 1979; Upton 1978a). The initial application, however, is to the 2^4 psychiatric data initially analysed by Wermuth (1976) and which is the basis of Aitkin's (1980) paper.

STP applied to the Wermuth (1976) data

The data consist of psychiatric patients cross-classified by four dichotomous 'state of mind' indices to produce a 2^4 table. Apart from Aitkin (1980) and Wermuth (1976), the data have also been previously analysed by Benedetti & Brown (1978). Table 3.6 contains the details.

Initially, what is required is an overall type I error rate $\gamma = 1 - (1 - \alpha)^k$ for the null hypothesis that all k effects to be tested in the model are null. Equivalently, one is testing that the pooled two-, three- and four-way interactions are null. With $\alpha = 5\%$, $\gamma = 0.431$.

The family type I error rates are next determined for the pooled two-way interactions (γ_2), three-way interactions (γ_3) and the four-way interaction (γ_4).

$$\gamma_2 = 1 - (0.95)^6 = 0.265$$
$$\gamma_3 = 1 - (0.95)^4 = 0.185$$
$$\gamma_4 = 1 - (0.95)^1 = 0.05$$

Table 3.6. *Wermuth's psychiatric data*

	D_1					
	C_1				C_2	
	B_1	B_2			B_1	B_2
A_1	15	9		A_1	23	14
A_2	30	32		A_2	22	16
	D_2					
	C_1				C_2	
	B_1	B_2			B_1	B_2
A_1	25	46		A_1	14	47
A_2	22	27		A_2	8	12

key: A = 'validity'. B_1 = hysteric. C_2 = extrovert.
       A_1 = energetic. B_2 = rigid. D = 'depression'.
       A_2 = psychasthenic. C = 'stability'. D_1 = acute depression.
       B = 'solidity'. C_1 = introvert. D_2 = none.

The type I error rate for pooled three- and four-way interactions is $\gamma_{3,4} = 1 - (0.95)^5 = 0.226$. These error rates are required to obtain relevant critical values appropriate for testing the significance of whole families of effects. The tests are based on what is called an analysis of deviance table obtained by fitting log–linear models in sequence and by recording in the table the change in goodness of fit Y^2, or deviance, that ensues. The analysis is based on Aitkin (1980) who uses 'GLIM' notation though the models he fits are identical to those given in Tables 3.7–3.11.

Table 3.7 indicates the reduction in Y^2 as extra parameters are added representing all two-way, three-way and four-way interactions. It is now possible to test the necessity for these interactions. The four-way interaction $\{\lambda_{ijkl}^{ABCD}\}$ is obviously not required since it produces absolutely no improvement in the goodness-of-fit at the cost of 1 df. Generally, the deviance would be compared with $\chi^2_{1,\,0.05}$.

In order to test the three-way interaction, both the three-way and four-way deviances are pooled and compared with $\chi^2_{5,\,0.226} = 6.93$. These pooled effects are significant, since $8.48 > \chi^2_{5,\,0.226}$.

The next step is to define what Aikin (1978, 1979; 1980) calls a 'minimal adequate' subset of the three- and four-way interactions. In the 2^4 table, there are 1 four-way and 4 three-way parameter sets altogether; an adequate subset would not normally include all of these.

A subset is deemed adequate if the deviance of the omitted terms (adjusted for those retained) does not exceed the critical value for the pooled set. There may be several adequate subsets with the property.

A minimal adequate subset is not only adequate, but it also contains no proper adequate subset. Thus if $\{\lambda^{ABC}\}$, $\{\lambda^{ABD}\}$ and $\{\lambda^{BCD}\}$ is an adequate subset and $\{\lambda^{ABC}\}$ alone is adequate, then the former is not minimal adequate whereas the latter is.

What this means in practice is that parameters are entered in a particular sequence and the reduction in deviance noted. If the omitted terms produce only a relatively small increase in deviance (adjusted for retained terms and

Table 3.7. *Analysis of deviance entering all two-way, all three-way and all four-way parameters*

Model	df	Y^2	Source	df	Deviance
$A/B/C/D$	11	68.89			
$AB/AC/AD/BC/BD/CD$	5	8.48	two-way	6	60.41
$ABC/ABD/BCD/ACD$	1	0	three-way	4	8.48
$ABCD$	0	0	four-way	1	0

compared with the critical χ^2 for the pooled set), then an adequate subset has been identified. It is minimal adequate if when only some of the parameters in the adequate subset are retained the adjusted deviance of the omitted terms is still comparatively small.

Aitkin (1980, p. 175) compares the sequence of models given in Table 3.8 in the search for a minimal adequate subset of the three- and four-way effects. (Note that in his original analysis the deviance associated with the ABD parameter is incorrectly given as 4.20.) Thus we see that including the 6 two-way interactions reduces Y^2 by 60.41. A minimal adequate subset appropriate to this sequence contains three parameter sets $\{\lambda^{ABC}\}$, $\{\lambda^{ACD}\}$ and $\{\lambda^{BCD}\}$. The deviance increase due to omitting $\{\lambda^{ABD}\}$ and $\{\lambda^{ABCD}\}$ is not significant compared with $\chi^2_{5,\,0.226} = 6.93$. However, although the retained set (ABC, ACD, BCD) is minimal adequate, none of the deviances associated with the retained parameters is large, whereas one of the omitted parameters (ABD) produces a large deviance.

This suggests that other minimal adequate subsets exist which are perhaps more parsimonious and which include ABD. It is sensible to enter this parameter first to see if it is itself minimal adequate.

The results of entering the effects in an alternative order commencing with ABD are given in Table 3.9 where it can be seen that by entering ABD first it is

Table 3.8. *Analysis of deviance entering three-way effects, order 1*

Model	df	Y^2	Source	df	Deviance
$A/B/C/D$	11	68.89			
$AB/AC/AD/BC/BD/CD$	5	8.48	two-way	6	60.41
$ABC/AD/BD/CD$	4	7.76	ABC	1	0.72
$ABC/ACD/BD$	3	7.44	ACD	1	0.32
$ABC/ACD/BCD$	2	4.35	BCD	1	3.09
$ABC/ACD/BCD/ABD$	1	0.003	ABD	1	4.35
			$ABCD$	1	0.003

Table 3.9. *Analysis of deviance entering three-way effects, order 2*

Model	df	Y^2	Source	df	Deviance
$AB/AC/AD/BC/BD/CD$	5	8.48	two-way	6	60.41
$ABD/AC/BC/CD$	4	3.27	ABD	1	5.21
$ABD/BCD/AC$	3	0.91	BCD	1	2.36
$ABD/BCD/ABC$	2	0.41	ABC	1	0.50
$ABD/BCD/ABC/ACD$	1	0.003	ACD	1	0.41
			$ABCD$	1	0.003

itself a minimal adequate subset, since $2.36 + 0.5 + 0.41 + 0.003 = 3.273 < 6.93 = \chi^2_{5, 0.226}$. This has more-attractive properties than the previous minimal adequate subset since none of the omitted terms are important. In general, the comparative reduction in deviance and the standardised values (for unsaturated models) indicate which parameter set should be entered first in subsequent permutations to see if they are minimal adequate. If the adjusted deviance of the omitted terms is still too large, then other important terms should be entered.

It is therefore necessary to include $\{\lambda^{ABD}\}$ in any subsequent model. The next step is to see which subset of the pooled two-, three- and four-way effects can be omitted, bearing in mind that including $\{\lambda^{ABD}\}$ implies 3 two-way effects.

In order to test whether the remaining two-, three- and four-way effects can be omitted, we compare the sequence of models given in Table 3.10. Entered in this order, both CD and AC need to be retained, since omitting all terms but CD gives a deviance of $13.43 + 0.27 + 3.27 = 16.97 > \chi^2_{11, 0.431} = 11.15$ for all 11 two-, three- and four-way effects. However, entering the effects as in Table 3.11 allows just AC to be retained.

Thus the excluded set (CD, BC and residual) produces a small deviance of $4.84 + 0.27 + 3.27 = 8.38 < \chi^2_{11, 0.431} = 11.15$. This gives us our final minimal model, ABD/AC. The model indicates that the combined occurrence of the levels of variables validity and solidity differs from what one would expect were

Table 3.10. *Analysis of deviance entering two-way effects, order 1*

Model	df	Y^2	Source	df	Deviance
equiprobability	15	87.21			
ABD/C	7	18.41	C, ABD and implied parameters	8	68.80
ABD/CD	6	16.97	CD	1	1.44
$ABD/CD/AC$	5	3.54	AC	1	13.43
$ABD/CD/AC/BC$	4	3.27	BC	1	0.27
			3 three-way, 1 four-way	4	3.27

Table 3.11. *Analysis of deviance entering two-way effects, order 2*

Model	df	Y^2	Source	df	Deviance
ABD/C	7	18.41			
ABD/AC	6	8.38	AC	1	10.03
$ABD/CD/AC$	5	3.54	CD	1	4.84
$ABD/CD/AC/BC$	4	3;27	BC	1	0.27
			residual	4	3.27

the occurrence of one of these states of mind independent of the other, and the relation between validity and solidity depends on whether or not the patient is depressed (*ABD*). Given this, validity is also related to stability (*AC*), but conditional on these relations there is no evidence in the data of the other possible two-way interactions between stability and depression (*CD*) and solidity and stability (*BC*), as they comprise part of the excluded set of Table 3.11.

Although we have arrived at a 'final' model *ABD*/*AC*, it must be stressed that we have not reached the end of the analysis. Further analysis generally entails the study of the residuals which are functions of the observed and expected frequencies in a search for missing factors responsible for organised patterns of positive and negative residuals (a topic we explore in Chapter 5) or for anomalously large differences between observed and expected frequencies. For example, the existence of a single 'deviant' cell in a contingency table may require one to fit a fairly complex model to the entire table to cope with the abnormal cell, even though the remaining cells may follow a fairly straight-forward trend which, when considered alone, could be reproduced by a relatively simple and easy-to-interpret model. Given that the 'final' model fitted to the Wermuth (1976) data is fairly complex, the last part of the analysis therefore involves attempts to fit a simple model to only part of Table 3.6. We delay this until after residuals have been discussed in more detail in Chapter 5. It is at this juncture that the 'routine' of Aitkin's STP approach breaks down, though, as will be seen in Chapter 5, the reasoning behind some of our methods of studying residuals has a very similar logical basis to that of the STP.

STP applied to the Upton & Fingleton (1979) data

As a further illustration of STP, let us reconsider the data initially presented in Table 2.5 and already discussed in Chapter 2 with respect to the saturated model and in association with screening earlier in this chapter. There are four dichotomous variables, and this leads to the following error rates.

If we set $\alpha = 0.10$, then the critical values for the subsets of pooled effects are as follows:

four-way	$\gamma_4 = 1 - (0.9)^1 = 0.10$	$\chi^2_{1,0.1} = 2.71$
three-, four-way	$\gamma_{3,4} = 1 - (0.9)^5 = 0.41$	$\chi^2_{5,0.41} = 5.05$
two-, three-, four-way	$\gamma = 1 - (0.9)^{11} = 0.686$	$\chi^2_{11,0.686} = 8.30$

Thus the family type I error rate is 68.6%, rather higher than Aitkin recommends. If we set $\alpha = 0.05$, the critical values are:

four-way	$\gamma_4 = 1 - (0.95)^1 = 0.05$	$\chi^2_{1,0.05} = 3.84$
three-, four-way	$\gamma_{3,4} = 1 - (0.95)^5 = 0.226$	$\chi^2_{5,0.226} = 6.93$
two-, three-, four-way	$\gamma = 1 - (0.95)^{11} = 0.431$	$\chi^2_{11,0.431} = 11.15$

The family type I error rate is now at an acceptable level.

Using these values, the analysis of deviance in Table 3.12 shows that the pooled three- and four-way interactions are not significant, since

$$5.51 + 1.18 = 6.69 < \chi^2_{5,\,0.226} = 6.93.$$

We can omit these terms.

The two-way interactions are considered next. We may enter these in a number of different orders, two of which are given in Tables 3.13 and 3.14. Since

$$12.33 + 4.42 + 6.69 > \chi^2_{11,\,0.431} = 11.15,$$

we cannot say that the first four parameters comprise a minimal adequate subset. In fact we need to retain all the two-way interactions apart from *CD*.

Table 3.12. *Analysis of deviance, all two-, three- and four-way effects*

Model	df	Y^2	Source	df	Deviance
A/B/C/D	11	87.76			
AB/AC/AD/BC/BD/CD	5	6.69	two-way effects	6	81.07
ABC/ABD/ACD/BCD	1	1.18	three-way effects	4	5.51
ABCD	0	0	four-way effects	1	1.18

Table 3.13. *Analysis of deviance entering two-way effects, order 1*

Model	df	Y^2	Source	df	Deviance
A/B/C/D	11	87.76			
AD/C/B	10	83.17	*AD*	1	4.59
AD/BD/C	9	81.00	*BD*	1	2.17
AD/BD/BC	8	39.96	*BC*	1	41.04
AD/BD/BC/AB	7	23.44	*AB*	1	16.52
AD/BD/BC/AB/AC	6	11.11	*AC*	1	12.33
AD/BD/BC/AB/AC/CD	5	6.69	*CD*	1	4.42
			residual	5	6.69

Table 3.14. *Analysis of deviance entering two-way effects, order 2*

Model	df	Y^2	Source	df	Deviance
A/B/C/D	11	87.76			
BC/A/D	10	46.73	*BC*	1	41.03
AB/BC/D	9	29.16	*AB*	1	17.57
AB/BC/AC/D	8	16.84	*AC*	1	12.32
AB/BC/AC/CD	7	9.40	*CD*	1	7.44
AB/BC/AC/CD/AD	6	6.90	*AD*	1	2.50
AB/BC/AC/CD/AD/BD	5	6.69	*BD*	1	0.21

If we enter the effects in the order of Table 3.14, we find that a more parsimonious model is obtained. The minimal adequate subset now consists of BC, AB, AC and CD, since $2.5 + 0.21 + 6.69 < \chi^2_{11,\,0.431} = 11.15$. Note that we can legitimately eliminate AD, even though it produced a significant reduction in deviance when entered first.

It is interesting that the stepwise selection procedure outlined earlier produces the same final model, as shown by the model-fitting sequence of Tables 3.15 and 3.16 which commences with the model of all two-way interactions. The order in which the parameters are eliminated is based on their standardised values resulting from fitting this model. Unlike BD and AD, CD cannot be eliminated since this produces a significant increase in Y^2. The following sequence shows that, using this same criterion, no other parameter of the model $AB/AC/BC/CD$ can be set to zero. The last model fitted illustrates that attempts to reintroduce previously eliminated parameters with the intention of significantly improving the fit are to no avail. We thus conclude that the minimal model, identified by STP and stepwise selection, is $AB/AC/BC/CD$.

Of course, the above analysis is somewhat contrived since, in reality, one would probably wish to distinguish between factors (A) age, (B) income and (C) car ownership, and the response (D) behaviour. In our earlier discussion of screening applied to this data set, we gave a brief justification, when the factor-response distinction is made, for fitting only models that include all the interactions between factors so as not to distort estimates of factor-

Table 3.15. *Results of the stepwise selection procedure*

Model	df	Y^2	Parameter	df	Y^2
$AB/AC/AD/BC/BD/CD$	5	6.69			
$AB/AC/AD/BC/CD$	6	6.90	BD	1	0.21
$AB/AC/BC/CD$	7	9.40	AD	1	2.50
$AB/AC/BC/D$	8	16.84	CD	1	7.44

Table 3.16. *The results of attempting to go beyond the finally selected minimal model*

Model	df	Y^2	Parameter	df	Y^2
$CD/AB/BC$	8	21.73	AC	1	12.33
$AC/BC/CD$	8	18.18	AB	1	8.78
$AB/AC/CD$	8	41.65	BC	1	32.25
$AB/AC/BC/CD/BD$	6	8.94	BD	1	0.46

response interactions. Further, more-detailed, consideration of this issue is given in Chapter 4.

Given that ABC and all its implied subordinates are represented in all models, the STP is slightly different, as can be seen by comparing Tables 3.12–3.14 with Tables 3.17–3.19. For example, because of the inclusion of parameters implied by ABC in all models, there are now only 7 two-, and three- and four-way effects that could be set to zero, as opposed to 11 previously. Such differences are reflected in the family type I error rates that are now adopted. Using these values, the analysis of deviance shows that the pooled three and four-way effects are not significant since $2.76 + 1.18 < \chi^2_{4,\,0.185} = 6.2$. These can be set to zero. However, we cannot legitimately set all two-, three- and four-way effects to zero since $10.13 + 2.76 + 1.18 > \chi^2_{7,\,0.302} = 8.36$.

The next stage is to find a minimal adequate subset of the two-way effects. One sequence in which they can be entered is as in Table 3.18. Since

$$1.13 + 4.41 + 3.94 = 9.48 > \chi^2_{7,\,0.302} = 8.36,$$

we cannot say that AD is a minimal adequate subset. In fact, we also need to retain BD. If the effects are entered in another order commencing with CD,

Table 3.17. *Initial analysis of deviance with three factors and a response*

Model	df	Y^2	Source	df	Deviance
ABC/D	7	14.07			
$ABC/AD/BD/CD$	4	3.94	two-way effects	3	10.13
$ABC/ABD/ACD/BCD$	1	1.18	three-way effects	3	2.76
$ABCD$	0	0	four-way effects	1	1.18

$$\gamma_4 = 1 - (0.95)^1 = 0.05 \qquad \chi^2_{1,\,0.05} = 3.84$$
$$\gamma_{3,4} = 1 - (0.95)^4 = 0.185 \qquad \chi^2_{4,\,0.185} = 6.20$$
$$\gamma = 1 - (0.95)^7 = 0.302 \qquad \chi^2_{7,\,0.302} = 8.36$$

Table 3.18. *Analysis of deviance with three factors and a response, two-way effects entered in order 1*

Model	df	Y^2	Source	df	Deviance
ABC/D	7	14.07			
ABC/AD	6	9.48	AD	1	4.59
$ABC/AD/BD$	5	8.35	BD	1	1.13
$ABC/AD/BD/CD$	4	3.94	CD	1	4.41
			residual	4	3.94

then this parameter alone becomes the minimal adequate subset; we now find that $2.5 + 0.2 + 3.94 = 6.64 < \chi^2_{7, 0.302} = 8.36$ (see Table 3.19).

Thus the minimal model is *ABC/CD*, exactly the same final model as that previously discovered by Upton & Fingleton (1979) via stepwise selection. Furthermore, the *CD* parameter is precisely the one unequivocally identified as significant by the earlier screening operation. Thus we conclude that car owners tend to by-pass their nearest centre. This in itself is a rather predictable result, although the absence of the *AD* and *BD* interactions was not.

Of course, we can never be fully satisfied that a 'final' model has been arrived at, since, as was intimated earlier, the presence or absence of 'significant' effects is very much a sample size phenomenon. Although there is no evidence in the data for *AD* and *BD* interactions, representing the 'effects' on behaviour of age and income respectively, this does not mean that such associations do not exist, for they could be revealed in a larger sample and may lie dormant in the present sample that only reveals the more prominent *CD* interaction.

This is not an argument for increasing the size of samples *ad infinitum*, for, not only would the cost of collecting the data escalate tremendously, but also many minor, uninteresting, complex (and hence difficult to describe), but statistically significant, 'effects' would be discovered. Given large sample data it would be more difficult to reduce to a parsimonious model like *ABC/CD* that outlines the broad trends in the data if conventional significance levels were adhered to, and thus difficult to derive simple statements of the main interactions in the data. In a large sample analysis in which the analyst gives more weight to the goal of broadly outlining the main trends in the data than to detecting 'significant' interactions, model selection techniques relying on significance tests may not be entirely helpful to the pragmatist searching for a 'useful' model. More detail of the large sample strategy is given in Chapter 6.

We have not reached the last stage of our analysis of Table 2.5, though it is probably unnecessary to search for deviant cells by analysing residuals, given

Table 3.19. *Analysis of deviance with three factors and a response; two-way effects entered in order 2*

Model	df	Y^2	Source	df	Deviance
ABC/D	7	14.07			
ABC/CD	6	6.64	*CD*	1	7.43
ABC/CD/AD	5	4.14	*AD*	1	2.50
ABC/CD/AD/BD	4	3.94	*BD*	1	0.20
			residual	4	3.94

such a simple final model. We see in Chapter 4 that extra information is hidden within this table, which can be extracted by multistage analysis.

STP applied to a 2^5 table

An exploratory application of the above techniques to a very large table is given below. The data, which are laid out in a compact format in Table 3.20, have been previously analysed by Upton (1978*a*) using stepwise selection techniques, and it is interesting to compare the two finally selected models, particularly as Upton found his only by 'bending the rules, albeit in a sensible fashion'. Thus what is being compared is an *ad hoc* approach in which the statistical significance of a particularly difficult-to-interpret parameter is overlooked, and a more automatic and regulated approach (STP) which ostensibly does not offer the analyst such latitude. The data set relate to the 1975 British referendum on entry into the EEC.

The per effect level of risk $\alpha = 0.025$, giving an overall type I error rate $\gamma = 1 - (0.975)^{26} = 0.482$. This indicates that there are 26 interaction effects: 10 two-way, 10 three-way, 5 four-way and 1 five-way. The overall type I error rate is within the limit of 0.5 regarded as appropriate by Aitkin (1979, p. 234; 1980, p. 173). The whole set of family error rates and critical values are as in Table 3.21.

The next step is to fit the sequence of models in Table 3.22. From Table 3.22 it is clear that we can reject the five-way effect. However, since

$$7.4 + 3.08 = 10.48 > \chi^2_{6, \, 0.141} = 9.64,$$

the pooled four- and five-way interactions are significant. It turns out that

Table 3.20. *A 2^5 table of voting preference data analysed by Upton (1978)*

A	B	C	D	E		A	B	C	D	E		A	B	C	D	E		A	B	C	D	E	
1	1	1	1	1	51	1	1	1	2	1	142	1	1	1	1	2	31	1	1	1	2	2	62
2	1	1	1	1	8	2	1	1	2	1	37	2	1	1	1	2	8	2	1	1	2	2	23
1	2	1	1	1	51	1	2	1	2	1	64	1	2	1	1	2	83	1	2	1	2	2	57
2	2	1	1	1	35	2	2	1	2	1	21	2	2	1	1	2	94	2	2	1	2	2	54
1	1	2	1	1	11	1	1	2	2	1	37	1	1	2	1	2	34	1	1	2	2	2	61
2	1	2	1	1	6	2	1	2	2	1	11	2	1	2	1	2	16	2	1	2	2	2	24
1	2	2	1	1	23	1	2	2	2	1	19	1	2	2	1	2	106	1	2	2	2	2	99
2	2	2	1	1	15	2	2	2	2	1	25	2	2	2	1	2	143	2	2	2	2	2	110

key: *A* 1 – in favour.   2 – not.
    B 1 – Conservative.   2 – not.
    C 1 – more than minimal legal schooling.   2 – only minimal schooling.
    D 1 – union member in household.   2 – none.
    E 1 – middle class.   2 – working class.

ABCD is a minimal adequate subset of these interactions, as shown by comparing the models in Table 3.23, since $1.81 + 4.23 = 6.04 < \chi^2_{6, 0.141} = 9.64$.

In order to examine the necessity for the three-way interactions, we next fit a model containing none except those implied by the significant four-way effect *ABCD*. The deviance of 9.87 in Table 3.24 is tested using the critical value of $\chi^2_{16, 0.333} = 17.83$. It can be seen that there is no need to retain any three-, four- or five-way interaction parameters in the model other than those already included. The Model *ABCD/AE/BE/CE/DE* fits well.

Table 3.21. *Error rates and critical values for STP*

$$\gamma = 1 - (0.975)^{26} = 0.482 \qquad \chi^2_{26, 0.482} = 25.66$$
$$\gamma_{3,4,5} = 1 - (0.975)^{16} = 0.333 \qquad \chi^2_{16, 0.333} = 17.83$$
$$\gamma_{4,5} = 1 - (0.975)^{6} = 0.141 \qquad \chi^2_{6, 0.141} = 9.64$$
$$\gamma_{5} = 1 - (0.975)^{1} = 0.025 \qquad \chi^2_{1, 0.025} = 5.05$$

Table 3.22. *Analysis of deviance entering all two-way, all three-way, all four-way and all five-way effects*

Model	df	Y^2	Source	df	Deviance
A/B/C/D/E	26	562.85			
AB/AC/AD/AE/BC/ BD/BE/CD/CE/DE	16	19.84	two-way interactions	10	543.01
ABC/ABD/ABE/ACD/ ACE/ADE/BCD/BCE/ BDE/CDE	6	10.48	three-way interactions	10	9.36
ABCD/ABCE/ABDE/ ACDE/BCDE	1	3.08	four-way interactions	5	7.40
ABCDE	0	0	five-way interactions	1	3.08

Table 3.23. *Analysis of deviance entering four-way effects*

Model	df	Y^2	Source	df	Deviance
ABC/ABD/ABE/ACD/ ACE/ADE/BCD/BCE/ BDE/CDE	6	10.48			
ABCD/ABE/ACE/ADE/ BCE/BDE/CDE	5	6.04	*ABCD*	1	4.44
ABCD/ACDE/ABE/BCE/ BDE	4	4.23	*ACDE*	1	1.81
			other four-, five-way interactions	4	4.23

To examine the necessity for the two-way interactions, the model $ABCD/E$, which sets to zero those not implied by the four-way effect, was fitted (Table 3.24). The Y^2 of 283.51 demonstrates the obvious necessity to include two-way interactions. The order of entry of the two-way effects given in Table 3.25 was chosen to attempt to identify a minimal adequate subset, using standardised values and deviance reductions as a guide.

Since, from Table 3.25, $10.46 + 9.87 = 20.33 < \chi^2_{26, 0.482} = 25.66$, then DE can be omitted, although it does make a rather large contribution to Y^2. Fitting in the sequence of Table 3.26 reaffirms the importance of DE and enables a minimal adequate subset to be created which excludes AE, since

$$13.59 + 9.87 = 23.46 < \chi^2_{26, 0.482} = 25.66.$$

Again, the excluded parameter, in this case AE, makes a seemingly important contribution to Y^2. The above sequence indicates that $ABCD/DE/CE/BE$ is the

Table 3.24. *Deviance for models with and without the two-way effects*

Model	df	Y^2
$ABCD/AE/BE/CE/DE$	11	9.87
$ABCD/E$	15	283.51

Table 3.25. *Analysis of deviance entering two-way effects, order 1*

Model	df	Y^2	Source	df	Deviance
$ABCD/E$	15	283.51			
$ABCD/AE$	14	231.13	AE	1	52.38
$ABCD/AE/BE$	13	135.09	BE	1	96.04
$ABCD/AE/BE/CE$	12	20.33	CE	1	114.76
$ABCD/AE/BE/CE/DE$	11	9.87	DE	1	10.46
			residual	11	9.87

Table 3.26. *Analysis of deviance entering two-way effects, order 2*

Model	df	Y^2	Source	df	Deviance
$ABCD/E$	15	283.51			
$ABCD/DE$	14	249.53	DE	1	33.98
$ABCD/DE/CE$	13	94.72	CE	1	154.81
$ABCD/DE/CE/BE$	12	23.46	BE	1	71.26
$ABCD/DE/CE/BE/AE$	11	9.87	AE	1	13.59
			residual	11	9.87

final model, but this does not fit the data, as $\chi^2_{12,\,0.05} = 21.03$. We thus return to the model suggested by Table 3.25, giving a final minimal model of *ABCD/ AE/BE/CE*. This is very similar to the model *ABCD/AE/BE/CE/DE* that Upton (1978*a*, p. 77) arrives at via stepwise selection. The marginally simpler model suggested by STP supports Aitkin's observation that backward elimination will, in certain circumstances, stop too soon and result in less parsimonious models than STP.

Unfortunately, both these models include the complex interaction *ABCD* and, as with the psychiatric data of Table 3.6 one might proceed to explore the possibility that this complex interaction is present simply to cope with one anomalous deviant cell that does not follow the general trend of the remainder of the table. Such an outlier would be identified using the methods described in Chapter 5 whereby a simpler model from which the complex parameter is absent is fitted to the complete table in the hope of identifying a large residual. Such a large difference between the observed and expected frequency would be due to the cell not following the general trend exhibited by the remainder of the table and encapsulated by the simple model.

Obviously, simply removing *ABCD* alone will still leave us with complex three-way interactions to interpret. Therefore, in an attempt to avoid these, it was decided to fit the model *D/AE/BE/CE* to Table 3.20, thus removing not only *ABCD* but also all its implied subordinate interactions. A poor fit can be expected from this model but this is not a prime concern at this stage – it is the source of the lack of fit which commands immediate interest. In fact, *D/AE/ BE/CE* fits very badly indeed ($Y^2 = 226.67 > \chi^2_{23,\,0.05} = 35.12$) and examination of the residuals does not enable us to attribute any large part of this lack of fit to an outlier eschewing the general trend. A more complex model is required.

Rather than persevering in an *ad hoc* search for models simpler than *ABCD/ AE/BE/CE* which account for the frequencies in most of the table, we now discuss an alternative way of removing troublesome effects than follows naturally from Upton's (1978*a*) stepwise selection strategy. He describes his final model *ABCD/AE/BE/CE/DE* thus, 'it cannot be improved significantly by the addition of any single parameter' and it 'is worsened significantly by the removal of any of the possible parameters. This looks like the end of the road.' However, he reexamines the necessity of the *ABCD* parameter at this stage, and by 'bending the rules' and excluding the 'significant' parameter, an even simpler model is arrived at. This is *AB/AC/AE/BC/BD/BE/CE/DE* (18 df, $Y^2 = 22.32$), which also fits the data well. Whether this is a 'better' model than *ABCD/AE/BE/CE* is, in the final analysis, a matter of opinion. The former is certainly easier to interpret and may as a result be of more practical value. The latter, based on the STP, would attract more support as an 'objective' representation of the relations in the data. Using STP, different analysts should come to the same conclusion about the data, given uniform error rates.

Interpretation of model $AB/AC/AE/BC/BD/BE/CE/DE$ is facilitated by concentrating on the interactions that are surprisingly absent rather than on those that are predictably present. Thus we note that there are direct relations between all pairings of the variables EEC referendum vote (A), political party (B), education (C), 'union membership' (D) and class (E), apart from the AD and CD interactions. Thus, conditional on all other interactions, 'union membership' does not interact with vote in the EEC referendum and is also independent of education. There is no need in this model to invoke higher-order interactions to explain the data. Thus the direct relation between, say, class and vote (AE) does not vary in magnitude or direction according to the level of other variables. Thus, complex interactions such as ABE are absent. Upton (1978a) gives a fuller account of this model.

The interpretation of our alternative and more-complex model $ABCD/AE/BE/CE$ can be aided by scrutinising the λ estimates, the ratio of these estimates to their standard errors, and the τ estimates of the equivalent multiplicative model given in Table 3.27. We also collapse Table 3.20 in order to highlight

Table 3.27. *Parameter estimates of the model ABCD/AE/BE/CE*

Parameter	λ estimate	Standard error	Ratio	τ parameter estimates
μ	3.56			35.23
A	0.33	0.036	9.22	1.39
B	-0.36	0.036	-9.97	0.70
C	0.14	0.036	3.91	1.15
D	-0.16	0.036	-4.50	0.85
E	-0.32	0.036	-8.97	0.73
AB	0.25	0.036	7.03	1.29
AC	0.09	0.036	2.57	1.10
AD	-0.03	0.036	-0.72	0.98
AE	0.12	0.036	3.26	1.12
BC	0.08	0.036	2.10	1.08
BD	-0.27	0.036	-7.61	0.76
BE	0.25	0.036	6.99	1.29
CD	-0.04	0.036	-1.03	0.96
CE	0.31	0.036	8.68	1.37
ABC	0.01	0.036	0.33	1.01
ABD	0.04	0.036	1.05	1.04
ACD	0.02	0.036	0.61	1.02
BCD	-0.09	0.036	-2.42	0.92
$ABCD$	0.07	0.036	1.91	1.07

the interactions present. The presence of the four-way interaction *ABCD* indicates that, even after allowing for all other interactions including complex three-way effects, there is still an effect needed in the model to increase the frequency of those in favour of the EEC who are also Conservative, well-educated 'union members', otherwise the model does not fit. Thus, in the multiplicative model we multiply by $\hat{\tau}^{ABCD} = 1.07$, as well as by the other relevant parameters, to obtain the expected frequency in cells denoting respondents at the first level of variables A, B, C and D. Similarly, we multiply by 1.07 or by 1/1.07 (so that the marginal constraints of a product of 1.0 are satisfied) to obtain the expected frequencies in other cells. Thus, for cells containing respondents at level 2 of variable B and level 1 of A, C, and D, we multiply by 1/1.07 to decrease the expected frequency of those in favour of the EEC who are not Conservative but are relatively well-educated 'union members'.

We attempt to clarify further the meaning of the *ABCD* interaction by collapsing Table 3.20, though, of course, in doing this we may be assuming away interactions that must be accounted for in the final analysis. Nevertheless, where the observed frequencies in collapsed tables provide evidence of inter-actions similar to the evidence given by the parameters of Table 3.27, they are of value, even though the parameters of Table 3.27 relate to the expected frequencies generated by the model rather than those observed. We thus commence by collapsing across the variables C, D and E to produce the two-way table of vote against party (Table 3.28).

From Table 3.28, we obtain a measure of the interaction between vote (A) and party (B) using the cross-product ratio, where

$$(429 \times 497)/(502 \times 133) = 3.19 \quad \text{and} \quad (3.19)^{1/4} = 1.33,$$

which compares well with $\hat{\tau}^{AB} = 1.29$ of Table 3.27. If we disaggregate Table 3.28 according to whether respondents are 'union members' or not, we find that the relation between party and vote is intensified for those who are 'union members', and mollified somewhat for those who are not. Table 3.29 illustrates the approximate relation between the variables and there we find that Conservatives who are 'union members' are more likely to vote in favour of EEC

Table 3.28. *Referendum vote by party supported*

	Conservative (B_1)	Not Conservative (B_2)
In favour of EEC entry (A_1)	429	502
Not in favour (A_2)	133	497

membership than those who are not. An indication of the influence of 'union membership' (D) on the relation between vote and party is given by the ratio of the cross-product ratios for the two subtables. For 'union members', we find that $(3.65)^{1/4} = 1.38$, and for 'non-unionists' $(2.79)^{1/4} = 1.29$; $(1.38/1.29)^{1/2} = 1.03$, which is equivalent to $\hat{\tau}^{ABD}$.

However, the existence of the $ABCD$ interaction means that the ABD interaction itself varies according to the level of education (C). From Table 3.30 we see that for the 'union members' the relation between party and vote is stronger for those with more education. We can quantify this interaction for the observed data. From Table 3.27, $\hat{\tau}^{ABCD} = 1.07$, which is equal to $[(1.49 \times 1.34)/(1.26 \times 1.21)]^{1/4}$, where the four bracketed terms are essentially the cross-product ratios for the four substrates of Table 3.30. For example, $[(82 \times 129)/(134 \times 16)]^{1/4} = 1.49$.

Apart from $ABCD$, our model also includes the two-way interactions between class (E) and the variables vote (A), party (B) and education (C).

Table 3.29. *Vote by party by 'union membership'*

	D_1				D_2	
	B_1	B_2			B_1	B_2
A_1	127	263		A_1	302	239
A_2	38	287		A_2	95	210

Table 3.30. *Table 3.20 collapsed over class (E)*

		C_1			C_2	
		B_1	B_2		B_1	B_2
D_1	A_1	82	134	A_1	45	129
	A_2	16	129	A_2	22	158
		C_1			C_2	
		B_1	B_2		B_1	B_2
D_2	A_1	204	121	A_1	98	118
	A_2	60	75	A_2	35	135

Given that $ABCD$ exists, these two-way interactions are simple since they are not conditional on the levels of the other variables. Table 3.31 allows an appraisal to be made of the interactions in conjunction with the interactions of Table 3.27. We find the strongest interaction in the education (C) by class subtable, where $[(409 \times 593)/(412 \times 147)]^{1/4} = 1.41$, which corresponds closely with $\hat{\tau}^{CE} = 1.37$ for the expected frequencies of the extended table. Allowing for the other influences, the middle class tend to have more than minimal legal schooling. The second strongest interaction is between party (B) and class. For this subtable, we find $[(303 \times 746)/(259 \times 253)]^{1/4} = 1.36$, where $\hat{\tau}^{BE} = 1.29$. Thus the subtable suggests what exists in reality, that Conservative party support and membership of the middle class are related attributes. Finally, the first subtable of Table 3.31 suggests that a favourable attitude towards the EEC is related to class, since the evidence in the collapsed table, where $[(398 \times 472)/(533 \times 158)]^{1/4} = 1.22$, is confirmed by the parameter estimate in Table 3.29, where $\hat{\tau}^{AE} = 1.12$.

Our final model arrived at by STP is somewhat complex with interactions that are difficult to describe. The particular challenge has been to give an account of the complex $ABCD$ interaction that is comprehensible and to facilitate this we have collapsed the observed data in various ways so that the collapsed tables contain relations approximating to the meaning of the model parameters.

In fact, STP does give the analyst more flexibility than is initially apparent, since the choice of α, and hence γ, is of course subjective. By setting $\alpha = 0.01$, the overall type I error rate $\gamma = 0.23$ and $\gamma_{4,5} = 1 - (0.99)^6 = 0.059$. Also, $\chi^2_{6,\,0.059} = 12.15$. Given this, $ABCD$ of the preceding analysis becomes insignificant. Furthermore, there is no necessity to stick dogmatically to one fixed α. There is 'no theoretical requirement for a constant α in all family tests. There

Table 3.31. *Class cross-tabulated by vote, party and education*

		Middle class E_1	Not middle class E_2
Vote	A_1	398	533
	A_2	158	472
Party	B_1	303	259
	B_2	253	746
Education	C_1	409	412
	C_2	147	593

key: as in Table 3.20.

may be occasions when high-order interactions are believed *a priori* to be negligible' (Aitkin 1978, p. 205), in which case a smaller type I error rate can be employed.

Despite this latitude, STP may in practice be implemented as a rigid auto-matic selection procedure, and the analyst must beware of abandoning critical thought and pragmatic commonsense approach. Often, only by personally intervening in the routine of model selection procedures does one arrive at a satisfactory and parsimonious model. On the other hand, STP has the advantage of a firmer foundation in statistical theory, a point reiterated by Professor Aitkin who writes, 'if the STP and stepwise selection choose the same model, I would regard this as validation of the model chosen by stepwise selection, not a demonstration that STP is unnecessary. If the two methods don't give the same answer, then I would regard the STP model as being more soundly based in statistical theory than the stepwise model (Aitkin, personal communication).'

The reason for this is that, 'STP uses a "basement" level of goodness-of-fit, based on the full model df k, and $\chi^2_{k, 1 - (1 - \alpha)k}$, while the backward elimina-tion method treats each goodness-of-fit term as χ^2_1, which it can't be, because we are always dropping the *smallest* of the available 1 df χ^2's. It is not surprising that the two methods will often give the same answer, if the table is not too large, and the sample sizes *are* large. In large tables, the backward elimination method may be expected to stop too soon, leaving terms in the model which the STP finds unnecessary. However, effective comparisons of the two methods are difficult (as I pointed out in the 1980 Biometrics paper) because we can't specify the overall type I error rate of the backward elimination model (Aitkin, personal communication).'

Because of these arguments and because of the lack of reference to Aitkin's STP approach outside the specialist statistical journals, considerable prominence is given to STP in this book. However, STP is not the final answer to the problem of selecting a minimal model, as has already been made clear in the various data analyses of this chapter, though its basic logic holds good when we turn to the study of residuals in Chapter 5. Furthermore, STP is ostensibly somewhat more complicated to apply than, say, stepwise selection, though the difficulty in obtaining $\chi^2_{d, \gamma}$, when γ takes an uncommon value, is easily circumvented by making use of the logical relationships between tabulated and untabulated critical values as in Chapter 5. Precise estimates of critical values from χ^2_d can be obtained by implementing appropriate computer sub-routines or by judicious use of standard program modules in programmable calculators that are capable of generating observations from theoretical probability distributions.

All this would be unnecessary were it true that STP and stepwise selection always produced the same 'final' model. This is not the case, however, and thus what we are calling for is an approach to model selection that gives some consideration to the problem of multiple significance testing for which STP is designed. Perhaps the best policy is to aim for models that are of practical value by jointly and critically adopting several approaches, particularly as screening is an automatic option on many installations and stepwise selection is easy to understand and implement.

We continue our study of STP in Chapter 5 where it is applied to a table involving polytomous variables. The analysis of polytomous variables does introduce another device, so far not considered, for the simplification of complex models. This is the reparameterisation of models by invoking simplifying parameters more tuned to trends within the data. We consider this option in Chapters 5 and 6.

4 Sample design and inference

Sampling models

Up to now we have been largely concerned with identifying structural models and have paid little heed to the fact that one particular sampling model is implicitly assumed. In fact, a number of sampling models could have been adopted, as outlined by Bishop *et al.* (1975, p. 435). This means that we have assumed that the observed data have been collected in one particular way, namely by choosing a sample of a predetermined size at random from a population. Such a scheme will produce an observed frequency in any cell of a multidimensional contingency table that reflects the underlying unknown probability that a randomly chosen member of the population will occupy the cell.

There are in fact three basic interrelated sampling models appropriate to a variety of data collection schemes. One such model is the Poisson distribution, which is applicable if we can assume that the frequency in each of N cells of the multidimensional contingency table is the outcome of N independent Poisson processes. This sampling scheme requires no *a priori* fixing of the total sample size and, therefore, would be appropriate if the phenomena of interest were observed for a fixed time period, at the end of which the frequencies in each cell, each the outcome of a Poisson process, could be totalled to arrive at a previously unspecified aggregate. Such a scheme would be approximately appropriate if we were conducting a traffic survey to investigate the relationship between vehicle type and whether or not the speed limit was broken, by observing a stretch of road for a given time period.

More usually, the analyst specifies the size of his sample prior to the investigation, in which case the simple multinomial distribution is appropriate. A third sample model, which will be discussed subsequently, is the product multinomial. The derivation of the simple multinomial from the Poisson distributions is presented by a number of authors such as Bishop *et al.* (1975, p. 447), and Plackett (1981), and these texts should be consulted by those interested in the theory. A very brief account follows. Let us consider that sampling has produced the observed frequencies $\{f_{ijk}\}$ in the cells of a three-way contingency table, but that the total sample size, f_{000}, was fixed beforehand.

Assuming that the frequency in each cell is the consequence of a Poisson process, conditional on fixed sample size, the probability or likelihood that the set of independent variates N_{ijk} produced by the set of Poisson processes $P(\mu_{ijk})$ exactly equals the observed frequencies f_{ijk}, given f_{000}, is

$$P\left(N_{ijk} = f_{ijk} \quad \text{for all} \quad i, j, k \, \middle| \, \sum_{ijk} N_{ijk} = f_{000}\right)$$

$$= \frac{\Pi(\mu_{ijk}^{f_{ijk}} e^{-\mu_{ijk}}/f_{ijk}!)}{\{(\Sigma \mu_{ijk})^{f_{000}} e^{-\Sigma \mu_{ijk}}/f_{000}!\}}$$

$\mu_{ijk} = $ mean of Poisson process in cell (i, j, k). In the same way that $P(B \setminus A) = P(B \text{ and } A) / P(A)$,

$$P\left(N_{ijk} = f_{ijk} \quad \text{for all} \quad i, j, k \, \middle| \, \sum_{ijk} N_{ijk} = f_{000}\right)$$

$$= \frac{f_{000}!}{\prod_{ijk} f_{ijk}!} \prod_{ijk} p_{ijk}^{f_{ijk}} \quad \text{(a multinomial distribution)}$$

since

$$\frac{\mu_{ijk}}{\Sigma \mu_{ijk}} = p_{ijk}$$

In just one dimension, the derivation is simpler to understand.

$$P(N_i = f_i \quad \text{for all} \quad i \mid \Sigma N_i = f_0)$$

$$= \frac{\Pi(\mu_i^{f_i} e^{-\mu_i}/f_i!)}{\{(\Sigma \mu_i)^{f_0} e^{-\Sigma \mu_i}/f_0!\}} \quad \text{say} \quad i = 1, \dots, 3$$

$$= \frac{(\mu_1^{f_1} e^{-\mu_1}/f_1!)(\mu_2^{f_2} e^{-\mu_2}/f_2!)(\mu_3^{f_3} e^{-\mu_3}/f_3!)}{(\mu_1 + \mu_2 + \mu_3)^{f_0} e^{-(\mu_1 + \mu_2 + \mu_3)}/f_0!}$$

$$= \frac{(\mu_1^{f_1} e^{-\mu_1})(\mu_2^{f_2} e^{-\mu_2})(\mu_3^{f_3} e^{-\mu_3})f_0!}{f_1! \, f_2! \, f_3! \, (\mu_1 + \mu_2 + \mu_3)^{f_0} e^{-(\mu_1 + \mu_2 + \mu_3)}}$$

$$= \frac{e^{-(\mu_1 + \mu_2 + \mu_3)} \mu_1^{f_1} \mu_2^{f_2} \mu_3^{f_3} f_0!}{f_1! \, f_2! \, f_3! \, (\mu_1 + \mu_2 + \mu_3)^{f_0} e^{-(\mu_1 + \mu_2 + \mu_3)}}$$

$$= \frac{\mu_1^{f_1} \mu_2^{f_2} \mu_3^{f_3} f_0!}{f_1! \, f_2! \, f_3! \, (\mu_1 + \mu_2 + \mu_3)^{f_0}}$$

since

$$\frac{\mu_1^{f_1} \mu_2^{f_2} \mu_3^{f_3}}{(\mu_1 + \mu_2 + \mu_3)^{f_0}} = p_1^{f_1} p_2^{f_2} p_3^{f_3}$$

$$= \frac{p_1^{f_1} p_2^{f_2} p_3^{f_3} f_0!}{f_1! \, f_2! \, f_3!}, \quad \text{a multinomial distribution}$$

Thus, given cell probabilities p_i, observed frequencies f_i and sample size f_0, the probability that the Poisson variates N_i will equal the f_i for all i is given to be the above formula.

Maximum likelihood estimation

The p_i or p_{ijk} are unknown theoretical probabilities which require estimation. One criterion that can be adopted (see Chapter 5 for a discussion of alternatives) is to use those estimates $(\hat{p}_{ijk})$ that maximise the likelihood (L)

$$L = \frac{f_{000}!}{\prod_{ijk} f_{ijk}!} \prod_{ijk} p_{ijk}^{f_{ijk}}$$

These maximum likelihood estimates, together with the associated estimated expected frequencies (e_{ijk}), can be obtained by differentiation of the log likelihood (see Bishop *et al.* 1975, p. 65).

Birch (1963) has shown that, provided we restrict ourselves to the (usually very large numbers of) hierarchical log-linear models, the maximum likelihood estimates of the expected frequencies (e_{ijk}) are obtained very simply on the basis of minimal sufficient (Haberman 1973*a*) statistics that turn out to be no other than the previously discussed margin totals.

Take, for example, the multinomial sampling model, and the following structural model

$$\log(p_{ijk}) = \mu + \lambda_i^A + \lambda_j^B + \lambda_k^C + \lambda_{ij}^{AB}$$

Because sets of parameters are implied by the inclusion of others the model can be written as AB/C in shorthand notation and thus, because included parameters are synonymous with equalised observed and expected margin totals, the minimal sufficient statistics for the maximum likelihood estimation of the expected frequencies are $\{f_{ij0}\}$ and $\{f_{00k}\}$. Similar minimal sufficient statistics can be derived for other hierarchical log-linear models and apply equally to Poisson or simple multinomial sampling.

Once the set of minimal sufficient statistics has been obtained, the results of Birch (1963) show that unique maximum likelihood estimates are the result, as discussed in Bishop *et al.* (1975, p. 69). Thus, if we wish to obtain the cell estimates generated by the model $\log(p_{ijk}) = \mu + \lambda_i^A + \lambda_j^B + \lambda_k^C + \lambda_{ik}^{AC} + \lambda_{jk}^{BC}$, and arbitrary constraints $\Sigma_i \lambda_i^A = \dots \Sigma_k \lambda_{jk}^{BC} = 0$, it is simply necessary to remember that the shorthand version AC/BC indicates the minimal sufficient statistics.

These are f_{i0k} and f_{0jk}

Therefore $e_{ijk} = \dfrac{f_{i0k} f_{0jk}}{f_{00k}}$

In general, the denominator is defined by the overlap of the minimal set. In fact, such direct estimates are not always so easily produced (see Bishop *et al.* 1975, p. 76) and an iterative algorithm must be used.

Product multinomial sampling: factors and responses

The adopted sampling scheme may differ from that outlined above, since not only may the total size of the sample be fixed beforehand, but the numbers in each subgroup, defined by various category combinations, may also be fixed. For example, it may be decided to interview 50 urban mortgage holders (A_1B_1) with respect to their political affiliations (C), and 50 rural (A_2B_1) mortgage holders, and so on, irrespective of the actual frequencies with which urban mortgage holders and rural mortgage holders occur in the population. In such a scheme we would be essentially interested in how political affiliation is influenced by residential environment (A) and residential tenure (B) and would not be concerned with how environment and tenure were interrelated. If the latter was of concern, such a sampling scheme would be impractical, since by fixing the numbers to be sampled within each of the variable A and B combinations, we are restricting natural variation that could indicate how they are related. By fixing the numbers in the multiway table when it is collapsed over variable C, one is simply investigating how C responds to variations in A and B, which are thus factors producing the response.

Given such a sampling scheme, it is in fact necessary to fit a particular class of models that include the parameter sets representing all the factor variables and their interactions. Thus, for the above hypothetical three-way table, any fitted model must include $\{\lambda_i^A\}$, $\{\lambda_j^B\}$ and $\{\lambda_{ij}^{AB}\}$, apart from any other parameter sets such as AC that are found to be necessary to produce a viable model. The necessity for the parameters representing the factor variables may be clarified by recalling that the parameters included are synonymous with equalised observed and expected table marginal totals. Since in the factor and response situation these marginal totals may be somewhat artificial when compared with the naturally occurring category frequencies, this must be taken into account, or controlled for, when generating expected frequencies. Otherwise, 'true' associations between factor and response variables, represented by, for example, $\{\lambda_{ik}^{AC}\}$, will assume distorted estimated values trying to cope with interactions between the factor variables that are somewhat unreal and only a product of the sampling scheme.

The above is a somewhat intuitive account justifying the necessity for parameters representing all possible interactions between factor variables when the distinction is made between factors and responses. The case can be argued from another point of view. Consider the structural model

$$\log(p_{ijk}) = \mu + \lambda_i^A + \lambda_j^B + \lambda_k^C + \lambda_{jk}^{BC}$$

with constraints

$$\sum_i \lambda_i^A = \dots \sum_k \lambda_{jk}^{BC} = 0$$

and a product multinomial sampling model in which A and B are factors and C is a response. As written, the structural model and sampling model conflict, since the former produces $\{e_{ijk}\}$ and hence marginal totals $\{e_{ij0}\}$ that will not necessarily agree with the marginal totals $\{f_{ij0}\}$ fixed by the sampling scheme. In order for both structural and sampling models to conform, so that what the model produced agrees with what is fixed by design, the parameter set AB must be included. Even when the multiway table collapsed over the response variable(s) is not fixed by design, it is usually a sensible approach to treat the factors as fixed. Unless the collapsed table includes zeros, very little is lost by this approach. Indeed, as will be seen subsequently, such an approach enables us to track down factor–response interactions more clearly, since a poorly fitting model that includes all factor interactions unequivocally points to the absence of factor–response interactions as the source of the deviance.

The discussion of factors and responses can be broadened somewhat by mentioning that there is no necessity for there to be simply one response and one, or a number of, factors as implied above.

Upton (1978b) distinguishes a number of variations on the basic theme. Consider the three-variable situation, with variables A, B and C. There are four different situations that can arise.

  (i) All three variables are factors, or all three variables are responses.

  (ii) Variables A and B are factors influencing the response variable C as above.

  (iii) Variable A is a factor influencing two response variables B and C.

  (iv) Variable A is a factor influencing the response B. Variables A and B then act as factors influencing the response C (multistage analysis).

In general, three classes of interaction can be distinguished, interactions between factors, interactions between responses, and interactions between factors and responses. 'The key interactions are these latter, since these identify a cause with an effect. Interactions between factors are of very minor interest – they usually represent known relationships and take on the status of "facts of life" (Upton 1981a, p. 6).' A convenient and sensible way of focussing attention on the factor-response interactions is to include in every model that is fitted to the data both the all-factor interactions and the all-response interactions. If these are insufficient to explain the data, then the model containing only these interactions will provide a poor fit to the data and it will immediately be clear that there are some important factor–response interactions. Hence, if A and B are factors in a four-dimensional table and the model AB/CD provides a poor fit, then there is a need to include factor–response interaction parameters such as AC.

Upton (1981a) goes on to analyse a 2^7 table in which the items of interest are Irish manufacturing units cross-classified according to ownership (O), size (S), market orientation (M), and according to whether they consider the freight-handling facilities at Aldergrove (A), Belfast (B), Larne (L) and Warrenpoint (W) as important to their business. O, S and M are treated as factors and A, B, L and W as responses (actually, to a postal questionnaire). Thus each model fitted to the data included the factor-interaction parameters MSO and, initially, the response–interaction parameters $ABLW$. After using the screening technique (Brown 1976) to identify important interactions, a stepwise procedure to conditionally test parameters produces the satisfactorily fitting model $MSO/AB/AL/BL/AW/LMO/AO/LWM/LMS$. Note that it has not been found necessary to include all the response variable interactions. Among those that are included is AW, indicating that firms stating proximity to Aldergrove was important also tended to say the same thing about Warrenpoint more frequently than if the two responses were independent. A typical factor–response interaction included in the model was AO, which indicates that non-Irish firms (O) tended to give the response that Aldergrove was an important advantage to location more frequently than if this factor–response pair were independent.

Multistage analysis

The distinction between factors and responses occurs quite commonly, and it is one that is essentially based on the temporal sequence of the variables, factors preceding responses, more than in their intrinsic nature. Some variables can in some contexts be factors and in others responses, and a variable may be a response to a previously occurring variable and a factor producing variation in a subsequent response. What is required for this type of data is a multistage analysis as outlined by Goodman (1973a, b).

Upton (1978a) performs a multistage analysis on data previously considered by Williams (1976) in which there are three variables, sex, education level and work status. Clearly, sex is a factor, but education level is considered both as a response to sex and as a factor alongside sex, producing variation in the response, work status. A similar analysis in Upton & Fingleton (1979, p. 111) of the data already discussed in Chapters 2 and 3 produces the following path diagram in which arrows start from factors and end at responses. It is seen that two variables, income (B) and car ownership (C) perform dual roles as responses and factors.

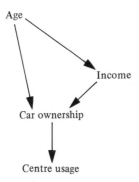

In the analysis of Williams' (1976) data, the analysis proceeds by collapsing an original multiway table over subsequent responses, such pooling being justified on the grounds that at the particular stage under consideration, subsequent responses 'have not yet happened' (Upton 1978*b*).

The Upton & Fingleton (1979) data is analysed from the reasonable point of view that while car ownership produces variations in the response centre usage, car ownership itself responds to the consumer's age (A) and income (B) and not according to which shopping centre is used (D). Thus, as is evident from Table 4.1, the data are pooled over response D and C is then treated as a response to A and B. Collapsing over C allows a further model to be fitted in which income (B) is considered as a response to age (A). Goodman (1973*b*) suggests a method of quantifying the arrows and of fitting composite models to this type of multistage data (see also Chapter 6).

Goodman's (1973*a*, *b*) method of arrow quantification and his suggestions about the tricky problem of interactions involving one or more polytomous variables have not been accepted unreservedly by writers such as Fienberg (1980), Duncan (1981) and Birnbaum (1982). The reservations derive mainly from the inability of path diagrams obtained from log–linear and logit model

Table 4.1. *Models fitted to Upton and Fingleton (1979) data*

Model	Interpretation	Data
ABC/CD	D as a response to A, B, C (only factor C significant)	2^4 table (Table 2.5)
$AB/AC/BC$	C as a response to A and B (both factors significant)	Above table collapsed over D to give 2^3 table
AB	B as a response (significant) to A	Above table collapsed over C

analyses to accomplish all that is accomplished in analogous quantitative variable analyses. In order to achieve path diagrams of comparable informativeness, Birnbaum (1982) goes beyond the methods we are concerned with to arrive at 'a calculus of causal effect for qualitative variables which is the direct counterpart of that used for quantitative variables'. Hence the effects of remotely connected variables can be inferred from the appropriate paths.

Quantified arrows *per se* can be misleading given the uncertain knowledge we have of the true value of an interaction. As is found later in the analysis of Table 6.24, optional but equally satisfactory models may exist. To avoid 'interaction sanctification', a policy of qualitative arrows is probably advisable, and where valid options exist it may be useful to display the competing path diagrams to make graphic the causal connections implied by each. Fienberg (1980) has some illustrations of these.

Sample designs and inferences

So far we have considered data gathered by simple random sampling, in other words we have invoked the simple multinomial sampling model with the sole *a priori* constraint of a predetermined sample size. Stratified samples, in which the levels of factor variables constitute strata within which sample sizes are fixed by design, have also been dealt with implicitly since these are consistent with the product multinomial sampling model. In this section we go on to briefly consider further aspects of sample design and its relation to inference including a discussion of cluster sampling and observations gathered over time and space. We omit reference to the details of sampling methods and refer interested readers to specialist texts such as Namboodiri (1978), Kish (1965) and Cochran (1977). Where the theory becomes intractable we simply cite the appropriate specialist literature and concentrate instead on those common sample designs with design effects that are particularly easy to comprehend and implement in our inferential procedure.

A simple random sample is a sample in which each different sample of the same size has the same probability of selection and each individual in the population is equally likely to become a sample unit. Although they are almost invariably representative of the population, such samples are relatively difficult to collect when the population to be sampled is large since they require the drawing up of a sampling frame from which the sample is ultimately selected.

This is also true of stratified sampling, though this has the advantage that if the proportionate size of the random sample chosen from each stratum is equal to the known proportion of the total population within each stratum (proportinally allocated stratified random sampling), then estimates of population parameters are always at least as precise as in random sampling. To put it another way, the sample level of precision can be achieved using a smaller sample. Disproportionate samples are used to ensure sufficient representation of elusive members of relatively infrequently occupied strata. We have already noted that stratification poses no real problem to the analyst if specific allowance is made in the statistical model for the sample design. Thus, following our discussion earlier in this chapter and Bishop *et al.* (1975, p. 36), if in a three-way table two variables A and B are required to describe the strata, then $\{\lambda^{AB}\}$ is necessarily included in our model. This is analogous to regression modelling in which the ordinary least squares (OLS) estimators of model parameters are biased unless a design variable is explicitly incorporated as an independent variable to allow for the stratification (Nathan & Holt 1980; Holt *et al.* 1980).

Although it is not typical of most of the small surveys analysed in this book, large social surveys are often based on more-complex sample schemes than those consistent with the simple or product multinomial model. The analyst is frequently presented with contingency tables which, at their simplest, comprise counts of individuals who are members of clusters drawn at random from a larger number. An example of this would be a sample comprising members of classes selected at random from among all the classes in a school. Very large surveys may be much more complex with multistage sample schemes involving clusters chosen from among units selected at random at an earlier stage. For example, the initial stage may involve the random selection of schools from among the total number within a city, and then a number of classes (clusters) may be chosen at random from within each school.

Though complex sample schemes are invariably advantageous in terms of cost and ease of data collection, they pose severe problems at the data analysis stage, for no completely acceptable strategy for dealing with the vagaries of complex sample design has, yet evolved, though some recent progress has been made by Altham (1976; 1979), Cohen (1976), Rao & Scott (1979; 1981), Fienberg (1979), Brier (1980), Fellegi (1980) and Holt *et al.* (1980). We discuss some of their innovations in more detail subsequently.

Several options are open to the analyst presented with contingency tables derived from complex sample schemes. One option is to proceed as if the data were obtained under multinomial sampling, that is, to treat the data as if it were representative of some population; though this is a rather unsatisfactory way of negotiating the difficulties, it has found some favour in the absence of practical alternatives.

A more acceptable option is to estimate in some way design effects due to complex sampling. Generally, the design effect is a measure of the efficiency of a sample design which is given by the ratio of the variance of an estimator obtained using the chosen design to the variance under simple random sampling.

Such effects normally exceed one, indicating that significance tests of inter-action effects based on simple random sampling assumptions are much more prone to type I error than the nominal 5% or 1% due to the underestimation of parameter standard errors. This underestimation is an inevitable outcome when sample units are not independent (as in simple random sampling) but are subject to intracluster correlation. Deflation to allow for design effects has been accomplished by reduction of the sample size to accommodate the lack of independent sampling units (see Kish & Frankel 1974; Penick & Owens 1976) and this is in many ways equivalent to the deflators developed by Altham (1976; 1979), Brier (1980) and Fingleton (1983a, b) which are discussed later.

The chi-squared test and complex samples

The effect of most complex sample schemes is to inflate the value of X^2 and of Y^2, both of which are no longer asymptotically distributed as χ^2 under the null hypothesis in independence, homogeneity and goodness-of-fit tests. This is reiterated by various authors' reports of experimental analyses (Fellegi 1980; Holt *et al.* 1980; Rao & Scott 1981) and has been the stimulus for recent research on the appropriate correction factors. Recent work by Holt *et al.* (1980) suggests that, 'the corrections work well for tests of goodness-of-fit and homogeneity, but tend to be very conservative in the independence case', for they report that this test is 'much less vulnerable than the corresponding tests for goodness of fit and homogeneity provided the variables cut across strata and clusters'.

Nevertheless we report the effects of cluster sampling on the independence chi-squared test as this combines probably the most common test on the two-way contingency table with the most immediate and obvious deviation from multi-nomial sampling for which a simple, if somewhat conservative, correction procedure exists.

Perhaps somewhat predictably, the inflating effect of complex sampling so that $E(X^2) > df$ (where $df = E(X^2)$ under simple random sampling and $E(X^2)$ signifies the mathematical expectation, the weighted mean of the random variable X^2 with weights equal to the probability of occurrence) does not hold with proportionally allocated stratified random sampling. With this scheme, the chi-squared test for independence is conservative so that $E(X^2) < df$ and thus, according to Holt *et al.* (1980); 'we would expect the ordinary chi-squared test to perform very well'.

The independence test with cluster sampling

The sample (given in Altham 1976) consists of Nk observations comprising $N = 71$ clusters, each of size $k = 2$, which were in fact hospitalised sibling pairs where each individual was either schizophrenic or not schizophrenic and either male or female. The observed data are given in Table 4.2.

Assuming that the individuals are independent and ignoring for the moment the fact that they are clustered into dependent sibling pairs, we find, ostensibly, a considerable degree of association between sex and diagnosis since

$$X^2 = [\log(f_{11}f_{22}/f_{12}f_{21})]^2/(f_{11}^{-1} + f_{12}^{-1} + f_{21}^{-1} + f_{22}^{-1})$$
$$= 2.37/0.14 = 16.87 > \chi^2_{1,0.05} = 3.84.$$

If, following Cohen (1976), we now assume his particular model for within-cluster dependence (see Cohen 1976 and Altham 1976 for details), we find that X^2 is deflated to 12.97. However, it is possible to reject the hypothesis of independence without invoking a model of how the siblings are related which is any more specific than simply assuming, quite plausibly, that the relation between members of the same cluster is positive. Given this very weak assumption about the nature of the within-cluster dependence, one can evaluate the minimum possible X^2 value assuming the maximum possible correlation. This is denoted as X^2_{td}. If $X^2_{td} > \chi^2_{1,0.05} = 3.84$, then one is wholly justified in attributing the 'significance' of X^2 to dependence between sex and diagnosis rather than to intracluster correlation. Without going into the details of the proof (see Altham 1976), we find that

$$X^2_{td} \approx [\log(f_{11}f_{22}/f_{12}f_{21})]^2 \bigg/ \left[\sum_i \sum_j (k/f_{ij})\right]$$
$$= X^2/k = 8.44 > \chi^2_{1,0.05} = 3.84.$$

This result indicates that diagnosis is related to the sex of the patient, with schizophrenia being more prevalent among males than females.

Note that, although the data in Table 4.2 consists of clusters of size two, k can assume any size, though it remains constant across clusters. Brier (1980) provides an alternative rationale for the results of Altham (1976) which facilitates an extension to varisized clusters. With unequal cluster sizes, we commence by assuming that we have a_1 clusters of size $n_1, \ldots, a_t$ clusters of size n_t. By also

Table 4.2. *Diagnosis and sex of hospitalised sibling pairs*

	Sex	
	male	female
Schizophrenic	43	32
Not schizophrenic	15	52

assuming that, instead of the usual multinomial sampling model, our data are generated by Dirichlet-multinomial distributions with different n (see Brier 1980), the asymptotic distributions of X^2 and Y^2 are as $B\chi^2$ rather than χ^2 to which they would approximate were the fitted model correct and multinomial sampling prevailed. Brier (1980) notes that

$$B = \left(\sum_{i=1}^{t} n_i a_i C_i \right) \Big/ \left(\sum_{i=1}^{t} n_i a_i \right)$$

and

$$1 \leqslant C_i = (n_i + R)/(1 + R) \leqslant n_i.$$

C_i thus depends on R which is a structural parameter representing clustering effects such that $\rho = 1/(1 + R)$, where ρ is the intracluster correlation coefficient.

An example of the inflation of X^2 due to cluster sampling with unequal cluster sizes is a survey of families in 20 neighbourhoods of Montevideo, Minnesota, USA (see Brier 1980). The survey concerns levels of satisfaction with housing. Individual families were cross-classified according to their levels of satisfaction on two trichotomous variables: A, satisfaction with housing in the neighbourhood, and B, satisfaction with their own home. Rather than being drawn at random from the population, the individual units, the families, are members of 20 neighbourhood clusters and it is reasonable to assume that the response of families within the same neighbourhood will be correlated. We present the raw data in Table 4.3 in which the rows denote the 20 clusters and the columns the nine responses to two trichotomous variables.

Table 4.4 is simply a collapsed version of Table 4.3, in which we temporarily ignore the existence of clusters and perform a conventional chi-squared test of independence assuming a simple random sample of 96 families. We find that $X^2 = 17.89$ and $Y^2 = 15.38$, both of which exceed $\chi^2_{4, 0.05} = 9.49$. Thus it seems, at least provisionally, that a family's level of satisfaction with its home is related to its level of satisfaction with housing in the neighbourhood generally.

It is possible to show that the apparent interaction between the variables could be due entirely to within-cluster correlation, especially if we adopt the earlier strategy of assuming maximum possible correlation. Thus we set $\rho = 1$ and thus $R = 0$. Given two cluster sizes, $t = 2$ and $C_1 = 5$ and $C_2 = 3$. Consequently, $B = [(5 \times 18 \times 5) + (3 \times 2 \times 3)]/[(18 \times 5) + (2 \times 3)] = 4.875$. We thus deflate by this factor giving $X^2/4.875 = 3.67$ and $Y^2/4.875 = 3.15$, both of which are less than $\chi^2_{4, 0.05} = 9.49$. We thus conclude that there is not totally unequivocal evidence that the level of satisfaction with one's home is related to the level of satisfaction with housing in the neighbourhood in general. Note that this correction is the same as that derived by Altham (1976) for equisize clusters, since for the data in Table 4.2, $B = (2 \times 71 \times 2)/2 \times 71) = 2 = k$.

Table 4.3. *Responses of families in 20 neighbourhood clusters*

A_1B_1	A_1B_2	A_1B_3	A_2B_1	A_2B_2	A_2B_3	A_3B_1	A_3B_2	A_3B_3
1	0	0	2	2	0	0	0	0
1	0	0	2	2	0	0	0	0
0	2	0	0	2	0	0	1	0
0	1	0	2	1	0	1	0	0
0	0	0	0	4	0	0	1	0
1	0	0	3	1	0	0	0	0
3	0	0	0	1	0	0	1	0
1	0	0	1	3	0	0	0	0
3	0	0	0	0	0	1	0	1
0	1	0	0	3	1	0	0	0
1	1	0	0	2	0	1	0	0
0	1	0	4	0	0	0	0	0
0	0	0	4	1	0	0	0	0
0	0	0	1	2	0	0	0	2
2	0	0	2	1	0	0	0	0
1	0	0	1	1	0	0	0	0
0	0	0	1	1	1	0	2	0
0	0	0	1	0	1	0	0	1
2	0	0	2	1	0	0	0	0
2	0	0	2	0	0	1	0	0

key: satisfaction with neighbourhood housing
    A_1 = unsatisfied.
    A_2 = satisfied.
    A_3 = very satisfied.

    satisfaction with own home
    B_1 = unsatisfied.
    B_2 = satisfied.
    B_3 = very satisfied.

Table 4.4. *Families cross-classified by housing satisfaction levels*

	B_1	B_2	B_3
A_1	18	6	0
	(12.5)	(9.75)	(1.75)
A_2	28	28	3
	(30.73)	(23.97)	(4.3)
A_3	4	5	4
	(6.77)	(5.28)	(0.95)

key: as above, the parenthesised terms are expected
    frequencies assuming independence.

Brier (1980) goes on to show how it is possible to estimate C_i rather than obtain a bound consistent with maximum possible intracluster correlation, though this is not simple and the source should be consulted for details. Also there are details of the (fairly weak) conditions under which the assumption of the Dirichlet-multinomial distribution is tenable and an intimation of how the model provides a convenient framework for the fitting and testing of general log–linear models in contingency tables.

The independence test with temporal and spatial data

The above corrections relate to cluster sampling in which there are N independent clusters, each with a number of dependent units. Very simple corrections to the basic chi-squared test for independence in contingency tables also exist for data gathered at successive points in time or at grid-line intersection points on maps that are sufficiently close together in time or space to fail to be uncorrelated as required by multinomial sampling. Such data are not infrequently encountered by behavioural and earth scientists, though the now-general awareness of difficulties caused by autocorrelated observations, combined with a lack of knowledge of appropriate corrections, may have dissuaded many from proceeding with their analysis. The corrections we present have much in common with those for cluster sampling in that there is a general need to deflate X^2, given positively related observations. Furthermore, we retain the philosophy of making minimal assumptions about the autocorrelation mechanism to obtain upper and lower bounds for the 'true' X^2 statistic based on the assumption of zero and maximum positive dependence between the observations. The upper bound corresponds to the usual X^2 statistic. The lower bound, assuming maximum correlation between observations less than r units apart and independence otherwise, is $X^2/(2r - 1)$ (see Altham 1979 for proof).

Consider, for example, that the behaviour of a mother and infant monkey has been observed over a period of time, allowing 5390 observations at discrete time intervals, and we wish to test the null hypothesis that two variables measured on the pair, the position of the infant's torso and the mother's gaze, are independent. The observed data are in Table 4.5 and are discussed in more detail in Altham (1979) and in Fingleton (1983a).

The basic chi-squared test for independence gives

$$X^2 = [\log (803 \times 2700)/(534 \times 1353)]^2/$$
$$[(1/803) + (1/534) + (1/1353) + (1/2700)]$$
$$= 285.6 > \chi^2_{1,\,0.05} = 3.84,$$

though we know that X^2 will be inflated in the presence of positively dependent observations. Since the analyst believes that any observations $r = 25$ units apart and more are pairwise uncorrelated, whereas less-distant pairs are correlated, we are able to say that $285.6/(2r-1) = 5.8 \leqslant X_t^2 \leqslant 285.6$ where X_t^2 is the 'true' chi-squared after allowing for the autocorrelation. Since $5.8 > \chi_{1, 0.05}^2 = 3.84$, we can say that even if the dependence between observations is at a maximum, it is insufficient to account for all the association that ostensibly exists between the behaviour of the animals. They do indeed interact.

With spatial data located at lattice intersection points so that some observations are correlated, a particularly easy-to-implement correction exists that is derived directly from the temporal analogue. We assume that observations at a distance d apart, or less, are positively dependent, whilst those more than distance d apart are pairwise uncorrelated. Making no other assumptions about the way in which observations on the lattice are related, apart from the stationarity condition which we mention later, and defining the distance d as the number of lattice edges between two points on the map taking the shortest possible route, it is possible to again derive upper and lower bounds for the 'true' chi-squared statistic corresponding to independent and maximally correlated observations. The independence chi-squared X^2 again demarcates the upper bound for X_t^2, whilst the lower bound is $X^2/[1 + 2d(d + 1)]$. (See Fingleton (1983a) for proof.) Table 4.6 contains data appropriate for this correction.

Treating Table 4.6 as a normal two-way contingency table with observations consistent with the multinomial sampling model, on the basis of the expected frequencies, assuming no association and given in parentheses, we find that $X^2 = 66.58 > \chi_{1, 0.05}^2 = 3.84$, providing considerable evidence that the occurrence of the two plants is positively related. This conclusion is of course based on the assumption that each observation is independent, though this is highly unlikely where seed dispersal mechanisms make plants growing in close proximity an inevitability. In fact, we suggest that observations $d = 2$, and less, steps apart are positively correlated simply on the grounds that, strictly, the presence or absence of the two plants are recorded for 446 grid squares and are only subsequently assigned to grid-square mid-points to be consistent with the theory. It

Table 4.5. *Time-dependent observations of mother and infant monkey behaviour*

| | | Infant's torso | |
		lowered	not lowered
Mother's gaze	looking	803	534
	not looking	1353	2700

can thus be argued that observations at 'points' centred on contiguous grid-squares will tend to be correlated by virtue of the likelihood of double-counting occurrences astride grid-square dividing lines, irrespective of seed dispersal mechanisms. Similarly, observations in grid-square corners will tend to produce dependence between lattice points two steps apart. Having settled on $d = 2$, we find that $X_t^2 \geqslant 66.58/[1 + 2d(d+1)] = 5.12 > \chi_{1, 0.05}^2 = 3.84$.

We conclude that, despite allowing for maximum possible positive correlation, there is still sufficient evidence of a relation between the plants, though if we extend pairwise correlation to a distance $d = 3$, the association is possibly more apparent than real since $X_t^2 \geqslant 2.66 < \chi_{1, 0.05}^2 = 3.84$.

The stationarity condition that was mentioned earlier is also required for time-dependent data, though it is mentioned explicitly here as it is a less easily satisfied assumption with spatial data. Without delving too much into the mathematical complexities of the topic, we note that, essentially, stationarity requires the pairwise association between observations to be solely a function of relative, as opposed to absolute, location so that, say, the correlation between two points three steps apart on the lattice will not vary with the region of the lattice the points occupy. Fortunately, the stationarity conditions required to simply derive bounds are not as stringent as those outlined above and the variable intersite correlations that would undoubtedly exist in many geographical data sets can be tolerated by the proposed correction procedure (see Fingleton 1983a, b). It would appear that a more serious problem is that of regional trends in the probability of occurrence of variables across the study area, so that plants may be less likely to occur in the north of a study region. This may restrict the adoption of the above method to localised study areas in which broad regional trends are not apparent, though trend could possibly be allowed for by introducing it as an explicit factor in a suitable multivariable model. In

Table 4.6. *Space-dependent observations of two types of flora in Hertfordshire*

| | | Foxglove | |
		present	absent
Wood sage	present	50 (21.07)	77 (105.93)
	absent	24 (52.93)	295 (266.07)

source: Silk (1979), see Seddon (1971) for further details.

Chapter 6 we extend the analysis to multiway tables describing temporally (and spatially) related observations.

In this chapter we have described a number of analyses involving factors and responses where the data are consistent with multinomial sampling, and have gone on to consider simple strategies that are available for tests of association in two-way tables when the basic assumption that observations are independent is violated, as in cluster sampling and time- and space-dependent data. We have favoured techniques where only very minimal assumptions are made of how observations are correlated. The chosen techniques are not the only ones available, though the corrections developed by various other authors for more-complex combinations of clustering and sampling have been omitted in the interests of simplicity.

5   Table design and inference

With dichotomous variables an n-variable analysis means 2^n cells in the ensuing n-way table, whereas the inclusion of polytomies among the set of n variables produces more than 2^n cells and less-compact marginal tables. A consequence is that even conceptually simple models may contain a surfeit of parameters corresponding to the enlarged marginal tables, thus making data interpretation somewhat more difficult. Also, the extra table cells may spread the sample too thinly to warrant the usual distributional assumptions about Y^2 and X^2.

This chapter is largely concerned with these and related problems arising from large unwieldy tables. It contains a description of some recent progress towards parsimonious modelling which involves the resolution of large sets of interaction parameters and takes account of the ordinal or higher-level values often attached to the levels of polytomies. Alternative strategies that are considered include the deletion of cells that are aberrant from the perspective of a simple model adequately fitting the majority of table cells, and category amalgamation and variable elimination. These latter ploys do have consequences which are discussed subsequently, though they remind us that table design is not an immutable phenomenon and that tables can be modified, not simply as a last resort to overcome the sparseness of observations and superfluity of parameters that often accompanies the analysis of polytomies, but as a means of illustrating and clarifying the meaning of interactions. The chapter is loosely organised as two halves. The first half mainly examines how simplification can be achieved via the models fitted to complex tables. The second half examines more-closely the role played by modifications to the table itself.

The simultaneous test procedure with polytomies

The presence of at least one polytomy among the set of variables analysed with the aid of the STP produces a minor necessary amendment to the scheme outlined in Chapter 3. This is illustrated by an analysis of the data in Table 5.1 which contains two polytomies and one dichotomy. The data describe the behaviour of consumers in the English Midlands and were collected and initially analysed in a different way by Williams (1979).

The starting point of the STP analysis is Table 5.2 and the overall type I error rate $\gamma = 1 - (1 - \alpha)^{2^r - r - 1}$ for an r-way table (see Aitkin 1979, p. 234), which should lie between 0.25 and 0.5. In this example this prerequisite means that $\alpha = 0.10$, $\gamma_3 = 1 - (0.9)^1$, $\gamma_{2,3} = 1 - (0.9)^4 = 0.34$. Since

$$4.14 < \chi^2_{4, 0.1} = 7.78,$$

the three-way effect can be set to zero. However, the combined deviance of the two- and three-way effects greatly exceeds the critical value of $\chi^2_{12, 0.34}$ indicating significant two-way interaction. Note at this juncture the essential difference between this application and the application of STP to dichotomies, which is that the number of effects no longer equals the number of degrees of freedom assigned to the appropriate critical χ^2 values. Having established the need for at least one two-way interaction, we enter them in two different orders in the search for a minimal adequate subset.

Table 5.3 demonstrates that only SF can be safely set to zero along with the three-way effect, since $4.88 + 4.14 = 9.02 = \chi^2_{12, 0.7} < \chi^2_{12, 0.34}$. Entered in the second order, all two-way interactions must be included since $107.61 + 4.14 = 111.75 > \chi^2_{12, 0.001} = 32.91 > \chi^2_{12, 0.34}$. Note that, in practice, with STP there is no general requirement to establish the exact critical value of χ^2. This is illustrated here by the use of logical relations between tabulated and untabulated χ^2 values to carry out significant tests.

In interpreting the fitted model SM/FM, the statement can be made that the size of centre patronised is related to the mode of travel, and trip frequency is

Table 5.1. *A three-way table with one dichotomous variable*

	M_1		M_2		M_3	
	F_1	F_2	F_1	F_2	F_1	F_2
S_1	102	28	2	3	9	10
S_2	48	12	10	11	3	15
S_3	43	18	27	45	22	89

key: $M_1 = $ walk; $M_2 = $ bus; $M_3 = $ car; mode of travel.
   $F_1 = $ frequent; $F_2 = $ seldom; frequency of trip.
   $S_1 = $ small; $S_2 = $ medium; $S_3 = $ large; size of centre visited.

Table 5.2. *Analysis of deviance entering all two-way and all three-way interactions*

Model	df	Y^2	Source	df	Deviance
S/F/M	12	288.47			
SF/SM/FM	4	4.14	two-way	8	284.33
SFM	0	0	three-way	4	4.14

also related to mode of travel. Given the existence of these interactions, trip frequency is independent of centre size since the *SF* parameter is legitimately set to zero.

Parameter trends

One difficulty of resorting to the parameter estimates of the model *SM/FM* to further aid interpretation of the data is the large number of parameters implied by the model, as can be seen in Table 5.4. What we in fact have are 21 parameters to interpret the original 18 numbers of Table 5.1 and, although these parameters are not all of the same importance and some are not

Table 5.3. *Analysis of deviance entering two-way effects in two different orders*

Model	df	Y^2	Source	df	Deviance
Order 1					
$S/F/M$	12	288.47			
SM/F	8	132.90	SM	4	155.57
SM/FM	6	9.02	FM	2	123.88
$SM/FM/SF$	4	4.14	SF	2	4.88
			residual	4	4.14
Order 2					
$S/F/M$	12	288.47			
FM/S	10	164.59	FM	2	123.88
FM/SF	8	111.75	SF	2	52.84
$SM/FM/SF$	4	4.14	SM	4	107.61
			residual	4	4.14

Table 5.4. *Parameter estimates of the model SM/FM fitted to Table 5.1*

Param.	Est.	sv	Param.	Est.	sv	Param.	Est.	sv
μ	2.80		λ_1^F	-0.07		λ_2^F	0.07	
λ_1^S	-0.48		λ_2^S	-0.27		λ_3^S	0.75	
λ_1^M	0.69		λ_2^M	-0.54		λ_3^M	-0.15	
λ_{11}^{FM}	0.67	7.4	λ_{12}^{FM}	-0.14	-1.1	λ_{13}^{FM}	-0.53	-4.8
λ_{11}^{SM}	0.99	6.9	λ_{21}^{SM}	0.01	0.1	λ_{31}^{SM}	-1.00	-8.8
λ_{12}^{SM}	-0.89	-4.0	λ_{22}^{SM}	0.34	2.1	λ_{32}^{SM}	0.55	3.9
λ_{13}^{SM}	-0.10	-0.5	λ_{23}^{SM}	-0.35	-2.2	λ_{33}^{SM}	0.45	3.6

key: param. = parameter.
  est. = estimate.
  sv = standardised value.

independent, this is hardly a satisfactory state of affairs and somewhat contrary to the stated goal of parsimony.

A reduction in the number of model parameters can be achieved by imposing extra constraints so that whole sets are represented by fewer parameters, a topic pursued in depth later. At this point we concentrate on an alternative simplifying device in which parameter sets are replaced by alternative sets of the same size designed to highlight essential features of the data latent in the original parameterisation. This approach makes various contrasts between parameters pertaining to category levels with a view to identifying the kind of trend existing in their values. With just three categories, two types of contrast are possible: one is a function of $\hat{\lambda}_1 - \hat{\lambda}_3$ and is designed to measure the strength of a linear trend in the original parameters; the other is a function of $\hat{\lambda}_1 - 2\hat{\lambda}_2 + \hat{\lambda}_3$ and its magnitude depends on the quadratic, that is, non-linear, trend in the original three parameters. We apply this to the parameters relating to the variable centre size with its distinguishable levels high to low. Table 5.5 gives the results of this and similar contrasts applied to all the variable S parameters together with standardised values obtained by methods described by Goodman (1971) and incorporated into the computer program ECTA.

We observe from the relative sizes of $\hat{\lambda}_L^S$ and $\hat{\lambda}_Q^S$ that, after controlling for other factors also influencing the frequencies, there is a predominantly linear increase in the attractiveness of centres with centre size category. However, the SM parameters of Table 5.5 indicate that the linear increase is not consistent but varies with travel mode. In fact, if one allows for the other influences, there is a linear decrease as centre size increases for pedestrians. The non-linear (quadratic) component $\hat{\lambda}_{Q_1}^{SM}$ is practically nil. This observation is consistent

Table 5.5. *Linear and quadratic effects*

Param.	Est.	sv
λ_L^S	−0.613	−6.27
λ_Q^S	0.137	2.52
$\lambda_{L_1}^{SM}$	0.991	8.91
$\lambda_{L_2}^{SM}$	−0.721	−4.30
$\lambda_{L_3}^{SM}$	−0.270	−2.08
$\lambda_{Q_1}^{SM}$	−0.005	−0.08
$\lambda_{Q_2}^{SM}$	−0.170	−2.06
$\lambda_{Q_3}^{SM}$	0.175	2.15

with the comparative inaccessibility to pedestrians of large, and hence widely spaced, centres. The reverse is true of bus travellers, for whom there is a linear increase in numbers with centre size category. The linearity of this trend is less conspicuous, and it becomes even less so when car travellers are considered.

Not only do the magnitudes of these deviations from linearity differ, but the direction differs also. For example, the attraction of small centres to bus passengers is much less than one would expect from a linear trend, probably reflecting routeing and fare policies, whilst they are much more attractive to car passengers than one would estimate from a linear trend. This is possibly a consequence of the relative cost and inconvenience of bus routes encouraging travellers to substitute car for bus travel.

We have confined the analysis to two kinds of parameter contrast simply because of the tripartite nature of the variable S. Given a larger number of categories, a variety of more subtle trends would be possible and different contrasts are available to detect them. If the number of categories increased to, say, five, then linear $(-2 -1\ 0\ 1\ 2)$, quadratic $(2 -1 -2 -1\ 2)$, cubic $(-1\ 2\ 0 -2\ 1)$ and quartic $(1 -4\ 6 -4\ 1)$ contrasts would be feasible. The numbers in brackets define the relation between parameters in the same way that linear $(-1\ 0\ 1)$ and quadratic $(1 -2\ 1)$ contrasts mean $(\lambda_1 - \lambda_3)$ and $(\lambda_1 - 2\lambda_2 + \lambda_3)$ in the above example. In general, if an ordinal variable has n categories, then contrasts up to degree $n - 1$ are possible.

Contrasts are also available that specify unequal distances between categories. For example, if the distance from the first to the second category is twice the distance from second to third, then the appropriate linear and quadratic contrasts become $(5 -1 -4)$ and $(1 -3\ 2)$. A variety of other contrasts can be obtained from standard tables such as those in Snedecor & Cochran (1974, p. 351, 572). The program documentation of ECTA (Goodman & Fay 1973) gives details of how to enter these to produce appropriate parameter estimates.

The presence of varied intercategory distances is considered in more detail in the following analyses utilising the GENSTAT program.

The uniform association model for the two-way table

The simple model SM/FM fitted to Table 5.1 ascribes six parameters, two of which are independent, to the FM interaction. We now demonstrate how this is reduced to a solitary uniform association parameter. Duncan (1979) and Goodman (1979a, b) give recent descriptions of the uniform association model, though it has origins in the work of Birch (1964, 1965) and others, as described by Plackett (1981). For the purposes of exposition, the analysis is based on Table 5.6, created by collapsing Table 5.1 over variable S. Treating the extended table as a two-way table can in fact be done, in this particular case, without any distortion of the estimates of the *FM* interaction parameters of Table 5.4, which are identical in the collapsed table. Rules describing the consequences of table collapsing are discussed in general terms later, and an analysis of the extended Table (5.1) is also given subsequently.

Replacing the *FM* interaction parameters by the single uniform association parameter $\hat{\phi}^{FM} = 1.238$ gives $Y^2 = 2.94 < \chi^2_{1,\,0.05} = 3.84$, compared with the perfect fit and zero degrees of freedom of the saturated model. Thus, constraining the *FM* association to a single parameter produces an insignificant loss of fit. Table 5.7 contains the expected frequencies. The independence model fits Table 5.6 very badly, with $Y^2 = 123.9 > \chi^2_{2,\,0.05} = 5.99$, but the inclusion of ϕ^{FM} brings about a highly significant improvement in fit of

$$123.9 - 2.94 = 120.96 > \chi^2_{1,\,0.05} = 3.84$$

Generally this is a test of the null hypothesis $\phi = 0$ that is a more powerful alternative to the usual chi-squared test of independence, given that the uniform association model is true (Goodman 1981*a*, p. 227). The significance of ϕ^{FM} is reaffirmed by its standardised value of 10.01.

The term 'uniform association' reflects the equality of the odds-ratio measure of association applied to the Table 5.7 frequencies, in which

$$(e_{11}e_{22}/e_{21}e_{12}) = (e_{12}e_{23}/e_{13}e_{22})$$

and $\log (e_{ij}e_{i+1j+1}/e_{ij+1}e_{i+1j}) = 1.238$.

Table 5.6. *The marginal two-way trip frequency (F) against travel mode (M) table*

		M		
		Walk (M_1)	Bus (M_2)	Car (M_3)
F	Frequent (F_1)	193	39	34
	Seldom (F_2)	58	59	114

Table 5.7. *Expected frequencies from the uniform association model fitted to Table 5.6*

	M_1	M_2	M_3
F_1	189.40	46.19	30.40
F_2	61.60	51.81	117.60

key: as for Table 5.6.

In contrast, if the independence model were fitted, one would find

$$\log \left(e_{ij} e_{i+1j+1} / e_{ij+1} e_{i+1j} \right) = 0.$$

The expected frequencies of Table 5.7 are obtained by substituting the parameter estimates of Table 5.8 into the following equation.

$$\log \left(e_{ij} \right) = \hat{\mu}' + \hat{\lambda}_i'^F + \hat{\lambda}_j'^M + v_i v_j \hat{\phi}^{FM} \qquad (i = 1, 2)$$
$$(j = 1, \ldots, 3)$$

where

$$\hat{\lambda}_1'^F = \hat{\lambda}_1'^M = 0$$

and

$$v_i = i \quad \text{and} \quad v_j = j.$$

The scores $\{v_i\}$ and $\{v_j\}$ assigned in this example to the levels of the (ordinal) row and column variables have the effect of equalising the local odds ratios derived from adjacent rows, as mentioned above. They can be used to reflect an assumption of equal intercategory distances.

As noted in Chapter 1, the GENSTAT program used to obtain these estimates involes a Plackett-style (1981) parameterisation with the 'first' level of each parameter set constrained to zero. The prime distinguishes these parameters from those subject to Goodman and ECTA-style constraints. Listing 2 (appendix) reproduces Tables 5.7 and 5.8.

As already intimated, scoring systems other than the one adopted above can be used to deal with unequal intercategory distances, though, sometimes, scores may be somewhat subjective and arbitrary because information is lacking regarding a latent variable on which to base the system. This potential arbitrariness does not, however, debar the use of scores. Agresti (1983) argues that they can 'provide information about the nature of the association without needing to regard them as indices of how far apart the ordered levels truly are'. The analysis of Table 5.11 is carried out with this exploratory approach in mind. Although not displaying constant association in the strictest sense, the models fitted to Tables 5.11 and 5.21 are referred to as uniform association models by virtue of their uniform response to change per unit of the designated category values.

Table 5.8. *Parameter estimates of the uniform association model fitted to Table 5.6*

Param.	μ'	$\lambda_2'^F$	$\lambda_2'^M$	$\lambda_3'^M$	ϕ^{FM}
Est.	4.01	−2.36	−2.65	−4.31	1.238
sv	33.03	−9.79	−13.03	−10.52	10.01

One option, given a lack of knowledge about the true category scores, is to estimate them from the data at hand. Plackett (1981) contains coms discussion on methods of category score estimation, and the general problem has also been considered by, among others, Andrich (1979), Andersen (1980), and Goodman (1979a, 1981a, b). Goodman (1979a) and Agresti (1983) describe an iterative method of score estimation. In this chapter we remain with preallocated scores, but intercategory distance estimation is reintroduced in Chapter 6 in the context of mobility tables.

The importance of the uniform association model, therefore, is that it fills a lacuna between the often unrealistically simple independence model and the usually unnecessarily complex saturated model for the two-way table, and that it introduces an important family of alternative and interrelated models (Goodman 1979a, b; Duncan 1979; Clogg 1982a, b) of which it is a special case with predesignated scores and constant local association. Variants exist in the literature in which the association is no longer uniform and which can depend on row and column effects. As we shall see, the model extends readily to the multiway table. The review by Agresti (1983) gives a comprehensive account of methods available for the analysis of cross-classifications having ordinal variables.

A further example of the application of the uniform association model to the two-way table is obtained by collapsing Table 5.1 over variable F. The data are given in Table 5.9.

Note that, as in the previous example, collapsing is a valid procedure which does not distort the interaction in the marginal table. The SM parameter estimates given in Table 5.4 and applying to Table 5.1 equal those which would be obtained on fitting the saturated model to Table 5.9. In order to achieve a model more parsimonious than the saturated model to capture the association in Table 5.9, we again fit the uniform association model, thus reducing the four independent SM parameters to one. The model, which generates the expected frequencies

Table 5.9. *The marginal two-way centre size (S) against travel mode (M) table*

		M		
		Walk (M_1)	Bus (M_2)	Car (M_3)
	Small (S_1)	130	5	19
S	Medium (S_2)	60	21	18
	Large (S_3)	61	72	111

key: S = size.
M = travel mode.

of Table 5.10, is less successful than for Table 5.6, with $X^2 = 28.7$ and $Y^2 = 31.78 > \chi^2_{3,0.05} = 7.82$. Note, however, that the inclusion of the extra parameter $\phi^{SM} (\hat{\phi}^{SM} = 0.766, sv = 9.6)$ has a considerable effect in reducing Y^2 from 142.09 for the independence model, a decrease of 110.31 for the loss of 1 df. Clearly, there is need for a model with an association component, but the assumption of constant association is too restrictive for Table 5.9.

The expected frequencies in Table 5.10 aid further comprehension of the uniform association model and indicate the source of lack of fit. Written as a model of dependence, $\log(e_{2j}/e_{1j})$, the expected log odds of the medium to small centre choice are, after allowing for rounding, a linear function with slope ϕ^{SM} of the level of mobility. A similar linear trend with the same slope exists for the expected log odds for large to medium centres, $\log(e_{3j}/e_{2j})$.

Plotting the log odds against j gives parallel lines, and so this model of dependence is called the parallel log-odds model by Goodman (1981a, p. 219; 1983). Clearly, this is a regression-like model with the log odds dependent on ordinal indices 1, 2, 3 assigned to the levels of factor M.

A large part of the lack of fit of this model to Table 5.9 is due to the observed frequencies in cells S_1M_2 and S_1M_3, which contribute 12.28 and 9.20 respectively to the overall X^2. There are more car travellers to small centres than expected from a consistent fall off in the odds of small to medium centre choice with extra mobility, as implied by the model, and far fewer bus passengers than expected. Both these conclusions are in line with those of the earlier analysis of the extended table based on linear and quadratic contrasts.

Quantitative category values for the two-way table

In this section we consider models in which $v_i \neq i$ and $v_j \neq j$ but which are assigned numerical values that are not necessarily equidistant. For example, the data in Table 5.11 describe the toxicity of the insecticide γ-benzene hexachloride as it affects the beetle *Tribolium castaneum*. The insecticide deposits are measured in mg per 10 cc but there is reason to believe that there will be a linear response to $\log_{10}$ deposit. Previous analysis of these data has been carried out by Hewlett & Plackett (1950) and Plackett (1981).

Table 5.10. *Expected frequencies from the uniform association model fitted to Table 5.9*

	M_1	M_2	M_3
S_1	123.3	21.1	9.6
S_2	57.3	21.1	20.7
S_3	70.4	55.8	117.7

Fitting the uniform association model, we obtain $Y^2 = 2.214 < \chi^2_{4, 0.05} = 9.49$. Table 5.12 gives the parameter estimates. The expected frequencies which are given in Table 5.13 are obtained using $v_i = i$ and $v_j = \log_{10}$ deposit.

It is possible to rewrite the uniform association model as a logit regression model, with the log odds of survival depending on the administered quantity of insecticide as follows:

$$\log(e_{2j}/e_{1j}) = \hat{\alpha} + \hat{\beta}(D_j - D_J) \qquad (j = 1, \ldots, J)$$

$$D_j = \log_{10} \text{ deposit in category } j$$

$$\hat{\alpha} = \log(e_{2J}/e_{1J})$$

The maximum likelihood estimate of the regression line slope $\hat{\beta}$ equals $\hat{\phi}^{SD}$, and indicates that as one approaches the maximum dose the log odds of survival fall at the rate of 3.96 per unit increase in $\log_{10}$ deposit.

Table 5.11. *A two-way table with a quantitative factor*

			$\log_{10}$ deposit (D)					
			1.082	1.161	1.212	1.258	1.310	1.348
Survival (S)	at most, six days	S_1	15	24	26	24	29	29
	more than six days	S_2	35	25	24	26	21	20

Table 5.12. *Parameter estimates of the uniform association model fitted to Table 5.11*

Param.	μ'	$\lambda_2'^S$	$\lambda_2'^D$	$\lambda_3'^D$	$\lambda_4'^D$	$\lambda_5'^D$	$\lambda_6'^D$	ϕ^{SD}
Est.	7.16	4.90	0.48	0.82	1.09	1.39	1.58	-3.96
Sv	5.4	2.98	1.79	2.33	2.54	2.68	2.72	-2.97

Table 5.13. *Expected frequencies from the logit model fitted to Table 5.11*

			$\log_{10}$ deposit (D)					
			1.082	1.161	1.212	1.258	1.310	1.348
Survival (S)	at most, six days	S_1	17.62	20.91	23.83	26.11	28.66	29.87
	more than six days	S_2	32.38	28.09	26.17	23.89	21.34	19.13

An indication of the appropriateness of the $\log_{10}$ transformation of the original deposits can be obtained by plotting $\log(f_{2j}/f_{1j})$ against D_j, which conform approximately to a straight line. The slope of the line provides a first approximation to the maximum likelihood estimate $\hat{\beta}$ or $\hat{\phi}^{SD}$. In general, a variety of transformations can be tried.

Fitting the uniform association model

The observed frequencies (f_{ij}) and the expected frequencies (e_{ij}) from a uniform association model or an equivalent logit regression model satisfy the following constraints

$$e_{i0} = f_{i0} \qquad (i = 1, \ldots, I)$$

$$e_{0j} = f_{0j} \qquad (j = 1, \ldots, J)$$

$$\sum_i \sum_j v_i v_j e_{ij} = \sum_i \sum_j v_i v_j f_{ij}$$

We note subsequently that these generalise to the multiway table.

The final constraint makes estimation difficult, though apparently not impossible, using ECTA or an equivalent program (Duncan 1979). Goodman (1979a) gives details of a method that provides parameter estimates, though one is required to write a computer program to solve the equations. The algorithm of Darroch & Ratcliff (1972) is one of several existing programs that can be used. Listing 3 (Appendix) gives the GENSTAT commands that reproduce the results pertaining to Table 5.11. It would be difficult to achieve these estimates in a much simpler way.

Uniform association models for multiway tables

The problem of an overabundance of parameters is magnified in multiway tables involving polytomies. Fortunately, the simplification produced when sets of parameters can be replaced by a single uniform association parameter extends to the multiway table. Consider for instance the three-way table and the three-way interaction parameters $\{\lambda_{ijk}^{ABC}\}$. Whichever constraint system is adopted, for the $I \times J \times K$ cell table, there are $(I-1)(J-1)(K-1)$ independent parameters in this set. A more parsimonious model than the saturated model

$$\log(p_{ijk}) = \mu + \lambda_i^A + \lambda_j^B + \lambda_k^C + \lambda_{ij}^{AB} + \lambda_{ik}^{AC} + \lambda_{jk}^{BC} + \lambda_{ijk}^{ABC}$$

is

$$\log(p_{ijk}) = \mu + \lambda_i^A + \lambda_j^B + \lambda_k^C + \lambda_{ij}^{AB} + \lambda_{ik}^{AC} + \lambda_{jk}^{BC}$$
$$+ v_i v_j \omega_k \phi^{ABC}$$

which Goodman (1981a) refers to as the uniform three-factor interaction model.

The constraint $\phi^{ABC} = 0$ is consistent with the model $AB/AC/BC$ and thus $\phi^{ABC} = \phi$ is denoted by $AB/AC/BC/\phi^{ABC}$. If the uniform three-factor interaction models hold true the difference between the Y^2 values of $AB/AC/BC$ and $AB/AC/BC/\phi^{ABC}$ is a more powerful test of the null hypothesis of no three-way interaction than the usual comparison of $AB/AC/BC$ with the saturated model. Since values of v_i, v_j and ω_k again represent category scores or values rather than parameters estimated from the data, there is 1 df for this test.

This is illustrated by an analysis of the data in Table 5.14 which are also analysed by Ashford & Sowden (1970), Mantel & Brown (1973), Plackett (1980) and Fienberg (1980).

Denoting age by A, breathlessness by B and wheeze by W, the model of zero three-way interaction $AB/WB/AW$ gives $Y^2 = 26.69 > \chi^2_{8, 0.05} = 15.51$, indicating the presence of differential association between wheeze and breathlessness with increasing age.

For example the log cross-product ratio for the youngest age group gives

$$\log\left[(9 \times 1841)/(7 \times 95)\right] = 3.22$$

compared with

$$\log\left[(372 \times 526)/(106 \times 132)\right] = 2.64$$

for the oldest group. As Plackett (1981) observes, if one places all the log cross-product ratios in order of increasing age, they conform roughly to a linear trend with slope -0.15. Fitting the uniform three-factor interaction model, one obtains the maximum likelihood estimate of this slope $\hat{\phi}^{ABW} = -0.1306$ with

Table 5.14. *Coal miners classified by age, breathlessness and wheeze*

Age group in years (A)	Breathlessness (B)		No breathlessness		
	wheeze (W)	no wheeze	wheeze	no wheeze	Total
20–24	9	7	95	1 841	1 952
25–29	23	9	105	1 654	1 791
30–34	54	19	177	1 863	2 113
35–39	121	48	257	2 357	2 783
40–44	169	54	273	1 778	2 274
45–49	269	88	324	1 712	2 393
50–54	404	117	245	1 324	2 090
55–59	406	152	225	967	1 750
60–64	372	106	132	526	1 136
Total	1 827	600	1 833	14 022	18 282

standardised value $= -4.43$. This model fits very adequately with

$$Y^2 = 6.8 < \chi^2_{7, 0.05} = 14.07.$$

The effect of incorporating the single parameter ϕ^{ABW} is to significantly reduce Y^2 by $19.89 = 26.69 - 6.80 > \chi^2_{1, 0.05} = 3.84$.

Estimation requires the solution of the following equations

$$e_{ij0} = f_{ij0} \qquad (i = 1, \dots, I; \ j = 1, \dots, J)$$

$$e_{i0k} = f_{i0k} \qquad (i = 1, \dots, I; k = 1, \dots, K)$$

$$e_{0jk} = f_{0jk} \qquad (j = 1, \dots, J; k = 1, \dots, K)$$

$$\sum_i \sum_j \sum_k v_i v_j \omega_k e_{ijk} = \sum_i \sum_j \sum_k v_i v_j \omega_k f_{ijk}$$

$$(v_i = i; \ v_j = j; \ \omega_k = k)$$

Listing 4 (Appendix) shows how these are solved using GENSTAT, which also automatically provides parameter estimates and standard errors. The estimate $\hat{\phi}^{ABW}$ is also obtainable from the expected frequencies of Table 5.15 since, in general

$$\hat{\phi}^{ABC} = \log \left[\frac{e_{ijk} e_{ij+1k+1}}{e_{ij+1k} e_{ijk+1}} \right] \Big/ \left[\frac{e_{i+1jk} e_{i+1j+1k+1}}{e_{i+1j+1k} e_{i+1jk+1}} \right]$$

Fitting the uniform three-factor interaction model $SM/SF/FM/\phi^{SFM}$ to Table 5.1 gives $Y^2 = 2.95 < \chi^2_{3, 0.05} = 7.82$ compared with

Table 5.15. *Expected frequencies of the uniform three-factor association fitted to Table 5.14*

		B_1		B_2		
		W_1	W_2	W_1	W_2	Total
		10.21	5.79	93.79	1 842.21	1 952
		21.21	10.79	106.79	1 652.21	1 791
		52.49	20.51	178.51	1 861.49	2 113
		121.39	47.61	256.61	2 357.39	2 783
A		169.29	53.71	272.71	1 778.29	2 274
		274.77	82.23	318.23	1 717.77	2 393
		393.34	127.66	255.66	1 313.34	2 090
		418.79	139.21	212.21	979.79	1 750
		365.51	112.49	138.49	519.51	1 136
Total		1 827	600	1 833	14 022	18 282

key: A = age category $\quad (i = 1, \dots, I)$.
$\quad\ \ B$ = breathlessness $\ (j = 1, \dots, J)$.
$\quad\ \ W$ = wheeze $\qquad\quad (k = 1, \dots, K)$.

$$Y^2 = 4.14 < \chi^2_{4,\,0.05} = 9.49$$

for the $SM/SF/FM$ model. Thus the constraint $\phi^{SFM} = 0$ incurs an insignificant loss of fit of $1.19 < \chi^2_{1,\,0.05} = 3.84$ and confirms the earlier conclusion of no three-way interaction.

Uniform conditional association

The previous analysis of Table 5.1 found that the model SM/FM fitted adequately. The absence of the SF and SFM interactions enables one to say that, for a given level of M, S and F are independent. This conditional independence can be denoted generally by $\Phi_{ij:k} = 0$ and corresponds to

$$\log\left[(e_{ijk}e_{i+1j+1k})/(e_{ij+1k}e_{i+1jk})\right] = 0$$

for

$$i = 1, \ldots, I-1; \quad j = 1, \ldots, J-1$$

An alternative proposition is that

$$\Phi_{ij:k} = \phi_k$$

This hypothesis is that the association between S and F is summarised by a single parameter (ϕ_k^{SF}) which assumes separate values at each of the K levels of variable M. Goodman (1981a, p. 233) calls this uniform conditional association and for Table 5.1 we write the model as

$$\log(e_{ijk}) = \hat{\mu}' + \hat{\lambda}_i'^{S} + \hat{\lambda}_j'^{F} + \hat{\lambda}_k'^{M} + \hat{\lambda}_{ij}'^{SM} + \hat{\lambda}_{jk}'^{FM} + v_i v_j \hat{\phi}_k^{SF}$$

or

$$SM/FM/\phi_k^{SF}$$

In fact, in order to fit this model to Table 5.1, we fit the uniform association model to the three two-way centre size (S) against frequency (F) tables existing at each of the three levels of variable M and sum the individual Y^2 to arrive at the aggregate $Y^2 = 2.82$ for the uniform conditional association model.

Compared with the model SM/FM there are three less degrees of freedom corresponding to the three extra parameters ϕ_k^{SF}, and thus the goodness-of-fit test is $2.82 < \chi^2_{3,\,0.05} = 7.82$. Although the uniform conditional association model fits very well, the ϕ_k^{SF} estimates of Table 5.16 suggest that adopting the

Table 5.16. *Parameter estimates of the uniform conditional association model fitted to Table 5.1*

Param.	ϕ_1^{SF}	ϕ_2^{SF}	ϕ_3^{SF}
Est.	0.19	0.22	0.56
sv	1.07	0.61	2.21

simpler *SM/FM* model ($Y^2 = 9.02 < \chi^2_{6,\,0.05} = 12.59$) incorporating the constraint that *S* and *F* are conditionally independent may not involve a significant loss of fit. The difference $9.02 - 2.82 = 6.20 < \chi^2_{3,\,0.05} = 7.82$ verifies that setting the three ϕ_k^{SF} parameters to zero is a legitimate simplification. Although this conditional independence has already been demonstrated by the earlier analysis, the present test, requiring the assumption that uniform conditional association holds true, is a more powerful test than the straightforward difference between the Y^2 of the *SM/FM* and *SM/FM/SF* models. The results of similar tests on the other two-way interactions are given in Table 5.18. Table 5.17 gives the expected frequencies from the two models.

Performing the same test of zero conditional association on the *FM* interaction requires a comparison of the models *SM/SF* and $SM/SF/\phi_i^{FM}$ which differ by the three parameters describing the (different amounts of) uniform association between *F* and *M* at each level of *S*. This is given in Table 5.18, and since $78.26 > \chi^2_{3,\,0.05} = 7.82$, these three parameters cannot be set to zero. A similar conclusion is obtained for the ϕ_j^{SM} parameters.

Uniform partial association

A further extension is to assume that the uniform conditional association model holds, and to test the proposition that the association is constrained to be

Table 5.17. *Expected frequencies generated by fitting SM/FM and $SM/FM/\phi_k^{SF}$ to Table 5.1*

	(i) *SM/FM*					
	M_1		M_2		M_3	
	F_1	F_2	F_1	F_2	F_1	F_2
S_1	99.96	30.04	1.99	3.01	4.36	14.64
S_2	46.14	13.86	8.36	12.64	4.14	13.86
S_3	46.90	14.10	28.65	43.35	25.50	85.50

	(ii) $SM/FM/\phi_k^{SF}$					
	M_1		M_2		M_3	
	F_1	F_2	F_1	F_2	F_1	F_2
S_1	103.18	26.82	2.44	2.56	7.90	11.10
S_2	45.64	14.36	9.12	11.88	5.20	12.80
S_3	44.18	16.82	27.44	44.56	20.90	90.10

key: as for Table 5.1.

constant as k varies. This can be represented as

$$\Phi_{ij:k} = \phi \qquad (k = 1, \ldots, K)$$

This condition implies no three-way interaction in the three-way table, and is called by Goodman (1981a, p. 234) the uniform partial association model.

This can be applied to, say, the *FM* interaction of Table 5.1 by fitting the $SM/SF/\phi^{FM}$ model, which states that there is uniform conditional association between F and M which does not vary in magnitude with the level of S. The goodness of fit of this model is given in Table 5.18, together with the goodness of fit of comparable models with uniform partial association applied to the *SM* and *SF* interactions.

The test of the constant ϕ_i^{FM} $(i = 1, \ldots, I)$ constraint, that is, zero three-factor interaction, is accomplished by comparing the Y^2 of two models that

Table 5.18. *Various uniform association and other models fitted to Table 5.1*

	Model	df	Y^2
1	SM/FM	6	9.02
2	$SM/FM/\phi_k^{SF}$	3	2.82
3	SM/SF	6	80.06
4	$SM/SF/\phi_i^{FM}$	3	1.80
5	SF/FM	8	111.75
6	$SF/FM/\phi_j^{SM}$	6	34.08
7	$SM/FM/\phi^{SF}$	5	4.29
8	$SM/SF/\phi^{FM}$	5	5.30
9	$SF/FM/\phi^{SM}$	7	34.10
10	$F/SM/\phi^{FM}$	7	11.97
11	$S/FM/\phi^{SM}$	9	40.81
12	$S/F/M/\phi^{FM}/\phi^{SM}$	10	43.75

Test		Models compared	df	Y^2
Zero conditional association	(SF)	1 − 2	3	6.20
	(FM)	3 − 4	3	78.26
	(SM)	5 − 6	2	77.65
Zero three-factor interaction	(SF)	7 − 2	2	1.47
	(FM)	8 − 4	2	3.50
	(SM)	9 − 6	1	0.02
Zero partial association	(SF)	1 − 7	1	4.73
	(FM)	3 − 8	1	74.76
	(SM)	5 − 9	1	77.65
Uniform partial association	(FM)	10 − 1	1	2.95
	(SM)	11 − 1	3	31.79

differ by this condition alone, such as models 8 and 4 in Table 5.18. Since $3.50 < \chi^2_{2,0.05} = 5.99$, it is legitimate to invoke the single ϕ^{FM} parameter, in place of the I ϕ_i^{FM} parameters, and thus there are $I - 1$ df for this test. Assuming uniform conditional association holds, these are more powerful tests than the usual zero three-factor interaction test, and they reaffirm the previous conclusion of zero three-factor interaction in Table 5.1.

The test of zero partial association is based on the assumption that the uniform partial association model holds true; in other words that, say, $SM/SF/\phi^{FM}$ holds true and the association between F and M is representable by a single parameter. The test is of the hypothesis that this single parameter is zero, and thus a comparison is made of two models (for example, SM/SF and $SM/SF/\phi^{FM}$) that differ solely by this parameter. Table 5.18 gives the details of this test; the ϕ^{FM} and ϕ^{SM} parameters cannot be set to zero and the ϕ^{SF} parameter, though significant, is probably unnecessary, as shown by the zero conditional association test that allows the ϕ_k^{SF} parameters to be nullified.

We therefore delete ϕ^{SF} but retain the SM and FM interactions, though not both in the form of partial associations since Table 5.18 shows that SM fails the test of uniform partial association. The final model is, therefore, $F/SM/\phi^{FM}$ for which $Y^2 = 11.97 < \chi^2_{7,0.05} = 14.07$. This concurs with the previous analyses of the marginal tables (Tables 5.6 and 5.9). Observe that the estimate $\hat{\phi}^{FM} = 1.238$ (sv = 10.01) retains its previous value in this extended table analysis.

The data in Table 5.19 describe the drinking of subjects living in group quarters; this was originally given by Bahr (1969) and analysed by Williams & Grizzle (1972) and Upton (1978a).

Table 5.19. *Drinking subjects living in group quarters*

Location (C)	No. of years in quarters (B)	Extent of drinking (A)		
		light	moderate	heavy
Bowery	0	25	21	26
	1–4	21	18	23
	5 +	20	19	21
Camp	0	29	27	38
	1–4	16	13	24
	5 +	8	11	30
Park slope	0	44	19	9
	1–4	18	9	4
	5 +	6	8	3

Variable A (drinking), is a response to variables B and C, and thus all models fitted to Table 5.19 (see Table 5.20) should contain the BC interaction (see Chapter 4). It is legitimate to drop the three-way ABC interaction, as indicated by the very adequate fit of $BC/BA/CA$ with $Y^2 = 5.48 < \chi^2_{8,\,0.05} = 15.51$. This is affirmed by the difference between this model and $BC/BA/CA/\phi^{ABC}$ for which $Y^2 = 2.96$, the single extra uniform three-factor interaction parameter does not significantly improve the fit for the loss of one df.

The model consisting solely of two-way interactions can be simplified further by representing the sets of interaction parameters by single uniform partial association parameters. The results of fitting various simplified models are also given in Table 5.20. This information was derived from GENSTAT listing 5 (Appendix). Note from Table 5.20 that though the BA interaction can be very adequately represented by the uniform partial association parameter ϕ^{BA}, the same is not true of the CA interaction. Observe also the extra power of the test of the BA interaction when the model $BC/CA/\phi^{BA}$ holds true. Comparing this with BC/CA, a significant loss of fit occurs, whereas the comparison of BC/CA and $BC/BA/CA$ does not produce the same conclusion. The estimate of ϕ^{BA} is 0.14 with standardised value 2.05, again indicating that it is a significant effect and that there is a steady rise in the number of heavy drinkers with increased years in quarters. The lack of fit of the model $BC/A/\phi^{BA}/\phi^{CA}$ is because of the inadequacy of the assumption of uniform partial association for the CA interaction. The main differences between the observed frequencies in Table 5.19 and the expected frequencies produced by this model illustrate the true nature of this CA interaction, for there is less light drinking and more heavy drinking than expected at location Camp. These conclusions are similar to those of Upton (1978a) who analysed the data using the related methods of linear and quadratic contrasts.

Table 5.20. *Uniform partial association and other models fitted to Table 5.19*

Model	df	Y^2
$BC/BA/CA$	8	5.48
$BC/BA/CA/\phi^{ABC}$	7	2.96
$BC/CA/\phi^{BA}$	11	6.25
$BC/A/\phi^{BA}/\phi^{CA}$	14	36.84
$BC/A/\phi^{CA}$	15	41.28
BC/CA	12	10.50

Uniform association models for multiway tables with
quantitative levels

The extension from the preceding analyses to multiway tables of
variables, some of which have quantitative levels, is very easily accomplished
even when the values assigned to levels are not equidistant. Table 5.21 is such
an example with unequal category distances which describes the response of
ingots to various amounts of heating and soaking. These data have been
analysed previously by Cox (1970) and by Fienberg (1980).

Since heating and soaking are factors, the *SH* interaction is again incorporated
in any model fitted to the data (see Chapter 4), and this sets

$$e_{ij0} = f_{ij0} \qquad (i = 1, \ldots, I)$$
$$(j = 1, \ldots, J)$$

This means that the total number of ingots tested at any combination of heating
and soaking times equates to the expected number not ready plus the expected
number ready. Note that no ingots were soaked for 2.8 minutes and heated for
51 minutes, and thus none are expected in this category. One of the *SH* parameters accounts for these two zero expected frequencies. Note also that the

Table 5.21. *The response of ingots to various amounts of heating and soaking*

Ready for rolling (R)	Soaking time (S)	Heating time (H)				
		7	14	27	51	Total
Not ready	1.0	0	0	1	3	4
	1.7	0	0	4	0	4
	2.2	0	2	0	0	2
	2.8	0	0	1	0	1
	4.0	0	0	1	0	1
	Total	0	2	7	3	12
						Total
Ready	1.0	10	31	55	10	106
	1.7	17	45	40	1	101
	2.2	7	31	21	1	60
	2.8	12	31	21	0	64
	4.0	9	19	15	1	44
	Total	55	155	152	13	375

note: heating and soaking times are not necessarily minutes but are, for simplicity,
referred to as such.

inclusion of the *HR* parameter in any model means that

$$e_{0jk} = f_{0jk} \qquad (j = 1, \ldots, J)$$
$$(k = 1, \ldots, K)$$

Since $f_{011} = 0$, then $e_{011} = 0$. This means that five expected frequencies $(e_{111} - e_{511})$ are zero, and accounted for by one parameter equivalent to the constraint $e_{011} = f_{011}$.

Fitting the model of zero three-way interaction $SH/SR/HR$ gives $Y^2 = 11.28$. Two of the parameters of this model set seven expected frequencies equal to zero for the reasons given above, and thus the remaining 33 expected frequencies are accounted for by the remaining 26 independent parameters. The difference, seven, is the number of degrees of freedom rather than the 12 that would be available in the absence of the zero marginal totals.

Although $SH/SR/HR$ fits adequately, further simplification can be achieved by using parameters specifying uniform partial association. For example, the model $SH/SR/\phi^{HR}$ fits only very marginally less well with $Y^2 = 12.17$ and 13 df. The extra degrees of freedom are because the exclusion of *HR* means that the constraint $e_{0jk} = f_{0jk}, j = 1, \ldots, J; k = 1, \ldots, K$ no longer holds and thus the zero in the *HR* margin no longer implies a zero expected marginal frequency and hence five expected frequencies of zero.

The model can be simplified further by also assuming uniform partial association for the *SR* interaction to give $SH/R/\phi^{SR}/\phi^{HR}$ with

$$Y^2 = 13.75 < \chi^2_{16,\,0.05} = 26.30.$$

For this model $\hat{\phi}^{SR} = -0.057$ (sv $= -0.17$) and $\hat{\phi}^{HR} = -0.082$ (sv $= -3.46$). Further simplification is achieved by removing the single insignificant parameter ϕ^{SR}, which only increases Y^2 by 0.03. This gives $\hat{\phi}^{HR} = -0.0807$ (sv $= -3.61$). Disregarding the sign, this is exactly the estimate obtained by Cox (1970) and Fienberg (1980). Observe the equivalence of these models to the logit regression model in which the parameter ϕ^{HR} is the change in the dependent logit (e_{ij1}/e_{ij2}) per unit change in heating time. This is comparable to the change in the observed log odds, which, for example, change from $\log(2/155)$ to $\log(7/152)$ after an extra 13 minutes of heating, a fall in the log odds of ingot readiness of 0.098 per minute.

The above analyses are only a sample of those possible. For example, various functions of the category values could replace the original ones, as in the parallel analysis for the two-way table (Table 5.11) given earlier. The equivalence of the uniform association model to some logit regression models estimated by maximum likelihood has been shown, and from this it is evident that the methods advocated are widely applicable to the analysis of rates and proportions that are commonly analysed by logit regression.

More generally, analyses can be extended to higher-dimensional tables, to tables in which several polytomous variables are specified, and to incomplete tables (Goodman 1979*a*). Goodman (1981*c*; 1981*d*) discusses other aspects of association models for tables with ordered categories.

Alternatives to maximum likelihood

All the parameters and expected frequencies estimated in this book are obtained by the maximum likelihood method, which was very briefly outlined in Chapter 4. However, logit regression models such as those just described, and indeed models for contingency tables in general, can also be estimated by criteria other than what amounts to the minimisation of Y^2. Before the advent of user-friendly computer packages, maximum likelihood estimation was probably less familiar to the non-mathematician steeped in regression analysis than the method of (non-iterative) weighted least squares, which, as the name suggests, bears a close relation to the often familiar methodology of least squares estimation. This method was originally developed by Berkson (1944, 1955) (see also Grizzle *et al.* 1969). Cox (1970), Plackett (1981) and Bishop *et al.* (1975) discuss the relative merits of the maximum likelihood and weighted least squares method.

Other alternatives also exist, as listed below, and though all are different functions of the observed and expected frequencies, Berkson (1980) argues that each is asymptotically distributed as χ^2. Neyman's (1949) chi-squared statistic has certain computational advantages over the more familiar Pearson chi-squared statistic, and Kullback's (Ireland *et al.* 1969) discriminant information statistic also has certain advantages compared with maximum likelihood estimation when testing some specialised models (see Chapter 6). Note that the relation between X_K^2 and Y^2 is similar to that between X_N^2 and X^2 with reversed positions of the observed and expected frequencies. Observe also from the formula for X_B^2 that, in common with ordinary least squares, the criterion is the minimisation of the (weighted) sum of the squared residuals.

(i) Pearson's chi-squared statistic $X^2 = \Sigma\left[(f-e)^2/e\right]$

(ii) Neyman's chi-squared statistic $X_N^2 = \Sigma\left[(f-e)^2/f\right]$

(iii) likelihood ratio statistic (maximum likelihood estimation)
$Y^2 = 2\Sigma f \log\left(f/e\right)$

(iv) Kullback's discriminant information (minimum modified discriminant information) $X_K^2 = 2\Sigma e \log\left(e/f\right)$

(v) Non-iterative weighted least squares (minimum logit chi-squared)
$X_B^2 = (\bar{\mathbf{L}} - \mathbf{L})'\mathbf{D}^{-1}(\bar{\mathbf{L}} - \mathbf{L})$

key: f = observed frequency
e = expected frequency

It is this which is the main alternative to maximum likelihood, involving, for the simple logit model outlined earlier, the solution of

$$\hat{B} = (X'D^{-1}X)^{-1}X'D^{-1}\bar{L}$$

which is a generalisation of the ordinary least squares estimating equation

$$\hat{B} = (X'X)^{-1}X'\bar{L}$$

The diagonal matrix D^{-1} is actually implied by the ordinary least squares estimating equation, but only needs to be made explicit when it is no longer an identity matrix. Its role then is to differentially weight each observation. For the single one-factor and one-dichotomous-response logit regression the vector of parameters B consists of α and β, the slope and intercept, respectively, of the regression line. The full model is written as $L = XB$, where $L = \log(p_{1j}/p_{2j})$. The design matrix X contains functions of the values of the factor x and can be simply ones and zeros for truly categorical factors. These equations generalise to the multivariate case, an example being Cox's (1970) weighted least squares analysis of the ingot data in Table 5.21. There are also a variety of functions of a response variable, for 'link' functions other than the logit are often used to stretch an untransformed 0-1 response variable onto the $-\infty$ to ∞ scale, and the choice of link is itself a major topic that we can do little more than mention in this brief description.

The reason for the augmented version of the ordinary least squares estimating equation is the violation of the assumptions of the Gauss–Markov theorem (Bibby 1977), which require the variance–covariance matrix V of the dependent logit to possess a main diagonal of equivalued variances σ^2 (homoscedasticity) and zero covariances in the off-diagonal cells. That is, ordinary least squares requires $V = \sigma^2 D$, where $D = I$. In the case of the binary response variable, it is possible to satisfy the condition $\text{Cov}(L_i, L_j) = 0$ $i \neq j$, but $\text{Var}(L_j)$ is not constant but fluctuates with the odds (p_{1j}/p_{2j}), in fact the estimate $\bar{L} = \log(f_{1j}/f_{2j})$ is approximately $N(L, 1/(f_{0j}p_{1j}p_{2j}))$ for large samples (Cox 1970; Theil 1970). Thus the matrix D^{-1} contains values $f_{0j}\hat{p}_{1j}\hat{p}_{2j}$ so that observations with a large variance carry little weight in the estimation process and vice-versa. With polytomous responses, the variance–covariance matrix will also contain non-zero covariances depending on the specification of the response variable.

The role of the weighted least squares estimating equation is to allow for these violations of the Gauss–Markov assumptions so that parameter estimates retain their optimal properties of unbiassedness and minimal variance. This requires estimates of **V** which are provided, approximately, by equations that appeal to large sample results (Cox 1970). In fact, this means that the method of weighted least squares is more susceptible to small sample problems than the method of maximum likelihood. Also, the dependent logit vector **L̄** is undefined when zero frequencies occur and 'working values' must be utilised (Berkson 1953; 1955; Grizzle *et al.* 1969). The effect of these has 'not been definitively investigated' (Bishop *et al.* 1975, p. 354), whereas sporadic zeros are of no consequence in maximum likelihood estimation.

Despite these drawbacks, there is the advantage in weighted least squares of inherent flexibility which enables the analyst to specify some models for which there are no equivalent hierarchical log–linear models estimated by maximum likelihood. The companion papers by Wrigley (1980) and Upton (1981*a*) illustrate the comparative virtues of both approaches. Wrigley (1980) uses the flexible GENCAT program (Landis *et al.* 1976) which relates closely to the work of Grizzle *et al.* (1969). As is evident in these analyses, the weighted least squares approach may involve the construction of complicated design matrices, whilst a very comprehensive account of the data can be obtained much more rapidly by remaining within the hierarchical family of log–linear models. A brief account of other aspects of this analysis was given in Chapter 4.

Further advantages of weighted least squares are that maximum likelihood estimates may not, for models in general, be as easy to obtain as for hierarchical log–linear models because the log likelihood function may not always possess the strict concavity necessary to guarantee the existence of a unique maximum. Also, infinite parameter estimates may be produced by very sparse arrays. It may therefore be convenient to invoke weighted least squares with a multimodal log likelihood function and a large sample.

There exists a much closer relation between weighted least squares and maximum likelihood estimation than has so far been indicated for the iterative version of weighted least squares, namely, iterative weighted least squares, gives what are, in fact, maximum likelihood estimates. The basis of this iterative approach is still the weighted least squares estimating equation but with the variance–covariance matrix of the dependent logit **V** successively reestimated on the basis of values from each iteration until there is convergence to the maximum likelihood estimate. This approach is fully described by Nelder & Wedderburn (1972) and Nelder (1974). By using this approach to obtain maximum likelihood estimates rather than the simple Deming–Stephan (1940) algorithm (iterative proportional fitting) of ECTA and like programs, one remains within the broad framework of the general linear model, a feature fully exploited in the versatile GENSTAT and GLIM packages.

The discussion in the first half of the chapter has concentrated on simplifying a single model fitted to an entire table as a means of drawing out the essence of a data set. With a large table describing polytomous variables, one simple model that satisfactorily accounts for the observed frequencies in their entirety may be difficult to find, and several different submodels may be necessary. Alternatively, a special effect, or effects, may need to be invoked which is attached to the model fitting the main part of the table. Special effects are part of the discussion in the remainder of the chapter. We also consider tables redesigned by reordering (Table 5.32), or breaking up, polytomies, the latter being referred to as Duncan's approach. The following account of continuation odds models develops the theme of multimodel tables.

Continuation odds models

With an I level polytomous response there are a number of optional specifications of the $I-1$ logit models necessary to account for the entire table. For example, for the two-way table, the options include

$$\log (p_{ij}/p_{Ij}) \qquad (i = 1, \ldots, I-1)$$

$$\log (p_{ij}/p_{i+1j}) \qquad (i = 1, \ldots, I-1)$$

$$\log \left(\sum_{k=i+1}^{I} p_{kj}/p_{ij} \right) \qquad (i = 1, \ldots, I-1)$$

Fienberg (1980) gives a number of other possibilities and the notation extends naturally to the multiway table. Observe that if the I levels are ordered, this information is utilised in the third logit, the so-called log continuation odds, which are often of substantive interest. To illustrate log continuation odds, consider the data in Table 5.22 which now reveal Table 5.11 as the outcome of merging the response categories. The observed continuation odds in this case are $(f_{2j} + f_{3j})/f_{1j}$, the odds of surviving more than six days, and f_{3j}/f_{2j}, the odds of

Table 5.22. *Toxicity to Tribolium castaneum of films formed by γ-benzene hexachloride*

		Log_{10} deposit					
		1.082	1.161	1.212	1.258	1.310	1.348
Period of	At most, 6	15	24	26	24	29	29
survival	7–9	5	4	7	6	4	4
(days)	More than 9	30	21	17	20	17	16

those surviving more than six days surviving more than nine days. The first of these odds corresponds to the previous analysis of Table 5.11, which found that the independence model failed to account for survival (beyond six days), with $Y^2 = 11.30 > \chi^2_{5, 0.05} = 11.07$. The uniform association model adequately accounted for the data, with $Y^2 = 2.21 < \chi^2_{4, 0.05} = 9.49$, enabling the interpretation that the log odds are linearly dependent on $\log_{10}$ deposit. However, this linear dependence does not necessarily carry over to the analysis of the survivors beyond six days, since their log continuation odds, $\log(f_{3j}/f_{2j})$, are also consistent with the simpler independence model ($Y^2 = 2.34 < \chi^2_{5, 0.05}$). In comparison, this uniform association model fits only marginally better ($Y^2 = 1.81 < \chi^2_{4, 0.05}$). Thus, while the odds of survival beyond six days depends on the deposit, the deposit does not determine whether this is more or less than nine days. Fienberg & Mason (1979) used continuation odds to discover that different levels of educational continuation also required different models.

Some logits, such as the first two given above, correspond exactly to log-linear models when estimated by maximum likelihood and when each of the component $I-1$ submodels are identical, in which case it is often just as easy to work with the whole table and fit a log-linear model with the factor–response distinction. On the other hand, the $I-1$ log continuation odds models are not always exactly equivalent to a log-linear model for the entire table, even if there are $I-1$ identical parameterisations. An important advantage, however, of using continuation odds is that they can be separately estimated and tested for goodness of fit for each increment in the response variable. Though the $I-1$ submodels may contain different effects, it can be demonstrated that if estimation is by maximum likelihood they jointly become a composite model for the entire table which is testable by simple addition of the $I-1$ individual Y^2 values (Fienberg & Mason 1979).

Proportional odds and proportional hazards models
McCullagh (1980) describes other models applicable to ordinal responses that are based on $(1 - \Sigma^i_{k=1} p_{kj})$ $i = 1, \ldots, I$, the probability of survival beyond category i given level j of the factor. Thus these models resemble the continuation odds models and also provide an alternative to analysis via association models. Two specifications are the proportional odds model, with response variable $\log[\Sigma^i_{k=1} p_{kj}/(1 - \Sigma^i_{k=1} p_{kj})]$ and the proportional hazards model with response $\log[-\log(1 - \Sigma^i_{k=1} p_{kj})]$. These models utilise the existence of a latent continuous response where appropriate and introduce the potential for conclusions to be stated without reference to the actual categories or category scores used in the sample, thus the models are robust and defy category redefinition. In the discussion of McCullagh's paper, Agresti

points out that this can be accomplished by log–linear methods so long as there is a sensible assignment of scores to response categories so that amalgamation effects are transcended by considering the cross-product ratio per unit distance on the response, and Fienberg notes that the response category boundaries may represent discontinuities in the response to factors that should be taken note of.

Extreme-ends and related models

As mentioned earlier, a submodel may represent only part of a table, and an additional element may be required if one is striving for a comprehensive model for the whole table. What is referred to here as the extreme-ends model is one such model created by adding a special effect to the independence model. The name derives from the presumption that, with two ordered polytomies, the cells at (one pair of) diagonally opposing corners of the two-way table, pertaining to responses at simultaneously the highest and lowest levels of the variables, should be treated differently from other cells.

In order to describe the model more fully, we continue the analysis of the data in Table 1.8 which describes the association between car availability and fatigue. It has already been shown in Chapter 1 that the independence model fails to adequately account for the observed frequencies

$$(Y^2 = 23.87, X^2 = 23.42 > \chi^2_{8, 0.05} = 15.51).$$

The rationale for the model is the presumption, after allowing for the varying marginal frequencies of Table 1.8, that there is a comparatively low probability that those with no car availability will disagree with the assertion that shopping is tiring, and a low probability that those with full car availability will agree with it. These two 'extreme ends' of the table are treated as equivalent to, but distinct from, the rest of the table. Table 5.23 contains the expected frequencies of the extreme-ends model. The model fits Table 1.8 quite well, with

Table 5.23. *Expected frequencies produced by the extreme-ends model fitted to Table 1.8.*

		Shopping fatigue (B)				
		B_1	B_2	B_3	B_4	B_5
Car availability (A)	A_1	55.93	11.56	17.94	17.03	96.54
	A_2	92.87	12.85	19.96	18.94	107.38
	A_3	98.20	13.59	21.10	20.03	76.07

key: A_3 denotes full car availability and B_5 full agreement that grocery shopping is very tiring.

$$Y^2 = 10.21 < \chi^2_{7,\,0.05} = 14.07,$$

and the introduction of the single extreme-ends parameter significantly reduces Y^2 from 23.87 for the independence model, a fall of

$$13.66 > \chi^2_{1,\,0.05} = 3.84.$$

Examination of Table 5.23 reveals that, unlike the uniform association models, the link between model parameters and equalised margins has been preserved, for not only are observed and expected row and column totals equalised, but so also are the totals in the two extreme cells. A logical consequence of this is the equalisation of the totals in the non-extreme cells, and so only one extra independent constraint has been imposed, compared with the independence model, which accounts for the lost degree of freedom.

The extreme-ends model and some relatives that are described later were fitted using GENSTAT, which, as listing 6 (Appendix) shows, accomplishes the task in a very compact way. The models can also be fitted via ECTA or an equivalent program and the two-way table treated as an incomplete multiway table, but this precludes the easy and automatic estimation of model parameters.

To fit the extreme-ends model using GENSTAT it is necessary to fit 'factors' allowing for the row and column totals, and a factor to control for the varying response in cells that are, or are not, in the extreme-end cells. Table 5.25 gives the layout of this factor. Table 5.24 gives the parameter estimates and standardised values of the parameters of the extreme-ends model.

Table 5.24. *Parameter estimates of the extreme-ends model fitted to Table 1.8*

Param.	μ'	$\lambda_2'^A$	$\lambda_3'^A$	$\lambda_2'^B$	$\lambda_3'^B$	$\lambda_4'^B$	$\lambda_5'^B$	$\lambda_2'^C$
Est.	4.02	0.11	0.16	-1.98	-1.54	-1.59	0.15	0.40
sv	33.82	1.06	1.66	-11.23	-10.44	-10.57	1.64	3.64

Table 5.25. *The layout of factors used to fit models by GENSTAT to Table 1.8*

(a) extreme-ends factor

1	2	2	2	2
2	2	2	2	2
2	2	2	2	1

(b) four-corners factor

1	2	2	2	3
2	2	2	2	2
3	2	2	2	1

Note that the standardised value of $\lambda_2'^C$ reinforces the earlier indication, based on the comparative Y^2 values of the independence model and the extreme-ends model, that an extreme-ends parameter makes a highly significant contribution to goodness of fit.

Note also that the quantity $\hat{\lambda}_2'^C = 0.40$ is added to the sum of the other parameter estimates to obtain the expected frequency in table cells that are not in the extreme ends. Extreme cells incur no increment, reflecting their comparative improbability.

A four-corners model

The extreme-ends model was based on the assumption that a single separate parameter was needed to account for the frequencies in one pair of diagonally opposite corners of Table 1.8. Intuition suggests that the other pair of corners could similarly require special treatment, but that their parameter should be distinct from that included in the extreme-ends model, for, in the context of the data in Table 1.8, one would expect the value of this parameter to enhance the frequencies since those with no car availability are more likely to agree that shopping is tiring, and those with full car availability are more likely to disagree. We call this the four-corners model. The model was fitted by again using GENSTAT and this time setting up a three-level factor in a 3×5 layout, as shown in Table 5.25(b), to represent the three separate influences, one for each pair of opposite corners and one for the remainder of the table.

Table 5.27 gives the expected frequencies of the model and Table 5.26 gives the parameter estimates. Note that the equalisation of various observed and expected cells totals consistent with the previous model is preserved, with the

Table 5.26. *Parameter estimates of the four-corners model*

Param.	μ'	$\lambda_2'^A$	$\lambda_3'^A$	$\lambda_2'^B$	$\lambda_3'^B$	$\lambda_4'^B$	$\lambda_5'^B$	$\lambda_2'^C$	$\lambda_3'^C$
Est.	4.03	−0.01	0.16	−2.07	−1.63	−1.68	0.14	0.53	0.38
sv	33.92	−0.03	1.64	−9.49	−8.33	−8.50	1.63	2.56	3.35

Table 5.27. *Expected frequencies of the four-corners model fitted to Table 1.8*

	B_1	B_2	B_3	B_4	B_5
A_1	56.02	11.99	18.62	17.67	94.69
A_2	94.67	11.92	18.51	17.57	109.33
A_3	96.31	14.09	21.87	20.76	75.98

key: as in Table 5.23.

additional constraint that the total of the observed and expected frequencies in the third and fourth corners of the table are also set equal. This amounts to one extra constraint and thus an extra degree of freedom is lost. The result is that the model has 6 df and fits the observed data very well;

$$Y^2 = 9.65 < \chi^2_{6, 0.05} = 12.59.$$

It is apparent from Table 5.26 that the expected positive $\lambda_3^{\prime C}$ estimate has materialised, though it only effects a minimal reduction in Y^2, as shown by comparison of $Y^2 = 9.65$ for the four-corners model, with $Y^2 = 10.21$ for the extreme-ends model, which is identical in every respect except that $\lambda_3^{\prime C}$ is absent. Since $Y^2 = 10.21 - 9.65 = 0.56 < \chi^2_{1, 0.05} = 3.84$, the additional parameter is unnecessary.

Quasi-independence for two-way tables

In this section, we revert to the extreme-ends model and consider further modifications. In particular, the possibility is investigated that just one cell, in this case a corner cell, requires a special parameter that is denoted by *. Since there is one parameter (or, analogously, factor level) associated with a single cell, because of the equalisation of observed and expected frequencies at each factor level, it follows that the observed frequency exactly equals the expected frequency in the single cell in question. This model is fitted to Table 1.8 by GENSTAT using the factor layout in Table 5.30(a). More generally, there may be more than one cell of variable location requiring a parameter *.

The expected frequencies produced by this model are given in Table 5.28 and the parameter estimates are in Table 5.29.

Table 5.28. *Expected frequencies of the quasi-independence model fitted to Table 1.8*

	B_1	B_2	B_3	B_4	B_5
A_1	*	12.64	19.62	18.62	93.12
A_2	100.59	13.29	20.63	19.58	97.91
A_2	91.41	12.08	18.75	17.79	88.97

key: as in Table 1.8, 5.23.

Table 5.29. *Parameters of the Table 5.28 model*

Param.	μ'	$\lambda_2^{\prime A}$	$\lambda_3^{\prime A}$	$\lambda_2^{\prime B}$	$\lambda_3^{\prime B}$	$\lambda_4^{\prime B}$	$\lambda_5^{\prime B}$	*
Est.	4.01	0.05	−0.05	−2.02	−1.58	−1.64	−0.03	−0.55
sv	29.72	0.45	−0.40	−11.22	−10.38	−10.52	−0.27	−3.01

A * is placed in the cell of Table 5.28 with expected frequency exactly equal to the observed frequency to identify the cell and to make the point that any value could be implanted in cell * with nil effect on the remaining expected frequencies generated by the model. Since the frequency in cell * could easily be zero, perhaps because observations have zero probability of occurring or because it is convenient to only fit models to a table with certain cells deleted, such tables are often referred to as incomplete.

The parameter estimates of Table 5.29 demonstrate that the effect of parameter * for the shopping fatigue data of Table 1.8 is to reduce the expected frequency in cell $(1, 1)$ down to the value 55. The remaining expected frequencies are obtained from a combination of parameters identical to that of the independence model; their source is thus a model of quasi-independence, a concept initiated by Goodman (1968).

In general, the quasi-independence model says that, apart from a selected cell or cells, the variables are independent. In the specific case of Table 1.8, one would say that the variables fatigue and car availability are independent, apart from an effect relating to cell $(1, 1)$, which reduces the number of untired shoppers with no car available to below what one would expect were the variables independent. Although this is a very believable proposition, it is unjustified as a complete account of the observed frequencies, since

$$Y^2 = 14.46 > \chi^2_{7, 0.05} = 14.07.$$

There are seven degrees of freedom in this example because, having removed the single parameter * and its associated cell, there are seven remaining parameters and 14 cells, and this is the difference. Despite its lack of complete veracity, the quasi-independence model does go a long way to explain the data, and the impact of parameter * can be assessed from the significant difference, $23.87 - 14.07 = 9.8 > \chi^2_{1, 0.05} = 3.84$, between the goodness of fit Y^2 of the independence and quasi-independence models.

An alternative modification to the extreme-ends model is to apply the parameter * to the other corner cell, though this quasi-independence model is more ill-fitting, with $Y^2 = 15.64 > \chi^2_{7, 0.05} = 14.07$.

A modification that involves a slight increase in complexity is to invoke individual * parameters for both the extreme cells. Table 5.30 illustrates this with Table 5.30(b) giving the layout required to fit two separate *'s via GENSTAT. The consequence of this is two expected frequencies set exactly equal to their observed counterparts giving a quasi-independence model for a 13-cell incomplete table with 6 df.

Fitting the 13-cell quasi-independence model gives

$$Y^2 = 10.13 < \chi^2_{6, 0.05} = 12.59,$$

a reasonably well-fitting model but one that does not significantly improve on the extreme-ends model since $10.21 - 10.13 = 0.08 < \chi^2_{1,0.05} = 3.84$. On a purely statistical basis it appears unnecessary to apply distinct effects of separate magnitude to each of the two diagonally opposing corner cells of Table 1.8 to approximate to the observed frequencies. However, in the final analysis, the quasi-independence model is to be preferred; in the context of Table 1.8 it is difficult to envisage a process that could bring about exactly equal effects. Substantive support for the extreme-ends model would come from identifying a mechanism for the equality phenomenon. A further challenge to do this in an electoral setting is presented by the equivalent bipolar loyalty model of Chapter 6. Were the present 13-cell quasi-independence model adopted, one would say that fatigue and car availability were unrelated apart from effects operating on the extreme-end cells which reduce the number of untired shoppers with no car availability, and the number of tired shoppers with full car avail-ability, to below what one would expect. This is an appealingly simple and credible account of the interactions in Table 1.8 which concurs with the interpretation from the extreme-ends model.

Uniform association models and reordered variables

The analysis of Table 1.8 has been carried out solely for the purpose of illustrating the above methods, for, originally, the table was a three-way table which has been collapsed over variable C, as described by Table 5.31, and it would be misleading not to recognise this fact.

Bowlby & Silk (1982) find that the model $AC/AB/BC$ adequately fits Table 5.31 with $Y^2 = 24.21 < \chi^2_{16,0.05} = 26.30$. However, this model can be simplified. One way to do this is by assuming uniform partial association for the AB inter-action, giving the model $AC/BC/\phi^{AB}$ with $Y^2 = 34.96 < \chi^2_{23,0.05} = 35.17$. This says that stage in life cycle (C) affects shopping fatigue (B), car availability (A) affects shopping fatigue, and that $\log(e_{ijk}/e_{ij+1k})$ varies linearly with i so that, for any two response categories, the log odds of a 'less tiring' to a 'more tiring' response improve by $-\hat{\phi}^{AB} = 0.10$ (sv $= -3.62$) for every increase in car availability level.

Table 5.30. *GENSTAT factor layouts producing quasi-independence models*

(a) the 14-cell incomplete table					(b) the 13-cell incomplete table				
2	1	1	1	1	1	2	2	2	2
1	1	1	1	1	2	2	2	2	2
1	1	1	1	1	2	2	2	2	3

Observe that a similar statement concerning the BC interaction is not possible, since the model $B/AC/\phi^{AB}/\phi^{BC}$ provides an inadequate fit with

$$Y^2 = 52.56 > \chi^2_{30,\,0.05} = 43.77,$$

and the gain of 7 df in imposing the uniform partial association constraint on the BC interaction brings about an unacceptable loss of fit of

$$17.60 > \chi^2_{7,\,0.05} = 14.07.$$

It is, however, possible to reorder the variable C categories and reexamine the uniform partial association assumption for the BC interaction, for, as far as shopping fatigue is concerned, a more natural ordering of life cycle levels is younger people with children, the middle aged and, finally, younger people without children. To test this assumption we compare the models $AC/AB/BC$ and $AC/AB/\phi^{BC}$ for which $Y^2 = 34.27 < \chi^2_{23,\,0.05} = 35.17$. The Y^2 difference between these two models is $10.06 < \chi^2_{7,\,0.05} = 14.07$. A second test is the comparison of $AC/BC/\phi^{AB}$ ($Y^2 = 34.96$, 23 df) and $B/AC/\phi^{BC}/\phi^{AB}$ ($Y^2 = 45.72$, 30 df), which also produces an insignificant Y^2 change. The model $B/AC/\phi^{BC}/\phi^{AB}$ generates the expected frequencies in Table 5.32. From these, apart from the previously described interaction ($\hat{\phi}^{AB} = -0.10$, sv $= -3.73$), one can also say that, for any two response categories, the log odds of a 'less tiring' to a 'more tiring' response improves by $-\hat{\phi}^{BC} = 0.07$ (sv $= -2.64$) for every increase in life cycle level, given the rearranged order. In fact, this is an overgeneralisation, for the $B/AC/\phi^{BC}/\phi^{AB}$ model just fails to satisfy conventional goodness-of-fit criteria, and there is some uncertainty about the placement

Table 5.31. *Agreement with the statement 'I find getting to grocery shops very tiring', by car availability and life cycle*

		Agreement (B)				
		'disagree'	'agree'			
Car availability (A)		1	2	3	4	5
Middle-aged (C_1)	1	22	1	9	6	36
	2	29	3	7	10	41
	3	27	3	6	1	24
Younger people without children (C_2)	1	14	8	4	6	22
	2	26	2	5	2	13
	3	27	7	3	3	16
Younger people with children (C_3)	1	19	2	3	5	42
	2	46	2	6	11	49
	3	37	10	16	12	37

of the lowest two life cycle levels, for, when rearranged, the $B/AC/\phi^{BC}/\phi^{AB}$ model fits nearly equally well, with $Y^2 = 47.32$. Nevertheless, this reordering tactic is generally quite useful as a means of achieving parsimonious models.

Triangular tables

Preceding analyses have amounted to fitting the independence model to part of the complete table, since the observed and expected frequencies were set equal in certain cells. Sometimes tables are designed to be incomplete from the outset, rather than being rendered incomplete to facilitate the fitting of a simple model. Usually, triangular tables are examples of such genuinely incomplete tables in which certain cells are impossible to fill because of the particular definitions given to the variables comprising the table margins. Table 5.33 is a typical example, comprising data originally analysed by Bishop

Table 5.32. *Expected frequencies of the* $B/AC/\phi^{BC}/\phi^{AB}$ *model fitted to Table 5.31*

Car availability (A)		Agreement (B)				
		1	2	3	4	5
Younger people with children (C_3)	1	17.26	3.18	5.86	6.55	38.15
	2	35.84	5.96	9.90	9.96	52.35
	3	44.03	6.60	9.89	8.97	42.52
Middle-aged (C_1)	1	21.62	3.71	6.35	6.59	35.73
	2	33.22	5.13	7.93	7.43	36.29
	3	27.48	3.83	5.34	4.50	19.85
Younger people without children (C_2)	1	18.66	2.97	4.74	4.57	23.06
	2	20.45	2.94	4.22	3.68	16.71
	3	28.44	3.68	4.77	3.75	15.35

Table 5.33. *Initial and final rating of 121 stroke patients*

		B				
		1	2	3	4	5
	1	5				
	2	4	5			
A	3	6	4	4		
	4	9	10	4	1	
	5	11	23	12	15	8

key: A = initial rating. B = final rating.

& Fienberg (1969), Haberman (1974), Altham (1975) and Goodman (1979*e*), in which the rows and columns are ordinal categories of the illness severity of hospitalised patients on entering and leaving hospital. Evidently, patients who deteriorate are never discharged and so there is zero probability that the upper right-hand triangle of cells will contain observations.

The quasi-independence model for Table 5.33 can be written

$$\log(p_{ij}) = \mu' + \lambda_i'^A + \lambda_j'^B \quad \text{for} \quad j \leqslant i \qquad (i = 1, \ldots, I)$$
$$p_{ij} = 0 \qquad \text{for} \quad j > i \qquad (j = 1, \ldots, J)$$

where p_{ij} is the probability that the patient will have initial rating i and final rating j. The result of fitting this model is $Y^2 = 9.60 < \chi^2_{6,\,0.05} = 12.59$. Table 5.34 gives the estimates of the expected frequencies and Table 5.35 the parameter estimates.

Note that Goodman (1979*e*) writes the model as

$$p_{ij} = a_i b_j \qquad \text{for} \quad j \leqslant i$$
$$= 0 \qquad \text{for} \quad j > i$$

Formulae for the estimates of the parameters a_i and b_j are given by Goodman (1979*e*) and there is discussion of the meaning of these parameters which is related to Altham's (1975) reparameterisation of an earlier version of the model in Goodman (1968).

As with other incomplete tables, model fitting can be accomplished by a variety of means to obtain maximum likelihood estimates of the expected

Table 5.34. *Expected frequencies for the data of Table 5.33*

		B				
		1	2	3	4	5
A	1	5				
	2	3.75	5.25			
	3	4.43	6.20	3.37		
	4	6.16	8.63	4.69	4.52	
	5	15.66	21.92	11.93	11.48	8

Table 5.35. *Parameter estimates and standard errors of the quasi-independence model fitted to the triangular table*

Param.	μ'	$\lambda_2'^A$	$\lambda_3'^A$	$\lambda_4'^A$	$\lambda_5'^A$	$\lambda_2'^B$	$\lambda_3'^B$	$\lambda_4'^B$	$\lambda_5'^B$
Est.	1.61	-0.29	-0.12	0.21	1.14	0.34	-0.27	-0.31	-0.67
sv	0.45	0.57	0.54	0.52	0.49	0.24	0.29	0.32	0.41

frequencies. In this example GENSTAT was again adopted with an 11-level factor, as in Table 5.36. This had the effect of constraining the expected frequencies in those cells with unique levels to be exactly equal to the 'observed' frequencies, which, in this case, were set to zero on account of the impossibility of those particular combinations of levels of the variables A and B.

The degrees of freedom appropriate to the quasi-independence model for the triangular table can be arrived at in two different ways. One can simply deduct the number of impossible cells (in general, h), from the total number of degrees of freedom that would have been available for the independence model $[(I-1)(J-1)]$ were it fitted to the complete table, that is,

$$df = [(I-1)(J-1)] - h = 6.$$

Alternatively, one can count the number of expected frequencies estimated, and deduct from this number the number of independent parameters associated with the estimates (in general, $(I+J-1)$), so that $df = 15 - 9 = 6$. This works because, in effect, the remainder of the table, comprising zeros, contains as many cells as parameters and these would be self-cancelling if one wished to consider the table as complete. Extra care should be taken in the calculation of the degrees of freedom for triangular tables when there are sampling zeros, that is, cells with observed frequencies of 0 but for which $p_{ij} > 0$.

Generally, the existence of sampling zeros in a table presents no problem for the calculation of degrees of freedom unless the zeros are so aligned that zero marginal frequencies occur in a marginal table consistent with, or implied by, the parameters of the model in question. It is then no longer the case that a one-to-one relation exists between zero cells and parameters responsible for the cells; this complicates the calculation of the degrees of freedom and considerable circumspection must be exercised. Bishop *et al.* (1975) discuss this topic in depth. Also, for incomplete tables in general, special care must be taken when the table is separable into subcomponents, as outlined subsequently.

Table 5.36. *Factor layout for the quasi-independence model fitted to Table 5.33*

1	2	3	4	5
1	1	6	7	8
1	1	1	9	10
1	1	1	1	11
1	1	1	1	1

Separable incomplete tables

Separability is defined as a property possessed by some incomplete tables which enables them to be broken down into their constituent subtables for the purposes of analysis. Members of the set of subtables, which together make up an incomplete table, are themselves complete and they are not interconnected with each other. Incomplete tables with this capacity for being broken down are referred to as separable, as opposed to the more usually encountered inseparable incomplete tables. When separability exists, each complete subtable is analysed as a table in its own right. Upton (1978*a*) gives some examples of separable incomplete tables and Bishop *et al.* (1975) discuss in detail issues relating to separability.

Treating a separable incomplete table as inseparable causes errors in the calculation of degrees of freedom, hence the importance of being able to detect separability. Bishop *et al.* (1975) observe that this relates to the existence or non-existence of cells linked in a continuous chain where the definition of a link derives from the constraints and parameters implied by the model in question. For example, the independence model defines a link to exist between a pair of cells when they occupy the same row (row margin constraint) or the same column (column margin constraint). Given this definition, Table 5.37(a) is separable since the resulting chain of cells is discontinuous, comprising two complete subtables. Tables 5.37(b) and (c), a triangular table and the often encountered diagonaless square table, are inseparable since all of their cells form a continuous chain belonging either to the same row or the same column.

Ignoring the fact that Table 5.37(a) is separable wrongly gives zero degrees of freedom for the independence model since, ostensibly, the five non-empty cells are accounted for by the five parameters pertaining to this table. Separating the table into its two component subtables, Table 5.38(a) and 5.38(b), which

Table 5.37. *Some incomplete tables*

	(a) Separable				(b) Inseparable triangular				(c) Inseparable diagonaless		
	B_1	B_2	B_3		B_1	B_2	B_3		B_1	B_2	B_3
A_1	f_{11}	*	f_{13}	A_1	*	f_{12}	f_{13}	A_1	*	f_{12}	f_{13}
A_2	*	f_{22}	*	A_2	*	*	f_{23}	A_2	f_{21}	*	f_{23}
A_2	f_{31}	*	f_{33}	A_3	*	*	*	A_3	f_{31}	f_{32}	*

key: * empty cells.

individually possess one and zero df, one obtains the correct value, 1, the sum of these individual df.

Bishop *et al.* (1975, p. 184) give a similar example and go on to discuss multiway incomplete tables in the context of models other than the independence model. In the case of a three-way table and the model AC/B, a pair of cells are linked in a chain either because they occupy the same row and layer (AC), or because they occupy the same column (B). Although a table may be separable by that criterion, replacing AC/B by BC/A redefines the basis on which cell pairs are considered linked and thus whether or not the table is separable.

Small samples

Tables describing polytomous variables are, by virtue of the large number of table cells, likely to contain small observed, and hence small expected, frequencies. This introduces the possibility that the X^2 and Y^2 statistics normally adopted to assess the goodness of fit of a model may fail to adhere approximately to the χ^2 distribution under the null hypothesis. This has not deterred the cautious analysis of sparse tables (e.g. Upton & Sarlvik 1981), and there is some encouragement for this in the work of Haberman (1977) which suggests that the change in Y^2 due to fitting hierarchical log–linear models to sparse tables will approximate as usual to the χ^2 distribution.

Possibly because of increased knowledge about the distributional consequences, there has been a downward trend in the admissible expected frequencies from around 10 to as low as 1 in certain instances (Yarnold 1970). Naturally though, because this is still a developing area of knowledge, there are differences of opinion on the minimum recommended expected frequency below which the exact X^2 or Y^2 distribution deviates too markedly from the χ^2 distribution. Certainly, there has been a flurry of recent research that has enhanced the body of knowledge on the small sample and sparse table problems, and which has tended to support a more liberal approach. Cox & Plackett (1980), for example, show that X^2 adheres approximately to χ^2 with very small frequencies, and Larntz (1978) also finds that X^2 approximates to χ^2 with average cell frequencies down to roughly 1.0. On the other hand, Kotze & Gokhale (1980) prefer Y^2, finding X^2 too conservative. Lawal & Upton (1980) give an approximation to the distribution of the X^2 goodness-of-fit statistic for use with small expectations

Table 5.38. *Complete subtables from the incomplete separable table*

		B_1	B_3			B_2
(a)	A_1	f_{11}	f_{13}	(b)	A_2	f_{22}
	A_3	f_{31}	f_{33}			

and Fienberg (1980) gives more detail on the small sample properties of chi-squared statistics. Hutchinson (1979) also cites some of the growing literature on this important research frontier.

For the data analyst, current evidence suggests that even with a minimum expected frequency of between 1 and 4, the approximation to the χ^2 distribution is probably tenable for both X^2 and Y^2, though possibly more so for X^2 (Larntz 1978; Fienberg 1980). When the average observed frequency exceeds 5 there need not be undue concern about distributional assumptions unless expected cell frequencies are highly concentrated in a few cells. Kotze (1982) advises that, 'a table will become too sparse when more than 20% of the cells have an expected count less than one'. In such cases, care must be taken not to blindly acccept the critical values produced by χ^2 tables, particularly in border-line cases. Where uncertainty exists, a less tedious solution than collecting more data is to amalgamate variable categories and, as a last resort, to eliminate variables entirely by collapsing the table and basing one's conclusion on the resulting marginal table. Both these tactics have the effect of increasing the observed frequencies in the (redesigned) table; done unwittingly, however, they may lead one to fallacious conclusions.

Table collapsing and category amalgamating

In Chapter 3, the 2^5 voting data (Table 3.20) was collapsed in various ways to facilitate the interpretation of a complex model fitted to the extended table. It was pointed out that the relationships between variables displayed in marginal tables, obtained by collapsing over one or more variables, may not exactly equal their 'true' relationship as elicited from the extended table in which the 'collapsed' variables and their effects were not ignored. As will be described later, rules exist (Bishop *et al.* 1975; Whittemore 1978; Reynolds 1978; Goodman 1979*d*) to indicate whether collapsing can be carried out with impunity or whether the relationship between variables inferred from a collapsed table will be a distortion of their 'true' value. The analyst should be aware of this possibility of parameter estimate distortion, though the fact that collapsing can occur with the 'true' interaction between variables preserved either exactly or approximately in marginal tables can and should be exploited in an analysis. Upton (1981) illustrates further how this can be done to avoid relying on possibly confusing alternative parameterisations. Similar comments are applicable to the amalgamation of polytomous variable categories.

However, in order not to give the impression that collapsing always produces meaningful marginal tables, a graphic illustration of the parameter instability that may occur is contained in Table 5.39, a hypothetical but illuminating data set also discussed by Kotze (1982).

The relevant (Goodman-style) parameter estimates of the saturated log-linear model fitted to Table 5.39 are given below, with standardised values in brackets.

$$\hat{\lambda}_{11}^{AB} = -0.737 \, (-12.54)$$
$$\hat{\lambda}_{11}^{AC} = -0.737 \, (-12.54)$$
$$\hat{\lambda}_{11}^{BC} = -0.067 \, (-1.14)$$
$$\hat{\lambda}_{111}^{ABC} = -0.011 \, (-0.20)$$

Collapsing over variable A and analysing the result marginal $B \times C$ table produces $\hat{\lambda}_{11}^{BC} = 0.325 \, (8.43)$, a value not only different from, but of opposite sign to, the 'true' λ_{11}^{BC}. This is a phenomenon often referred to as Simpson's paradox (Simpson 1951; Birch 1963; Blyth 1972; Kotze 1982).

The conditions under which collapsing changes parameter estimates are dealt with by Bishop *et al.* (1975). Essentially, their theorem divides variables into three sets, R, I and C. Set C contains the variable or variables to be collapsed; set I contains variables that are conditionally independent of those in set C; and set R contains other variables. It is legitimate to collapse over variables in C with respect to interactions involving variables in set I or a mix of variables from R and I. However, interactions involving variables only from set R will assume different values in the collapsed and extended tables.

These rules are illustrated by returning to the analysis of the 2^5 voting preference data of Table 3.20. The model $ABCD/AE/BE/CE$ indicates that set C contains variable E, set I contains variable D, and set R contains variables A, B and C, when Table 3.20 is collapsed over variable E to create the marginal Table 3.30. The collapsibility theorem (Bishop *et al.* 1975) predicts that any parameter involving variable D will not assume a distorted value in the marginal table, whereas other parameter estimates will be, to some extent, affected. This is verified by fitting the saturated model to Table 3.30, in which all parameter

Table 5.39. *An illustration of Simpson's paradox*

	A_1			A_2	
	B_1	B_2		B_1	B_2
C_1	10	100	C_1	100	50
C_2	100	730	C_2	50	20

key: A_1 = male. A_2 = female.
     B_1 = treat patient. B_2 = do not treat patient.
     C_1 = recovery. C_2 = death.

estimates involving variable D ranging from $\hat{\lambda}_1^D = -0.16$ to $\hat{\lambda}_{1111}^{ABCD} = 0.07$ equal those of the extended table, whilst parameters comprising variables entirely from set R, such as $\hat{\lambda}_{11}^{AB} = 0.28$, differ from the comparable estimates listed in Table 3.27.

If set I is empty the above rule suggests that no parameter estimate will remain undistorted by table collapsing, though Whittemore (1978) has demonstrated that even in this case it is possible to occasionally encounter 'perfect' tables in which collapsing preserves parameter estimates exactly. It has been suggested above that collapsing is sometimes legitimate and even where it does change parameter estimates it is still of practical value, and Whittemore's (1978) observation amounts to further liberalisation of the conditions under which collapsing can take place. Goodman (1972*b*, 1979*d*) has introduced a sign-rule to predict how two-way interactions change as a result of collapsing tables of dichotomies.

The amalgamation of levels of a polytomous variable to create a variable with a lesser number has very similar ramifications to those outlined above. The effects of category amalgamation are illustrated in the context of the travel data of Table 5.1. In particular, the two levels, medium and small, of the variable S, centre size, are amalgamated to create the composite category 'not large', as illustrated by Table 5.40.

The model *SM/FM* which fitted Table 5.1 ($Y^2 = 9.02 < \chi^2_{6,\,0.05}$) indicates that variables S and F are conditionally independent, and one therefore finds on fitting the same model to Table 5.40 ($Y^2 = 4.75 < \chi^2_{3,\,0.05}$) that the variable F parameter estimates given in Table 5.41 remain undisturbed by the amalgamation process.

Table 5.40. *Category amalgamation applied to Table 5.1*

		Walk (M_1)		Bus (M_2)		Car (M_3)	
		F_1	F_2	F_1	F_2	F_1	F_2
Not large	(S_1)	150	40	12	14	12	25
Large	(S_2)	43	18	27	45	22	89

key: F_1 = frequent.
$\quad\ \ F_2$ = seldom.

Table 5.41. *Parameter estimates of the model SM/FM fitted to Table 5.40*

Param.	μ	λ_1^F	λ_1^S	λ_1^M	λ_2^M	λ_{11}^{SM}	λ_{12}^{SM}	λ_{13}^{SM}	λ_{11}^{FM}	λ_{12}^{FM}	λ_{13}^{FM}
Est.	3.38	-0.07	-0.16	0.43	-0.33	0.74	-0.35	-0.39	0.67	-0.14	-0.53

Kotze (1982) also gives an example of category amalgamation. Goodman (1981*b*) gives some criteria and methods of category amalgamation in the context of the two-way table and variants of the uniform association model.

Duncan's approach to polytomous variables

Duncan (1975) amalgamates the categories of polytomies by treating each level as a separate dichotomous variable and assessing the necessity for its inclusion in a model. This also turns out to be a plausible way of devising models unburdened by the large number of parameters usually associated with interactions involving polytomies. Instead, a selection is made of an appropriate subset of parameters deemed responsible for the interaction. This can be accomplished, in a rather tricky way, using ECTA, but it is easier to use GENSTAT, thus rendering the incomplete table approach redundant and at the same time making parameter estimates feasible. The parameter estimates can play a role in the selection of a final model, and thus they are employed in a reanalysis of Duncan's (1975) snow-shovelling data to see if the same final model is suggested.

The data are given in Table 5.42 and are designed to detect whether respondents' religion affected their attitude to girls as well as boys doing hard manual labour, controlling for time. In this case religion is a four-level polytomy, whilst time and snow-shovellers' sex are dichotomies. There is evidence that the respondent's attitude is associated both with their religion and with the year the question was posed. This is, however, a rather imprecise statement that Duncan (1975) improves upon by treating the four-level religion variable as four dichotomies that can either be included as separate effects or set to zero depending on their individual significance. So as not to distort these factor–response interactions, as usual each alternative model contains the interfactor time–religion interaction.

Table 5.42. *Duncan's snow-shovelling data*

	Y_1		Y_2	
	A_1	A_2	A_1	A_2
R_1	104	42	165	142
R_2	65	44	100	130
R_3	4	3	5	6
R_4	13	6	32	23

key: $Y_1 = 1952.$ $Y_2 = 1971.$
R_1 = Protestant; R_2 = Catholic; R_3 = Jew; R_4 = other.
A_1 = only boys should shovel snow.
A_2 = boys and girls should shovel snow.

Listing 7 (Appendix) contains GENSTAT commands that reproduce some of Duncan's published results including the equivalent of the simplest hierarchical model which fits the data but which contains redundant interactions. This is the model $RY/RA/YA$ for which $Y^2 = 0.4 < \chi^2_{3,\,0.05} = 7.82$. The term 'equivalent' is used because in the listing the polytomous religion variable is represented as a set of dichotomies.

The standardised values of the relevant parameters of this model are given in Table 5.43. They indicate that, of the religion variable, only whether or not the respondent is a Catholic has any effect on the response. Thus the four levels of the religion polytomy can be amalgamated into just two, Catholic and non-Catholic. Note that the absence of the λ'^{OA} estimate is simply because its presence is implied by the presence of the other interactions. Note also that attitudes are strongly time dependent.

Table 5.44 contains the relevant parameters of the final model suggested by the significant interactions of Table 5.43. A more structured approach using the STP could have been attempted and Duncan (1975) selects a final model using a stepwise strategy. The final model of Table 5.44 is identical to Duncan's final model and fits very well with $Y^2 = 1.37 < \chi^2_{5,\,0.05} = 11.07$, thus, compared with the $RY/RA/YA$ model, a loss of fit of only 0.97 is incurred for the gain of 2 df.

These estimates reflect the growth of the sexual equality movement over the years. Notwithstanding this, non-Catholics have tended to view shared snow shovelling with more disdain than have Catholics. The appropriate marginal tables illustrate these observations.

Table 5.43. *Parameter estimates of the equivalent of the $RY/RA/YA$ model fitted to Table 5.42*

Param.	λ'^{AY}	λ'^{PA}	λ'^{CA}	λ'^{JA}
Est.	−0.69	0.10	−0.55	−0.54
sv	−4.53	0.40	−2.07	−1.01

Table 5.44. *Some parameter estimates of the final model for Table 5.42*

Param.	λ'^{AY}	λ'^{CA}
Est.	−0.68	−0.44
sv	−4.50	−3.14

Residuals and incomplete tables

Polytomies and multivariate analyses produce tables with many cells. A consequence of this is that cells containing observed frequencies deviating considerably from the expected frequencies are inevitable even when the model generating the expected frequencies holds true. The reason for this is the same as that underlying the inevitability of encountering truly null, but ostensibly significant, interactions when long lists are purposefully examined and which Aitkin's (1980) simultaneous test procedure is designed to compensate. As we have already noted, the existence of a non-zero residual is tantamount to setting to zero the * parameter specific to that cell since the equalisation of the observed and expected frequency means that * is not zero. Thus, as with parameters pertaining to more than one cell, a certain amount of random variation can be expected even when * is truly null.

Though large deviations between observed and expected frequencies can quite naturally be expected for no other reason than random variation, there comes a point when the deviation is too large to ascribe to chance. It is therefore necessary to quantify the deviations as the first stage in assessing whether they are indeed too large. Each cell contributes a certain amount to the overall X^2 or Y^2, and these individual contributions are reasonable indications of which, if any, * parameters ought not to be set to zero. Considering the absolute differences between the observed and expected frequencies alone could be misleading, but the contributions to X^2 scale the difference to allow for the greater likelihood of large differences in cells with large frequencies. It is convenient to work with the square root of the contributions to X^2 denoted r_{ij} for cell (i, j), for these amount to a very simple formula for each cell (which is automatically calculated by GENSTAT)

$$r_{ij} = (f_{ij} - e_{ij})/e_{ij}^{1/2} \qquad (i = 1, \ldots, I)$$
$$(j = 1, \ldots, J)$$

The $\{r_{ij}\}$ are often called standardised residuals (Haberman (1973b), Plackett (1981)). As they are square roots of X^2 variables, they approximate to standard normal deviates, and so any one exceeding 1.96 would, by conventional criteria ($\alpha = 0.05$), be significant. However, since there is not 1 df per cell, the individual X^2 contributions, and hence the $\{r_{ij}\}$, are not independent but interrelated, and thus it is wrong to adhere strictly to this convention. More nearly approximately normal functions can be invoked (Nelder 1974; Anscombe 1953), but with loss of simplicity. Bishop *et al.* (1975, p. 137) describe some alternative standardised residuals, the most obvious being the components of Y^2, but the components of X^2 have more convenient distributional properties (Larntz 1978). Haberman (1978) also describes an alternative standardised residual.

Given that the above method identifies a cell with a large standardised residual, the question of whether this can be attributed to a non-zero * parameter must now be tackled. A way of doing this is to note the difference between the Y^2 of a model plus * and an identical model minus *. This, in fact, amounts to fitting the model minus * to the complete table and then to the (incomplete) table from which the deviant cell has been removed. Clearly, we cannot compare this Y^2 change with $\chi^2_{1,\,0.05} = 3.84$ for reasons already mentioned, α must be reduced to below 0.05 to make significance more difficult to achieve. As Upton (1981*a*) points out, in an N cell table with potentially N* parameters, the probability of bringing about a given change of Y^2, or greater, by the introduction of a single * parameter will be roughly N times what it would be for a single cell since there are N opportunities to encounter the Y^2 change. In fact, the interrelatedness of the Y^2 will reduce this, but the choice of N is suitably conservative. Alternatively, since the probability of trying all the (truly null) * parameters and none of them being significant is approximately $(1-\alpha)^N$, the probability that at least one of them will be is $1-(1-\alpha)^N$. This is therefore an approximate indication of the overall level of risk which for $N > 1$ will exceed the per effect level α. This may be unrealistically large, and thus Upton (1981*b*) suggests adopting a per effect level $\alpha = 1-(1-r)^{1/N}$ where r is the overall level of risk set at an acceptable level.

To illustrate the method, we return to the suspended analysis of Wermuth's (1976) psychiatric data and study the residuals generated by a model fitted to the complete table. In Chapter 3, some dissatisfaction was expressed with the 'final' model ABD/AC because of its comparative complexity arising from the presence of the three-way ABD interaction. We now explore the possibility that a similar model devoid of ABD fits part of Table 3.6 adequately, even though it does not satisfactorily account for the observed frequencies of the entire table. That is, we are investigating whether the simpler model plus * fits the full table. Table 5.46 gives the comparative goodness of fit of ABD/AC and $AB/AD/BD/AC$, which differ solely by ABD, and reaffirms the necessity for ABD in a model fitting the complete table.

The standardised residuals produced by the ill-fitting model $AB/AD/BD/AC$, and shown in Table 5.45, indicate that the cell most likely to require a * parameter is cell $(1, 1, 2, 2)$ which possesses the largest standardised residual. Table 5.46 describes the impact of the * parameter, which, by conventional criteria, is highly significant since $7.48 > \chi^2_{1,\,0.05} = 3.84$.

However, from the above discussion $\alpha = 0.05$ implies an inflated overall level of risk r. If r is reduced to 0.10 then $\alpha = 0.0066$. Since $7.48 = \chi^2_{1,\,0.0062} > \chi^2_{1,\,0.0066}$, the * parameter is still significant, but now only marginally. Upton (1980) examines data with a much more prominent deviant cell.

One advantage of persevering with this line of attack is that further simplification is possible, for Table 5.46 shows that the removal of the *AB* has an inconsequential effect on the goodness of fit. None of the other parameters can be set to zero, and so *AD/AC/BD/** is chosen as a final model. Fitting *AD/AC/BD* to Table 3.6 gives $Y^2 = 13.87$ and accurately identifies the deviant

Table 5.45. *Expected frequencies and standardised residuals produced by fitting AB/AD/BD/AC to Table 3.6*

	D_1					
	C_1			C_2	
	B_1	B_2		B_1	B_2
A_1	16.22 (−0.30)	13.81 (−1.29)	A_1	16.73 (1.53)	14.24 (−0.06)
A_2	37.47 (−1.22)	28.21 (0.71)	A_2	19.58 (0.55)	14.74 (0.33)

	D_2					
	C_1			C_2	
	B_1	B_2		B_1	B_2
A_1	21.68 (0.71)	43.29 (0.41)	A_1	22.37 (−1.77)	44.66 (0.35)
A_2	16.39 (1.39)	28.93 (−0.36)	A_2	8.56 (−0.19)	15.12 (−0.80)

key: standardised residuals in brackets.

A_1 = energetic; B_1 = hysteric; C_1 = introvert; D_1 = acutely depressed.
A_2 = psychasthenic; B_2 = rigid; C_2 = extrovert; D_2 = not acutely depressed.

Table 5.46. *Models fitted to Table 3.6*

Model	df	Y^2	Parameter	Y^2 change	df
ABD/AC	6	8.38			
AB/AD/AC/BD	7	13.57	*ABD*	5.19	1
AB/AD/AC/BD/*	6	6.09	*	7.48	1
AD/AC/BD/*	7	6.24	*AB*	0.15	1
C/AD/BD/*	8	21.12	*AC*	14.88	1
AC/BD/*	8	39.82	*AD*	33.58	1
B/AD/AC/*	8	13.78	*BD*	7.54	1

cell $(1, 1, 2, 2)$ with, in this case, a standardised residual of -1.88; the introduction of parameter $*$ to control for this reduces Y^2 by 7.63. The model $AD/AC/BD/*$ indicates two-way interaction between validity (A) and depression (D), validity and stability (C) and solidity (B) and depression. Therefore, compared with what would hold were these symptoms unrelated, there are, for example, more patients jointly psychasthenic and acutely depressed, more energetic and extrovert, and less rigid and acutely depressed (see Table 5.47). Given these, there is no interaction between validity and solidity, solidity and stability, and stability and depression. Also, the $*$ parameter indicates that there are fewer than expected patients simultaneously energetic, hysteric, extrovert and not acutely depressed! The expected frequency obtained by fitting the $AD/AC/BD$ model is 23.01, compared with the observed 14. In the final analysis it is probably a matter of opinion which of $AD/AC/BD/*$ and ABD/AC is the more useful model, though one advantage of a final model involving only two-way interactions is that it is easier to collapse the extended table to obtain a simple display, as in Table 5.47, which may equate exactly or, in this case approximately, to the true two-way interactions obtained from $AD/AC/BD/*$.

Table 5.47. *Two-way tables illustrating the main interactions in Table 3.6*

	D_1	D_2		C_1	C_2
A_1	61	132	A_1	95	98
A_2	100	69	A_2	111	58
	D_1	D_2			
B_1	90	69			
B_2	71	132			

key: as in Table 5.45.

6 Counts from temporal observations

This chapter describes methods of analysing table counts obtained by categorising the same individual on at least two occasions. A sample comprising a number of such individuals yields what are normally referred to as panel data, and these are a common source of information on mass changes in opinion, status or behaviour. As a result of attrition of the panel and the difficulties associated with high-dimensional tables, panels are more often two-wave (i.e. two-occasion) than multiwave, and univariate rather than multivariate, and although these more-complex data are not ignored, we naturally commence with the simple one-variable two-wave panel.

A variety of models are introduced, initially in the context of this two-way table, to deal with features commonly associated with counts from temporal observations. Three common phenomena are the preponderance of identical responses at different times (loyalty or inertia), the dependence of transitions between categories on intercategory distances (distance), and the directional balance of intercategory transitions (symmetry). Loyalty, distance and symmetry effects are often in evidence together and in association with other traits in two-way tables, and are the fundamental components of the various models discussed in the text. They are also important elements of models devised for multiwave and multivariate panels described in the second half of the chapter.

As well as internal coherence, an attempt is made to provide wider integration by drawing together themes introduced in previous chapters. These include screening, STP, incomplete table analysis and uniform association. The topic of many repeated observations in close sequence producing dependent observations (see Chapter 4) is also briefly reconsidered.

Counts from observations made over time, or their equivalent, give rise to samples and tables of distinctive design. The methods described in this chapter reflect this fact whilst aiming not to lose sight of a broad unity of approach that permeates the book. Markov chain models provide an alternative method (see, for example, Markus 1979 and Logan 1981) that is somewhat dissimilar to the one considered here, though they are not unrelated, as described by Bishop *et al.* (1975).

The main diagonal model

This model is designed to account for a recurring feature of panel data, the inflation of the observed frequencies in the cells comprising the main diagonal of the square table that results from observing a single variable twice.

This phenomenon is clearly evident in Table 6.1 which describes the voting behaviour of a panel in the two British general elections held in 1974. For simplicity, the table is confined to the three main political parties. The close timing of the two elections probably enhances the possibility that an identical response will occur on the two occasions, a feature that would have, in any case, been evident due to the well-known tendency to remain loyal to one party. Comparison with the expected frequencies consistent with the independence hypothesis confirms the presence of inflated observed frequencies in the main diagonal cells and the commensurate deflation of the off-diagonal observed frequencies. Clearly, the independence model accounts inadequately for the data, with $Y^2 = 613.1 > \chi^2_{4, 0.05} = 9.49$, but it can usefully guide us towards an appropriate model.

Table 6.1. *The voting behaviour of a panel in the two 1974 British elections*

(a) Observed frequencies

		October vote		
		C	Lib	L
February vote	C	170	20	3
	Lib	22	70	28
	L	6	12	227

(b) Expected frequencies, independence hypothesis

		October vote		
		C	Lib	L
February vote	C	68.5	35.3	89.2
	Lib	42.6	21.9	55.5
	L	86.9	44.8	113.3

key: C: Conservative party.
    Lib: Liberal party.
    L: Labour party.

source: ESRC Survey Archive, Essex University.

In order to capture the loyalty or inertia effect evident from a comparison of Table 6.1(a) and (b), a single diagonal parameter is added to the parameters of the (log–linear) independence model to inflate the expected frequencies in the main diagonal cells. The main diagonal model is therefore

$$\log(p_{ij}) = \mu' + \lambda_i'^A + \lambda_j'^B + \lambda_2'^D \qquad (i=j)$$
$$= \mu' + \lambda_i'^A + \lambda_j'^B \qquad (i \neq j) \qquad\qquad (i,j = 1, \dots, I)$$

with constraints

$$\lambda_1'^A = \lambda_1'^B = \lambda_1'^D = 0$$

automatically imposed by the GENSTAT program. The extra diagonal parameter has the effect of reducing the degrees of freedom to one below the number for the independence model, thus $df = (I-1)(I-1) - 1$.

Upton (1980) gives a multiplicative and log–linear parameterisation of what is the equivalent of this model, despite the different name, that is consistent with Goodman-style ECTA constraints, and Goodman (1979b) writes the model out in multiplicative form but with only two parameters accounting for the independence component of the model. Note that temporal data are not a necessary condition for large main diagonal frequencies and invocation of the main diagonal model, for they are sometimes the outcome of cross-sectional surveys relating to variables such as left and right eyesight grades, father and son's socio-economic status, and so on. Note also that deflated cell frequencies can occur in situations of status disinheritance or analogous phenomena in other contexts, though these also come within the orbit of the model.

As with the majority of models considered in this book, the presence of a parameter in a model sets the total of a specific set of expected frequencies equal to the total of the equivalent set of observed frequencies. Comparison of the frequencies in Tables 6.1(a) and 6.2 'confirms' this equalisation, for, in addition to the usual row and column totals constraints consistent with the independence model, the sum of the expected frequencies on the main diagonal of Table 6.2 is set equal to the total of the main diagonal observed frequencies. The corollary of this is the equalisation of the off-diagonal frequencies totals.

Model fitting is easily accomplished via GENSTAT by laying out a diagonal 'factor' as follows for the three-level party variable

$$
\begin{array}{ccc}
2 & 1 & 1 \\
1 & 2 & 1 \\
1 & 1 & 2 \\
\end{array}
$$

To fit the model by ECTA or an equivalent program, one treats the two-way table as an incomplete three-way table with the two layers C_1 and C_2 containing the observed frequencies apart from the main diagonal frequencies, and the main diagonal frequencies, respectively. Fitting the model $A/B/C$ to this table satisfies the above-mentioned constraints, but parameter estimates may not be automatically forthcoming.

It is obvious from a comparison of Tables 6.1(a) and 6.2 that the expected frequencies of the main diagonal model are now largely in line with their observed counterparts. It is true that the fit of the model is only approximate ($Y^2 = 53.17 > \chi^2_{3,\,0.05} = 7.82$) and a more refined model is necessary to meet conventional goodness-of-fit criteria, none the less the impact of the diagonal parameter is enormous. The effect of introducing this one parameter λ'^D is to bring about a highly significant fall in Y^2 of

$$613.1 - 53.17 = 559.93 > \chi^2_{1,\,0.05} = 3.84.$$

The significance of λ'^D is reaffirmed by the standardised value of Table 6.3. There is every indication that no adequate model will be found for Table 6.1(a) from which a diagonal effect or its equivalent is absent.

The mover–stayer and related models

A refinement that follows on immediately from the main diagonal model is to attribute the inflated main diagonal frequencies to inertia or loyalty effects that differ according to the diagonal cell in question. This differentiated main diagonal effect is encapsulated in what is sometimes referred to as the mover–stayer model, the name originating from social mobility analysis.

Table 6.2. *The expected frequencies of the main diagonal model fitted to Table 6.1(a)*

		October vote		
		C	Lib	L
February vote	C	164.43	8.51	20.06
	Lib	16.00	84.31	19.69
	L	17.57	9.18	218.25

key: as for Table 6.1.

note: fitting terminates when only approximate equality is achieved.

Table 6.3. *Parameter estimates of the main diagonal model for Table 6.1(a)*

Param.	μ'	λ'^A_2	λ'^A_3	λ'^B_2	λ'^B_3	λ'^D_2
Est.	2.79	−0.02	0.08	−0.65	0.21	2.31
sv	22.30	−0.11	0.50	−3.70	1.41	19.50

Because of this concern with exact replication of the main diagonal frequencies, the mover–stayer model possesses I parameters for the I main diagonal cells of an I^2 table, $I - 1$ more than the main diagonal model. The model is equivalent to Goodman's (1965; 1968) quasi-independence or quasi-perfect mobility model, and was first suggested by Blumen *et al.* (1955). The I main diagonal parameters equalise the observed and expected main diagonal cell frequencies, and consequently their totals, so the mover–stayer and main diagonal models are hierarchically related. The former must fit any square table at least as well as the latter but with $I - 1$ less degrees of freedom. The degrees of freedom are $I^2 - 3I + 1$. Upton (1978a) discusses the failure of the mover–stayer model and the estimation of the number of movers and number of stayers in a population.

Table 6.5 shows that the fit of the mover–stayer model to the voting data in Table 6.1(a) is significantly better than the fit of the main diagonal model. The estimates and standardised values of the model parameters, with $*_1$, $*_5$ and $*_9$ representing the main diagonal parameters, are given in Table 6.4. Observe that $\hat{*}_1 = \log (e_{11} e_{32}/e_{12} e_{31})$, $\hat{*}_5 = (e_{13} e_{22}/e_{12} e_{23})$ and $\hat{*}_9 = \log (e_{12} e_{33}/e_{13} e_{32})$ (Duncan 1981).

The $*$ parameter estimates show the presence of interparty loyalty variations that were assumed away in the main diagonal model, and suggest a more parsimonious model with party loyalty applicable only to the political extremes. Invoking loyalty effects of separate magnitude produces the square table equivalent of variants of the extreme-ends model encountered previously, which is fitted by similar methods. In Table 6.5 this is labelled the differentiated bipolar

Table 6.4. *Parameter estimates of the mover-stayer model fitted to Table 6.1(a)*

Param.	μ'	$\lambda_2'^A$	$\lambda_3'^A$	$\lambda_2'^B$	$\lambda_3'^B$	$*_1$	$*_5$	$*_9$
Est.	1.57	1.61	-0.23	1.31	0.07	3.56	-0.24	4.01
sv	3.94	4.16	-0.72	3.22	0.25	8.75	-0.58	9.77

Table 6.5. *Variants on the mover-stayer model fitted to Table 6.1(a)*

Model	df	Y^2
Main diagonal	3	58.17
Mover–stayer	1	3.09
Differentiated bipolar loyalty	2	3.43
Bipolar loyalty	3	4.38
Right wing loyalty	3	225.8
Left wing loyalty	3	173.5

loyalty model. The loss of Liberal loyalty increases the degrees of freedom by 1 for only a small increase in $Y^2 = 3.43 - 3.09 = 0.34 < \chi^2_{1,\,0.05} = 3.84$. Amalgamating the remaining two loyalty parameters gives the so-called bipolar loyalty model of Table 6.5; this shows that the assumption of equal and high levels of loyalty to both parties of the political extremes is a tenable assumption. This model is actually equivalent to the extreme-ends model (Chapter 5), but for this application there is possibly more substantive justification. It can be argued that voters adhere to their views with increasing and equal tenacity as one moves towards the political extremes, irrespective of direction! The final two models of Table 6.5 show that loyalty to only one of these parties is insufficient for a successful model.

Note from Table 6.6 and Table 6.1(a) the equalisation of the totals in the subset of main-diagonal cells represented by a single parameter. In general, the * parameter estimates of the mover–stayer model can provide information on which * parameters can be set equal and thus the members of the subsets of main-diagonal cells. Duncan (1981) also performs this kind of analysis and makes useful comments.

Minor diagonals models

It is equally possible to fit a 'main diagonal' model with expected frequencies identical to those of Table 6.2 by subtracting the λ'^D_2 parameter estimate from the off-diagonal cells rather than adding it to the main diagonal. This is accomplished by reversing the positions of the levels 1 and 2 in the layout of the GENSTAT factor given earlier as a diagonal 'factor', and refitting the model. Viewed from this perspective, λ'^D_2 takes on the role of a 'deflation factor' (Goodman 1979b), a barrier effect which inhibits mobility but which remains constant irrespective of the origin and destination. A natural development of this model is to replace the monolithic barrier by a set of barriers that are differentiated according to the type of movement. What are referred to here as minor diagonals models are one class of model arising from this development, as outlined by Goodman (1972c). This has a diagonal effect like the main

Table 6.6. *Expected frequencies of the bipolar loyalty model fitted to Table 6.1(a)*

	C	Lib	L
C	172.07	15.14	5.79
Lib	21.31	71.40	27.29
L	4.61	15.46	224.93

key: as for Table 6.1(a).

diagonal model, but applied to subsidiary or minor diagonals rather than to the main diagonal, hence the use of the plural term and occasional prefix indicating the number of parameters. Writing the model as

$$\log(p_{ij}) = \mu' + \lambda_i'^A + \lambda_j'^B + \lambda_k'^D \qquad (i \neq j, k = |i-j|)$$
$$= \mu' + \lambda_i'^A + \lambda_j'^B \qquad (i=j)$$
$$(i,j = 1, \ldots, I)$$

one sees the replacement of $\lambda_2'^D$ by $I-1$ subsidiary diagonal parameters, giving

$$df = (I-1)(I-1) - (I-1) = I^2 - 3I + 2.$$

The model is easily fitted by GENSTAT or an equivalent program using the following factor layout for the typical 3^2 table (Table 6.7). This equalises the observed and expected frequency totals on each of three diagonals. Fitting the model by ECTA, or an equivalent iterative proportional fitting routine, requires incomplete table methodology.

Variants on this basic model include the restriction of diagonal effects to only a subset of the subsidiary diagonals. This type of refinement is considered in another context subsequently. Another variant is the incorporation of separate parameters to differentiate between subsidiary diagonals either side of the main diagonal, giving $2(I-1)$ subsidiary diagonal parameters in all. For the 3^2 table, this amounts to specifying five separate diagonals rather than three.

Although variations like this are easy to specify, an exact understanding of what the different models actually mean with respect to a process under study may be more difficult to achieve. A powerful reason for the inclusion of particular diagonal parameters, or parameters in general, is when their presence is invited on the basis of credible theories about the system of interest. In a social science context such theories are rather scarce and more often than not one has to resort to purely inductive methods.

Distance models

An assumption of the minor diagonal model is that transitions represented by cells on the same subsidiary diagonal are subject to identical inertia, distance, or barrier effects. In an electoral context, the ideological stances of the parties may render this a somewhat untenable assumption, for example in

Table 6.7. *A typical 3^2 table*

1	2	3
2	1	2
3	2	1

a simple three-party contest a right-wing Conservative party and a leftward inclined 'Centre' party will make the 'Centre' to Conservative transition comparatively more difficult to accomplish than a move from the 'Centre' to Socialist party. More appropriate therefore are distance models that, among other things, allow for the influence of varied interparty distances on voting behaviour. Distance models can also be applied to the study of social and spatial mobility.

A simple distance model for the two-way table can be written in log–linear terms as follows:

$$\log(p_{ij}) = \mu' + \lambda_i'^A + \lambda_j'^B + \lambda_{ij}'^D \qquad (i,j = 1, \ldots, I)$$

$$\lambda_{ij}'^D = \begin{cases} \sum_{r=i}^{j-1} d_r & (i < j) \\ 0 & (i = j) \\ \sum_{r=j}^{i-1} d_r & (j < i) \end{cases}$$

$$\lambda_1'^A = \lambda_1'^B = 0 \qquad \lambda_{ij}'^D = \lambda_{ji}'^D$$

The constraints imposed on $\{\lambda_{ij}'^D\}$ are simplifying collinearity and quasi-symmetry conditions. Goodman (1972c) and Bishop *et al.* (1975) call this class of model crossing-parameter models, and we refer to it later as a pure distance model.

To explicate the collinearity constraint, we consider a 4^2 table and the difference between the distance parameter applicable to cell (2,4),

$$\lambda_{24}'^D = d_2 + d_3,$$

and the parameter for cell (1,4),

$$\lambda_{14}'^D = d_1 + d_2 + d_3,$$

where the parameters d_1, d_2 and d_3 are the distances from categories 1 to 2, 2 to 3, and 3 to 4 respectively. The fact that the difference between $\lambda_{14}'^D$ and $\lambda_{24}'^D$ is d_1 implies that the categories are aligned (that is, collinear) with intervals d_1, d_2 and d_3. In general, the distance $\lambda_{ij}'^D$ between category pair i and j is the sum of the intervening intercategory distances d.

Note that when fitted to the 3^2 table, the pure-distance model is indistinguishable from the differentiated bipolar loyalty model in terms of expected frequencies, Y^2, and degrees of freedom. Likewise, the mover-stayer model for the 3^2 table generates exactly the same expected frequencies, Y^2, and degrees of freedom as the loyalty–distance and quasi-symmetry models which are introduced subsequently. These examples act as a warning not to accept too readily one particular line of reasoning.

In electoral studies, whilst interparty distances are an appealing concept, there is also a demonstrable need to subject hypothesised voting behaviour to the influence of party loyalty. To accommodate both loyalty effects, as represented in the main diagonal model, and the above-mentioned distance effects, Upton & Sarlvik (1981) have introduced a loyalty–distance model and applied it to the Swedish political system of the 1960s which evidently possessed parties aligned at various positions along a single left–right ideological axis. Hence the collinearity constraint is particularly appropriate. Written as a log–linear model for the two-way table, the loyalty–distance model is

$$\log(p_{ij}) = \mu' + \lambda'^A_i + \lambda'^B_j + \lambda'^C_k + \lambda'^D_{ij} \qquad (i, j = 1, \ldots, I)$$

This model is identical in constraints and parameters to the pure distance model, except for the presence of the loyalty parameter λ'^C_k, where

$$\lambda'^C_k = \begin{cases} \lambda'^C_2 & (i = j) \\ 0 & (i \neq j) \end{cases}$$

so that main diagonal cells of the table of expected frequencies receive the increment λ'^C_2 representing loyalty in the second election to the party supported in the first election.

Upton & Sarlvik (1981) describe the model in alternative multiplicative terms and in the context of the multiway table. Loyalty-distance models for multiwave panel data are discussed later. They also mention the possibility of related models for multidimensional political systems, and Pontinen (1982) discusses pure-distance models in the presence of the multidimensional ordering of employment categories. Migration and other forms of spatial behaviour may

Table 6.8. *Voting of a panel in the 1964 and 1970 Swedish elections*

		1970 vote				
		Comm	SD	C	P	Con
	Comm	22	27	4	1	0
	SD	16	861	57	30	8
1964 vote	C	4	26	248	14	7
	P	8	20	61	201	11
	Con	0	4	31	32	140

key: Comm: Communist party.
  SD: Social Democratic party.
  C: Centre party.
  P: People's party.
  Con: Conservative party.

also be treated as responses to the joint influence of (place) loyalty and (multidimensional) distance.

Table 6.8 describes the voting behaviour of Upton & Sarlvik's (1981) panel and Table 6.9 summarises the results of fitting various models to these data. Although the loyalty–distance model is the best of these simple models, it fails to satisfy conventional goodness-of-fit criteria, a topic we defer discussing until later. For the moment, it is accepted as an adequate and simple account of the main features of Table 6.8.

Table 6.10 gives the distance parameter estimates $(\hat{d}_i)$ produced by the pure distance and loyalty–distance models, and shows the inflation of the distance estimates of the former in an attempt to reduce the off-diagonal expected frequencies (and hence inflate those on the main diagonal), given the absence of a loyalty parameter. Such a parameter is essential, as indicated by its highly significant standardised value ($\lambda'^C_2 = 1.4$, standardised value $= 9.95$) when

Table 6.9. *Various models fitted to the Swedish voting data*

Model	df	Y^2
Independence	16	2260
Main diagonal	15	141.6
Mover–stayer	11	101.1
(five) Minor diagonals	12	51.07
(nine) Minor diagonals	9	44.80
Pure distance	12	129.4
Loyalty–distance	11	33.77
Distance/*$_1$/*$_7$/*$_{13}$/*$_{19}$/*$_{25}$	9	32.27
Quasi-symmetry	6	23.38

Table 6.10. *Interparty distance estimates obtained from Table 6.8*

Model		d_1	d_2	d_3	d_4
Pure distance	est.	-1.61	-2.01	-1.24	-1.69
	sv	-9.56	-23.19	-13.87	-13.39
Loyalty–distance	est.	-0.42	-1.10	-0.43	-0.82
	sv	-2.1	-9.09	-3.56	-5.42

key: $d_1 =$ Communist - Social Democrat.
$d_2 =$ Social Democrat - Centre.
$d_3 =$ Centre - People's party.
$d_4 =$ People's party - Conservative.

incorporated in the loyalty–distance model, and by the significant improvement in fit when added to the pure distance and independence models. Comparison of the fit of the loyalty–distance and distance $/*_1/*_7/*_{13}/*_{19}/*_{25}$ models of Table 6.9 quashes any suggestion of separate degrees of loyalty to individual parties.

Listing 8 (Appendix) gives the GENSTAT commands required to fit this sequence of models. It can also be fitted by a program such as ECTA to obtain the maximum likelihood estimates by iterative proportional fitting. In the case of the loyalty–distance model, the use of ECTA involves treating the I^2 table as an incomplete $I^2 \times 2^I$ table. This is laborious and produces an unwieldy table for large I and no automatically produced parameter estimates. In the absence of GENSTAT, or an equivalent package, with a large table it is worth writing a special program with iterations that terminate when there is simultaneous equalisation (to a specified level of error) of the totals of the observed and expected frequencies in the following sets:

  (i) all cells in the table;
  (ii) all cells on the main diagonal;
  (iii) all cells in the same row;
  (iv) all cells in the same column;
  (v) all cells denoting transitions that include a move between category i and category $i + 1; i = 1, \ldots, I - 1$.

The constraints (i)–(v) are satisfied by the expected frequencies in Table 6.11.

The degree of freedom for the loyalty–distance model can be deduced from these constraints, which are of course equivalent to parameters. In general, there are $1 + 1 + (I - 1) + (I - 1) + (I - 1)$ independent parameters, corresponding to constraints (i)–(v), responsible for the expected frequencies in the I^2 cells of the two-way table, giving $I^2 - 3(I - 1) - 2$ df.

Table 6.11. *Expected frequencies generated by the loyalty–distance model*

	Comm	SD	C	P	Con
Comm	22	22.43	6.53	2.41	0.64
SD	22.13	859.44	61.67	22.72	6.03
C	2.40	22.96	245.44	22.29	5.91
P	2.31	22.06	58.10	205.12	13.42
Con	1.16	11.11	29.27	25.46	140

key: as in Table 6.8.

Large samples

Although the loyalty–distance model is informative and parsimonious, according to conventional goodness-of-fit criteria it fails to successfully account for the data in Table 6.8, since $Y^2 = 33.77 > \chi^2_{11, 0.05} = 19.68$. This 'lack of fit' should not be a cause of undue concern, for simple models that are only approximately true cannot be expected to 'fit' a table containing a large sample. This derives from our knowledge that goodness of fit declines with increasing sample size when the model fitted is not exactly true (Bishop *et al.* 1975, p. 329). Therefore, via the usual criteria, 'successful' models will be comparatively complicated unless alternative rules are employed.

In large surveys or analyses of census data (for example, Fienberg & Mason 1979), it has therefore become an acceptable practice to examine the percentage of the total Y^2 available to be accounted for by explanatory (factor–response) interactions, which is actually accounted for by any particular model containing a subset of these interactions. The total Y^2 available is the deviance of a model with the complete set of factor–response interactions nullified. In the case of the Table 6.8 this is $Y^2 = 2260$, the independence model deviance. Inclusion of the explanatory loyalty and distance effects accounts for

$$98.5\% = [(2260 - 33.77)/2260] \times 100$$

of the total available deviance. Note that this approach is not devoid of theoretical substantiation, for it is equivalent to measuring the % of the information content of a table that is explained by a given model.

Quasi-symmetry models

The discussion so far has developed two of the major themes, loyalty and distance, which pervade this chapter. We now come to the third, symmetry. It is actually more convenient to approach this in a roundabout way commencing with quasi-symmetry, which is the presence of symmetry plus row and column effects which distort what would otherwise be pure symmetry among the cell counts of a square table. In general, tables like this possessing an underlying symmetry that is conditioned by other effects so as not to be overt are said to display weak symmetry. One reason for introducing quasi-symmetry first is that it is just one step removed from the loyalty–distance model fitted to the square two-way table with at least 16 cells. The details of the difference between these two models are given below. Caussinus (1965) was the instigator of the quasi-symmetry model. Apart from the usual fitting constraints necessary for unique estimates and constraints establishing the quasi-symmetry condition, there are no other assumptions made about parameter values. Thus the model is close in spirit to the saturated model, which is devoid of assumptions about parameter values, and somewhat removed from previously considered models, such as the main diagonal model which sets equal all main diagonal and all off-diagonal parameters. The log–linear quasi-symmetry model for the two-way table is

$$\log(p_{ij}) = \mu' + \lambda_i'^A + \lambda_j'^B + \lambda_{ij}'^{AB} \qquad (i, j = 1, \ldots, I)$$

and the usual Plackett-style fitting constraints anchor a subset of these parameters to zero. The most natural assignation of zeros is to the parameters $\lambda_1'^A$, $\lambda_1'^B$ and $\lambda_{ii}'^{AB}$, $i = 1, \ldots, I$, though this is not accomplished via GENSTAT without judiciously placing appropriately labelled parameters on the main diagonal. The constraint

$$\lambda_{ij}'^{AB} = \lambda_{ji}'^{AB} \qquad \text{for all} \quad i, j$$

establishes quasi-symmetry which, when relaxed, returns us to the saturated model.

Model fitting via GENSTAT or an equivalent program is carried out by equalising the totals in parallel sets of observed and expected frequencies that correspond to the model parameters. Listing 9 (Appendix) gives the details for the 4^2 table. The constraints mean that, in general, there are $(I-1)(I-2)/2$ degrees of freedom. Bishop *et al.* (1975) and Upton (1978*a*) show how the same thing can be done using ECTA or an equivalent, and Tables 6.12 and 6.13 demonstrate the constraints $f_{ij} + f_{ji} = e_{ij} + e_{ji}$, which are tantamount to $\lambda_{ij}'^{AB} = \lambda_{ji}'^{AB}$.

The model was fitted to Table 6.12 which originates from the published migration reports of the 1971 British census. These data describe the place of residence on two occasions of a subgroup of migrants (who happen to be British residents who were born in the New Commonwealth). The two occasions are the 1966 and 1971 censuses, the data comprise a 10% sample, and the table categories are an amalgamation of the more important centres of population, the Metropolitan Counties.

Table 6.12. *Observed migrant behaviour*

	B_1	B_2	B_3	B_4
A_1	118	12	7	23
A_2	14	2127	86	130
A_3	8	69	2548	107
A_4	12	110	88	7712

key: A: 1966.   1: Central Clydeside.
     B: 1971.   2: Urban Lancashire and Yorkshire.
                3: West Midlands.
                4: Greater London.

The quasi-symmetry model fits Table 6.12 extremely well with

$$Y^2 = 2.60 < \chi^2_{3, 0.05} = 7.82,$$

indicating that the migrant flows would be symmetrical were it not for other influences associated with differential regional 'push' and 'pull' effects.

As Upton & Sarlvik (1981) observe, the quasi-symmetry model fitted to the two-way table imposes one less constraint than the loyalty–distance model on the 'distance' parameters $\{\lambda'^{AB}_{ij}\}$, for the collinearity constraint is relaxed. It is therefore possible to write quasi-symmetry + collinearity = loyalty–distance, and use the Y^2 difference as a conditional test of collinearity. Fitting the loyalty–distance model to Table 6.12 gives $Y^2 = 10.54 < \chi^2_{5, 0.05} = 11.07$, and the Y^2 difference $10.54 - 2.60 = 7.94 > \chi^2_{2, 0.05} = 5.99$ indicates that, assuming quasi-symmetry to be true, the absence of collinearity is the reason for the 'poor' fit of the loyalty–distance model. Notwithstanding the approximate north–south geographical alignment of the regions, one cannot assume that the regions are perceived to be arranged linearly so that the distance between any pair is the sum of the intervening distances. This analysis contrasts with that of Table 6.8 (see Table 6.9) where relaxing the collinearity constraint does not significantly improve the fit.

Symmetry and marginal homogeneity

Defined in terms of theoretical probabilities in a two-way table, symmetry is the condition whereby

$$p_{ij} = p_{ji} \qquad (i, j = 1, \dots, I)$$

An equivalent statement is

$$\log(p_{ij}) = \mu' + \lambda'^{AB}_{ij} \qquad (i, j = 1, \dots, I)$$

where

$$\lambda'^{AB}_{ij} = \lambda'^{AB}_{ji}$$

and

$$\lambda'^{AB}_{11} = 0$$

Table 6.13. *Expected migrant behaviour according to the quasi-symmetry model*

	B_1	B_2	B_3	B_4
A_1	118	13.45	8.20	20.34
A_2	12.55	2127	82.08	135.38
A_3	6.80	72.92	2548	104.28
A_4	14.66	104.62	90.72	7712

key: as Table 6.12.

Note the absence from this statement of $\{\lambda_i'^A\}$ and $\{\lambda_j'^B\}$, which previously removed true symmetry about the main diagonal from the expected frequencies of the quasi-symmetry model.

Symmetrical expected frequencies for cell (i, j) and cell (j, i) are obtained very simply since $e_{ij} = e_{ji} = (f_{ij} + f_{ji})/2$. Using GENSTAT, one simply fits the 'factor' responsible for the symmetry of the quasi-symmetry model.

In general, the symmetry model for the I^2 table possesses $I(I-1)/2$ degrees of freedom, $I-1$ more than for the quasi-symmetry model because of the latter's extra parameters controlling for marginal heterogeneity.

Marginal homogeneity is the condition

$$p_{i0} = p_{0i} \qquad (i = 1, \ldots, I)$$

Observe that the existence of symmetry implies the existence of marginal homogeneity, since if $p_{ij} = p_{ji}$, then $\Sigma_j p_{ij} = \Sigma_j p_{ji}$. Quasi-symmetry, on the other hand, is symmetry without the concomitant marginal homogeneity, and thus we can write quasi-symmetry + marginal homogeneity = symmetry. Since the difference between these two forms of symmetry model is marginal homogeneity, the Y^2 difference resulting from fitting both models to the same table is a conditional test of marginal homogeneity on the assumption that quasi-symmetry holds.

Unconditional tests of marginal homogeneity demand expected frequencies that total to the same values across row i and down column i for $i = 1, \ldots, I$ without necessarily being symmetrical. Maximum likelihood estimates with this condition are not easy to achieve. Plackett (1981) gives an example and Bishop *et al.* (1975) also discuss their calculation. Ireland *et al.* (1969) obtain estimates by minimising the modified version of the minimum discriminant information statistic rather than Y^2. Bhapkar (1979) gives a method based on weighted least squares which removes the need for complex iterations. Such unconditional tests are of value where the data deviate significantly from quasi-symmetry.

Fitting the symmetry model to Table 6.12 gives

$$Y^2 = 9.13 < \chi^2_{6, 0.05} = 12.59,$$

an adequate fit. The imposition of the marginal homogeneity assumption in progressing from quasi-symmetry to symmetry brings about a fairly large, but insignificant, increase in deviance of $9.13 - 2.60 = 6.53 < \chi^2_{3, 0.05} = 7.82$. Before making any conclusions, we note that although symmetry is consistent with Table 6.12, a significant reduction in Y^2 can be achieved using a variant of the diagonals-parameter symmetry model that possesses an appealingly simple interpretation.

Diagonals-parameter symmetry models

If the minor diagonals and symmetry effects are combined, one arrives at the diagonals–parameter symmetry model introduced, together with simplified versions, by Goodman (1979c). Like the quasi-symmetry model, these models say that one would have symmetry were it not for other influences, in this case the various diagonals parameters that introduce differential odds pertaining to the subsidiary diagonals. The basic model is therefore

$$\log(p_{ij}) = \mu' + \lambda_{ij}'^{AB} + \lambda_k'^{D} \qquad (k = i - j)$$
$$(i = 1, \ldots, I)$$
$$(j = 1, \ldots, I)$$

with

$$\lambda_{ij}'^{AB} = \lambda_{ji}'^{AB} \qquad (i \neq j)$$
$$\lambda_{11}'^{AB} = 0$$
$$\lambda_k'^{D} = 0 \qquad (k = 0, \ldots, I-1)$$

There are $I - 1$ extra (diagonal) parameters compared with the symmetry model, and thus there are $(I-1)(I-2)/2$ degrees of freedom.

Goodman (1979c) gives methods of direct maximum likelihood estimation of the expected frequencies and parameters of the model without recourse to iterative methods. These estimates can also be obtained very simply via GENSTAT or an equivalent program by combining a symmetry 'factor' with a diagonals-parameter 'factor' to introduce the varying subsidiary diagonal odds. The layout for the 2^4 table is given in Table 6.14. Listing 10 (Appendix) gives more detail on fitting this and the allied models, described below.

Variants of the above model impose conditions on the diagonals parameters $\{\lambda_k'^{D}\}$ so that some of them are set equal either to each other or to zero. The entire set constrained to zero, of course, returns us to the symmetry model. These more parsimonious models amount to hypotheses about the true values of the diagonals parameters such as, for example, the hypothesis that

$$\lambda_k'^{D} = 0 \qquad (k < 0)$$

Table 6.14. *Diagonals parameters laid out for GENSTAT*

1	2	3	4
1	1	2	3
1	1	1	2
1	1	1	1

holds for a specified subset of size K of the $I - 1$ parameters. Compared with the unmodified version of the model, a diagonals-parameter symmetry model incorporating this constraint will possess an extra K degrees of freedom since the subset of parameters of size K is not estimated from the data, thus giving $K + [(I - 1)(I - 2)]/2$ degrees of freedom.

The hypothesis that

$$\lambda_k^{\prime D} = \lambda_s^{\prime D} \quad (k < 0)$$

$$\lambda_s^{\prime D} = \text{equalized subset}$$

is an alternative that sets equal a specified subset of size K of the $I - 1$ diagonals-parameters. Since K parameters are replaced by one, there are $K - 1$ more degrees of freedom than for the unadulterated diagonals-parameter symmetry model, that is,

$$(K - 1) + [(I - 1)(I - 2)]/2 = K + \tfrac{1}{2}I(I - 3).$$

The conditional symmetry model is the special case in which all $I - 1$ diagonals-parameters are replaced by a single parameter, giving

$$(I - 2) + [(I - 1)(I - 2)]/2 = (I + 1)(I - 2)/2$$

degrees of freedom, one less than for the symmetry model.

Table 6.15 gives the results of fitting examples of these models to the data in Table 6.12. The diagonals-parameter symmetry model significantly improves on the fit of the symmetry model since $9.13 - 1.12 = 8.01 > \chi^2_{3,\,0.05} = 7.82$, and simplifications of this bring about no inordinate loss of fit. The conditional symmetry model is the simplest successful model and this is also a significant improvement on the symmetry model, since

$$9.13 - 2.97 = 6.16 > \chi^2_{1,\,0.05} = 3.84.$$

Table 6.15. *Diagonals-parameter symmetry and related models fitted to Table 6.12*

Model	df	Y^2	Diagonals-parameter estimates (sv in parentheses)
Symmetry	6	9.13	
Diagonals-parameter symmetry	3	1.12	0.18 (1.75), 0.15 (1.19), 0.65 (1.83)
$\lambda_k^{\prime D} = 0$	4	2.53	0.18 (1.75), 0, 0.65 (1.83)
$\lambda_k^{\prime D} = \lambda_s^{\prime D}$	4	1.16	0.17 (2.11), 0.17 (2.11), 0.65 (1.83)
Conditional symmetry	5	2.97	0.19 (2.48)

Accepting this as the final model for Table 6.12, because it also has a sensible interpretation, we conclude that the migrant flows would be symmetrical were it not for a significant pull towards the south. The odds of a southward rather than a northward move are $e^{\hat{\lambda}'^D_s} = 1.21$ to 1. Listing 10 (Appendix) reproduces these results.

Multiwave panels and loyalty models

The two-way table deriving from two-wave panel data and describing responses to a single stimulus has dominated the discussion thus far in this chapter. From this point on we consider data resulting from observing individuals more than twice (multiwave panels) and data from multivariate panels involving more than one variable per wave. For simplicity, we are restricted to simple versions of these more complex panels, though the methods described can be easily extended to larger tables. We commence with multiwave panels and loyalty models. Models featuring the two other themes, distance and symmetry, are dealt with subsequently.

An n-wave panel responding to a single I category stimulus results in the creation of an I^n-cell table that can be usefully recast as a two-way $I^n \times I$ table like Table 6.16. An earlier version of these data is given in Table 6.1 which is the result of ignoring the final wave of May 1979. The current investigation is concerned with the relationship between the 1979 vote and the two 1974 votes.

Table 6.16. *The choices of a panel of voters over three elections*

Feb. 1974 (A)	Oct. 1974 (B)	May 1979 (C)		
		C	Lib	L
C	C	164	4	2
	Lib	15	4	1
	L	1	0	2
Lib	C	15	6	1
	Lib	22	42	6
	L	5	5	18
L	C	3	0	3
	Lib	4	4	4
	L	18	15	194

key: as in Table 6.1.

source: ESRC Survey archive, Essex University.

Table 6.17 describes the fit of various models to these data. The model AB/C contains the factor interaction AB but no factor–response interaction relating the latest vote to previous ones, and it is thus an appropriate model with which to begin to search for dependence. The AB/C model fails to account for Table 6.16 and so we turn next to the multiway equivalent of the previously discussed main diagonal model which is denoted by $AB/C/L1/L2$ in Table 6.17. This is referred to here as the pure-loyalty model. This greatly improves on the previous model, but since $Y^2 = 27.65 > \chi^2_{14, 0.05} = 23.68$, there is still need for some further elaboration to satisfy the conventional goodness-of-fit criteria. This is accomplished by the introduction of additional loyalty parameters to allow for the fact that there are some panel members who voted consistently for one party in all three elections. It therefore seems appropriate to treat these differently from floating voters and allot them special parameters $*_1$, $*_{14}$ and $*_{27}$. We call the resulting model a mover–stayer loyalty model and denote it by $AB/C/L1/L2/*_1/*_{14}/*_{27}$ in Table 6.17. It fits Table 6.16 tolerably well with $Y^2 = 16.95 < \chi^2_{11, 0.05} = 19.68$. Note that, in this case, the mover–stayer loyalty model possesses three degrees of freedom less than the pure-loyalty model, on account of the three extra $*$ parameters, and that these bring about a significant improvement in fit of $27.65 - 16.95 = 10.70 > \chi^2_{3, 0.05} = 7.82$. In general, there are $[(I^{n-1} - 1)(I - 1)] - (n - 1)$ df for the pure-loyalty model, and $[(I^{n-1} - 1)(I - 1)] - (n - 1) - I$ df for the mover–stayer loyalty model.

Some simplification of the mover–stayer loyalty model is achieved by nullifying the $*_1$ and $*_{27}$ parameters which are shown in Table 6.18 to be insignificant. The standardised value of the parameter $*_{14}$ is close to the critical value of 1.96

Table 6.17. *Models fitted to Table 6.16*

Model	df	Y^2
AB/C	16	554.6
$AB/C/L1/L2$	14	27.65
$AB/C/L1/L2/*_1/*_{14}/*_{27}$	11	16.95
$AB/C/L1/L2/*_{14}$	13	17.53

Table 6.18. *Relevant parameters of a mover–stayer loyalty model*

Param.	λ^{L1}	λ^{L2}	$*_1$	$*_{14}$	$*_{27}$
Est.	1.41	1.66	0.15	-1.37	-0.27
sv	3.87	4.74	0.17	-1.94	-0.38

derived from a $N(0,1)$ distribution, and is therefore retained to give a final model $AB/C/L1/L2/*_{14}$. The difference between the Y^2 of this and the pure-loyalty model is $27.65 - 17.53 = 10.12 > \chi^2_{1,0.05} = 3.84$. This difference has an approximate probability of 0.001 assuming $*_{14}$ to be truly zero and, therefore, $*_{14}$ clearly differs from zero.

Using the estimates in Table 6.19, the interpretation of Table 6.16 is that there was loyalty to parties selected in both 1974 elections, with stronger loyalty to the most recently chosen party. There is no need to consider consistent voters separately, except that those who voted Liberal in all three elections were significantly fewer in number than one would expect.

Although the model $AB/C/L1/L2/*_{14}$ provides a plausible fit to Table 6.16, it is devoid of distance effects which could be a real entity in the voting transition process. One problem with fitting distance models to 3^3 tables is, as with 3^2 tables, they may not take on a unique identity. In this case, the loyalty–distance model is indistinguishable from a model with loyalty and symmetry alone. Incidentally, that model fits rather well, with $Y^2 = 10.85 < \chi^2_{12,.05} = 21.03$, though, illogically, it signifies very significant loyalty to the vote cast in February 1974 and indifference to the October 1974 vote. This is another reason to prefer the model $AB/C/L1/L2/*_{14}$.

Multiwave panels and loyalty–distance models

The equations below identify the parameters and constraints of a version of the previously described loyalty–distance model that is appropriate to the three-way table. The notation is easily extended to handle higher-dimensional tables, and Upton & Sarlvik (1981) give equivalent multiplicative and log-linear parameterisations that are derivable from this specification of the model.

$$\log(p_{ijk}) = \mu' + \lambda'^{AB}_{ij} + \lambda'^{C}_{k} + \lambda'^{L1}_{l} + \lambda'^{L2}_{m} + \lambda'^{D}_{jk}$$

$$(i, j, k = 1, \ldots, I)$$
$$(l = 1, 2)$$
$$(m = 1, 2)$$

Table 6.19. *Parameter estimates of the final model* $AB/C/L1/L2/*_{14}$ *fitted to Table 6.16*

Param.	λ^{L1}	λ^{L2}	$*_{14}$
Est.	1.35	1.61	-1.26
sv	8.83	10.04	-3.19

The following constraints (or their equivalents) are also required

$$\lambda'^{AB}_{11} = 0$$

$$\lambda'^{C}_{1} = 0$$

$$\lambda'^{L1}_{i} \begin{cases} \lambda'^{L1}_{2} & (j=k) \\ \lambda'^{L1}_{1} = 0 & (j \neq k) \end{cases}$$

$$\lambda'^{L2}_{m} \begin{cases} \lambda'^{L2}_{2} & (i=j) \\ \lambda'^{L2}_{1} = 0 & (i \neq k) \end{cases}$$

$$\lambda'^{D}_{jk} \begin{cases} = \sum_{r=j}^{k-1} d_r & (j<k) \\ = 0 \\ = \sum_{r=k}^{j-1} d_r & (k<j) \end{cases} \qquad \lambda'^{D}_{jk} = \lambda'^{D}_{kj} \quad \text{for all} \quad j,k$$

In general, there are $[(I^{n-1} - 1)(I-1)] - (n-1) - (I-1)$ degrees of freedom for the loyalty–distance model fitted to an n-way table with an I category variable. This is $I-1$ less than the degrees of freedom of the pure-loyalty model on account of the $I-1$ distance parameters. The longhand version of the pure-loyalty model derives directly from the above equation on setting the distance parameters to zero, which then becomes

$$\log(p_{ijk}) = \mu' + \lambda'^{AB}_{ij} + \lambda'^{C}_{k} + \lambda'^{L1}_{i} + \lambda'^{L2}_{m}$$

with constraints identical to those given above imposed on the parameters common to both models. The model

$$\log(p_{ijk}) = \mu' + \lambda'^{AB}_{ij} + \lambda'^{C}_{k} + \lambda'^{L1}_{i} + \lambda'^{L2}_{m} + \lambda'^{D}_{jk}$$

with constraints

$$\lambda'^{D}_{jk} = \lambda'^{D}_{kj}$$

$$\lambda'^{D}_{jk} = 0 \qquad (j=k)$$

in addition to the other constraints, can be referred to as a loyalty quasi-symmetry model for obvious reasons. The constraints also imply $\lambda'^{L1}_{2} = 0$ and thus the model is denoted as $AB/C/L2/SYMM$ in Table 6.21. Note that this model has $[(I-1)(I-2)] - 1$ degrees of freedom less than the pure-loyalty model for the three-way table.

The data in Table 6.20 describes the major parties preferred by a panel of Swedish voters in three elections which was originally analysed by Upton (1978a). The results of fitting these and other models to these data are summarised in Table 6.21, and are reproduced using GENSTAT by listing 11 (Appendix). As Upton found, the loyalty–distance model provides an adequate fit to the data. However, some simplification can be achieved by setting to zero the parameter d_2 representing the distance between the Centre party and the People's party. This possibility is evident from the standardised value of the d_2 parameter given in Table 6.22 and by the small Y^2 difference between the models $AB/C/L1/L2/d_1/d_2/d_3$ and $AB/C/L1/L2/d_1/d_3$ of

$$55.99 - 55.01 = 0.98 < \chi^2_{1,0.05} = 3.84$$

A similar hypothesis that the true value of d_3 is zero produces a marginally

Table 6.20. *Swedish voting behaviour in 1964, 1968 and 1970*

		C (1970)			
A (1964)	B (1968)	SD	C	P	Con
SD	SD	812	27	16	5
	C	5	20	6	0
	P	2	3	4	0
	Con	3	3	4	2
C	SD	21	6	1	0
	C	3	216	6	2
	P	0	3	7	0
	Con	0	9	0	4
P	SD	15	2	8	0
	C	1	37	8	0
	P	1	17	157	4
	Con	0	2	12	6
Con	SD	2	0	0	1
	C	0	13	1	4
	P	0	3	17	1
	Con	0	12	11	126

key: as in Table 6.8.

Table 6.21. *The results of fitting various models to Table 6.20*

Model		df	Y^2
Loyalty–distance	$AB/C/L1/L2/d_1/d_2/d_3$	40	55.01
Pure-loyalty	$AB/C/L1/L2$	43	93.75
Pure-distance	$AB/C/d_1/d_2/d_3$	42	311.70
Loyalty quasi-symmetry	$AB/C/L2/SYMM$	38	54.36
	$AB/C/L1/L2/d_1/d_3$	41	55.99
	$AB/C/L1/L2/d_1$	42	59.89

significant Y^2 increase. Though the outcome of these tests is conditional on the pair of models involved, none the less it is apparent that the major political cleavage of Table 6.20 is that separating the Social Democrats from the three parties of the right. This is shown by the comparative goodness of fit of the models $AB/C/L1/L2/d_1$ and $AB/C/L1/L2$ in Table 6.21, and by the standardised value of d_1 in Table 6.22. Apart from this, it can be argued that the ordering of the parties is not strict.

The distance estimates of Table 6.22 can be attributed to 1969, mid-way between the 1968 and 1970 elections since the party positions on both occasions have a bearing on the interparty distance estimates. Similarly, the distances derived from the previous analysis involving five parties and the 1964 and 1970 elections (Table 6.8) are attributable to 1967. At that time, the People's party was significantly on the right of the Centre party and the Conservatives were significantly further to the right. Evidently, the detectable right to left ordering of all the parties had broken down by the end of the decade. Although Upton & Sarlvik (1981) do not test the effect of setting distance parameters to zero, this conclusion is corroborated by their comprehensive analysis of a wide array of similar data which presents a picture of a converging non-Socialist bloc in the late 1960s which emerged to form three-party coalitions in the 1970s.

A feature of their parameterisation is the set of attraction parameters $\{\alpha_k\}$ which represent the intrinsic party attractions. More specifically, the parameters represent the probability of voting for each party in 1970 in the absence of loyalty and distance effects. Since loyalty and distance effects are not absent, these probabilities are not the same thing as the observed voting probabilities. None the less, it is informative to observe which parties retained popular support in 1970 by means other than their intrinsic attractiveness. The $\{\alpha_k\}$ parameters are equivalent to the parameters labelled $\{\lambda'^{C}_{k}\}$ above. The relation between the two parameterisations is given by

$$\alpha_k = e^{\lambda'^{C}_{k}} \Big/ \sum_{k=1}^{I} e^{\lambda'^{C}_{k}}$$

and from this we obtain the estimates of Table 6.23.

Table 6.22. *Parameter estimates of the loyalty-distance model fitted to Table 6.20*

Param.	λ'^{C}_{2}	λ'^{C}_{3}	λ'^{C}_{4}	λ'^{L1}_{2}	λ'^{L2}_{2}	d_1	d_2	d_3
Est.	0.67	0.25	−0.64	1.52	1.35	−1.18	−0.16	−0.40
sv	4.03	1.44	−3.19	7.34	13.26	−5.90	−0.99	−2.04

From Table 6.23 it is clear that the majority support for the Social Democrats was largely derived from strong party-loyalty effects and from the party's ideological separation on the left-to-right axis, and was not due to other influences which would also attract support and which are encapsulated by the comparatively small α_k estimate. With no improvement in loyalty or intrinsic attractiveness and with the gradual leftward encroachment of the right wing parties, it is possible to foresee the demise of the Social Democrat Government. Such a defeat actually occurred in the 1976 election.

Multivariate panel data

When panel members respond to more than one question on each of n occasions, models may be called for in which simultaneous responses interact and also depend on previous responses. Such a survey is described by Table 6.24

Table 6.23. *The intrinsic attractiveness of the four Swedish parties, estimated via the loyalty–distance model*

	α_1 (SD)	α_2 (C)	α_3 (P)	α_4 (Con)
Intrinsic attractiveness	0.21	0.41	0.27	0.11
Observed proportions	0.52	0.23	0.16	0.09

key: as in Table 6.8.

Table 6.24. *Votes and attitudes in October 1974 and May 1979*

		C_1 D_1	C_2 D_1	C_1 D_2	C_2 D_2
A_1	B_1	0	9	0	1
A_2	B_1	1	180	0	16
A_1	B_2	3	20	59	120
A_2	B_2	2	67	12	133

key: A_1: for more nationalisation in 1974.
A_2: against more nationalisation in 1974.
B_1: for the Conservative party in 1974.
B_2: against the Conservative party in 1974.
C_1: for more nationalisation in 1979.
C_2: against more nationalisation in 1979.
D_1: for the Conservative party in 1979.
D_2: against the Conservative party in 1979.

source: ESRC Survey archive, Essex University.

which is typical of many multivariate panels published in the literature and which is suited to the techniques described by Goodman (1972*b*; 1973*a*, *b*).

The data in Table 6.24 derive from the panel used earlier to draw up Table 6.16. To facilitate the present exposition we focus on two responses at the time of the October 1974 and May 1979 elections: attitudes towards a particular social and economic policy (for or against further nationalisation), and vote in favour of or against the Conservative party. Since the Conservative party has traditionally taken a stance against nationalisation in favour of free enterprise, one would expect there to be an association between the responses made at any one time. However, attitude towards nationalisation (C) may also be influenced by previous attitude on that matter (A), and it may also depend on previous vote (B). Similarly, the vote cast in 1979 (D) may to some extent depend on previous vote and attitude.

The analysis focusses on the 1979 responses and thus 1974 attitudes and votes are treated as factors. Since there is no obvious 'causal' ordering of the two simultaneous responses, we refrain from labelling one as factor and the other as response. This has a bearing on the models that are fitted to the data, each of which includes the interfactor AB interaction.

The significant interactions in Table 6.24 and their approximate relative importance are identified by jointly implementing STP, screening and stepwise selection. The results of STP are summarised in Tables 6.25, 6.26 and 6.27. Note that, since every model includes the interfactor interaction AB, there are five other optional two-way interactions and five optional higher-order interactions: thus there are, in all, ten potentially nullifiable interactions and so we establish that the overall type I error rate $\gamma = 1 - (0.95)^{10} = 0.40$, giving the critical value for this test as $\chi^2_{10,0.4}$. The critical value for the pooled three- and four-way effects is $\chi^2_{5,0.23}$ since $\gamma_{3,4} = 1 - (0.95)^5 = 0.23$.

Since $1.79 < \chi^2_{5,0.85} < \chi^2_{5,0.23}$ the three- and four-way effects can be safely nullified. However, $434.48 + 1.79 = 436.27 > \chi^2_{10,0.001} > \chi^2_{10,0.4}$ and thus there are significant two-way interactions. Table 6.26 shows the results of entering these in an order determined by the standardised values of the parameters of the model containing all two-way interactions. From this order we find that

Table 6.25. *Initial analysis of deviance for two-wave two-variable panel data*

·Model	df	Y^2	Source	Deviance
$AB/C/D$	10	436.27		
$AB/AC/AD/BC/BD/CD$	5	1.79	two-way effects	434.48
			three-, four-way effects	1.79

none of the two-way effects can be nullified since

$$17.69 + 1.79 = 19.48 > \chi^2_{10,\,0.05} > \chi^2_{10,\,0.4}.$$

However, the interactions can be entered in the revised order of Table 6.27 which allows a more parsimonious model to be selected.

Since $7.03 + 1.79 = 8.82 < \chi^2_{10,\,0.4} = 10.47$, the BC interaction can be set to zero and the final model designated as $AB/AC/CD/AD/BD$.

An alternative and supplementary insight into the data is obtained from the results of screening (see Chapter 3) given in Table 6.28.

Table 6.26. *Analysis of deviance with the panel data of Table 6.24*

Model	df	Y^2	Source	df	Deviance
$AB/C/D$	10	436.27			
$AB/BD/C$	9	135.35	BD	1	300.92
$AB/BD/BC$	8	77.55	BC	1	57.80
$AB/BD/BC/AC$	7	34.95	AC	1	42.60
$AB/BD/BC/AC/CD$	6	19.48	CD	1	15.47
$AB/BD/BC/AC/CD/AD$	5	1.79	AD	1	17.69
			residual	5	1.79

Table 6.27. *Analysis of deviance of Table 6.24 with revised order*

Model	df	Y^2	Source	df	Deviance
$AB/C/D$	10	436.30			
$AB/AC/D$	9	355.20	AC	1	81.10
$AB/AC/CD$	8	296.20	CD	1	59.0
$AB/AC/CD/AD$	7	208.10	AD	1	88.10
$AB/AC/CD/AD/BD$	6	$-$ 8.82	BD	1	199.28
$AB/AC/CD/AD/BD/BC$	5	1.79	BC	1	7.03
			residual	5	1.79

Table 6.28. *The results of screening Table 6.24*

Interaction	df	Marginal contribution	Partial contribution
AC	1	81.0	34.1
AD	1	127.8	17.7
BC	1	57.8	7.0
BD	1	300.9	187.0
CD	1	59.1	7.0
ABC	1	0.5	0.4
ABD	1	1.2	0.7
ACD	1	0.1	0.0
BCD	1	0.7	0.4
$ABCD$	1	0.0	0.0

The results collated in Table 6.28 concur with the STP analysis that all three- and four-way interactions are nullifiable and that all of the two-way interactions are (ostensibly) significant with respect to the $\chi^2_{10,\,0.05}$ critical value, though the adjusted STP significance level allows *BC* to be set to zero. From this it can be inferred that 1974 vote is not directly related to 1979 attitude, whilst 1974 attitude evidently has a significant direct relation to 1979 vote.

It is possible to obtain evidence of the relative magnitude of other interactions from Tables 6.26, 6.27 and 6.28. These indicate that the *CD* interaction is the weakest of those retained, suggesting that the 1979 vote and 1979 attitude were largely responses to earlier votes and attitudes and that their contemporaneous mutual interaction was of relatively minor importance. In fact, *CD* could have been nullified instead of *BC*. There is reason to believe that the strongest interaction is *BD* which represents the association between 1979 vote and 1974 vote.

The models that fit Table 6.24 are conveniently devoid of three-way interactions and so, as in Chapter 4, a simple path diagram can be of use to display the direct and indirect interactions inherent in the data. The diagram above summarises the interactions of the suggested final model *AB/AC/CD/AD/BD*. A double-headed arrow denotes that the pair of variables is not separated into factor and response.

Some weak symmetry models for multivariate panel data

Duncan (1980, 1981) has introduced some models embodying the symmetry concept which are specific to multivariate panels. Most of the examples cited are confined to the two-variable two-wave panel, though the analysis extends naturally to a larger number of variables. Essentially, the method treats the multiway table as a two-way table with time 1 responses and time 2 responses constituting the rows and columns respectively. With two dichotomous variables, the layout is as in Table 6.24. It is then possible to proceed to examine this two-way table for the presence of symmetry and quasi-symmetry using the methods already described. However, since the rows and columns of the two-way table are designated as joint variables *AB* and *CD* (in Table 6.24), forms of weak symmetry other than quasi-symmetry may be present which allow marginal heterogeneity to be attributed solely to changes in attitude over time, to changes in vote over time, to changes in vote and attitude over time, or to changes in the relation between vote and

attitude over time. This partitioning enables one to test the hypothesis
that $AB = CD$.

In Table 6.29, the model $A/C/SYMM$ is consistent with expected frequencies
in which the condition of symmetry is approached as closely as possible, given
that the observed and expected frequencies are equalised in the marginal table
obtained by collapsing over variables B, C and D, that is, at the two levels of
A and, therefore, by implication, at the two levels of C. This means that the
model includes a parameter explicitly representing the growth in the total
number of respondents against more nationalisation. Without this parameter,
one would have marginal homogeneity and the condition that the 1974
responses frequencies (in all four vote-by-attitude categories) were replicated
in 1979. This is clearly not the case, since $Y^2 = 175.8 > \chi^2_{6,0.05} = 12.59$, though
it is an oversimplification to attribute the lack of fit solely to attitude changes
($Y^2 = 47.63 > \chi^2_{5,0.05} = 11.07$). Account must also be taken of the change in
the size of the pro-Conservative vote. Invoking both attitude and vote changes
give us the model $A/B/C/D/SYMM$ which fits Table 6.24 adequately. The data
in Table 6.29 can be reproduced via GENSTAT by using listing 12 (Appendix).

One could (mistakenly) arrive at the impression that the relationship between
attitude and vote differed in 1974 and 1979, by quantifying the CD interaction
and then collapsing the table and quantifying the AB interaction in the ensuing
2^2 table. A similar conclusion is reached from Table 6.30 which cross-classifies
1974 consistency by 1979 consistency, where consistent respondents either
voted for the Conservatives and against more nationalisation or voted against
the Conservatives and for more nationalisation.

From Table 6.30, $Y^2 = 11.96 > \chi^2_{1,0.05} = 3.84$, indicating heterogeneous
table margins (homogeneous margins imply symmetry in the 2^2 table) and
significantly less consistency in 1979. This would be evidence that the interaction between vote and attitude had changed over time were the drifting votes
and attitudes, identified earlier, also allowed for.

A test of the hypothesis that $AB = CD$ is given by the difference between the
Y^2 of the models $A/B/C/D/SYMM$ and $AB/CD/SYMM$. Consistency symmetry
is imposed in the former and relaxed in the latter. The loss of fit produced by

Table 6.29. *Various symmetry models fitted to Table 6.24*

Model		df	Y^2
Symmetry	$SYMM$	6	175.8
AC asymmetry	$A/C/SYMM$	5	47.63
AC, BC asymmetry	$A/B/C/D/SYMM$	4	3.63
Quasi-symmetry	$AB/CD/SYMM$	3	2.33

imposing consistency symmetry is $3.63 - 2.33 = 1.30 < \chi^2_{1, 0.05} = 3.84$, thus the simpler $A/B/C/D/SYMM$ model can be adopted. It is therefore possible to account for the marginal heterogeneity of Table 6.24 without resort to the AB (and hence, by implication, CD) interaction of the redundant $AB/CD/SYMM$ model. The AB interaction sets equal the observed and expected frequencies in the marginal table corresponding to the four 1974 categories and, therefore, controls for the interaction between vote and attitude at that time. We have shown that such a parameter is superfluous and that the interaction between vote and attitude remained stable despite changing attitudes and votes.

Duncan (1980, 1981) gives much more detail on these and related tests, and illustrates how the above type of analysis corresponds to cross-sectional analyses in which one investigates the legitimacy of setting to zero the three-way AVT (attitude by vote by time) interaction.

Bishop *et al.* (1975) and Bhapkar (1979) consider weak forms of symmetry for three-way tables. Maximum likelihood estimates for such models are obtainable by a straightforward extension of what has already been outlined using the GENSTAT program.

Direction of causation in multivariate panels

When variables are ordered in a temporal sequence, earlier variables are potential factors influencing later responses, but later variables cannot influence

Table 6.30. *1974 consistency by 1979 consistency*

		Observed frequencies	
		1979	
		Consistent	Inconsistent
1974	Consistent	259	140
	Inconsistent	88	136

		Expected frequencies-symmetry	
		1979	
		Consistent	Inconsistent
1974	Consistent	259	114
	Inconsistent	114	136

earlier ones, and the logic of this argument allows one to unequivocally distinguish between factors and responses. With multivariate panels, however, variables that are contemporaneous are less easily sorted into factors and responses without the guidance of theory. None the less, it is often of interest in the typical two-variable situation to establish which variable is dominant and which is subordinate. For example, is a Conservative vote a result of being anti-union or does a Conservative vote produce anti-union sentiment? Duncan (1980) argues that, 'the only evidence on direction of causation must come from the cross-lagged associations', that is, AD and BC interactions where A and B occur earlier and are thus undoubted potential factors. The relative magnitude of these interactions in Table 6.24 from the evidence in Tables 6.27 and 6.28 suggests that BC is nullifiable and that attitude is the dominant variable. Duncan & McRae (1979) and Duncan (1980, 1981) adopt an alternative approach based on the loss of fit ensuing from setting the cross-lagged AD and BC interactions equal.

Simplifying polytomous multivariate panel data

In this section the discussion focusses on simplifying or nullifying cross-lagged and other across-time associations involving at least one polytomous variable. The techniques described in Chapter 5 dealt precisely with the problem of polytomous variable interactions in a non-temporal context, and some of the simplifications described here are achieved by adopting these earlier methods. Since much of the material has been introduced earlier, the presentation can therefore be brief. To expound the methods, consider Table 6.31 which has been analysed previously by Duncan (1981) and Knoke (1976). This is, in fact,

Table 6.31. *Presidential vote and Party identification in 1956 and 1960*

			1960					
		Party:	Dem	Dem	Ind	Ind	Rep	Rep
		Vote:	Dem	Rep	Dem	Rep	Dem	Rep
	Party	Vote						
	Dem	Dem	127	29	17	2	0	0
	Dem	Rep	15	24	4	4	0	3
1956	Ind	Dem	11	3	9	5	0	1
	Ind	Rep	1	6	21	52	1	33
	Rep	Dem	1	0	3	0	1	1
	Rep	Rep	2	0	2	16	9	181

key: Dem: Democratic.
Ind: Independent.
Rep: Republican.

a table describing the responses of non-Catholics, previous analysts also considered Catholic responses.

Denoting party identified with in 1956 as $P1$, and 1956 Presidential vote as $V1$, and the 1960 choices as $P2$ and $V2$, a model that fits table 6.31 is that invoking all two-way interactions, $P1V1/P2V2/P1P2/V1V2/V1P2/P1V2$ for which $Y^2 = 22.56 < \chi^2_{16,\,0.05} = 26.30$. The fit is not particularly close and improvements can be made if some attention is given to the detail of STP. However, rather than opting for more-complex interactions to significantly improve on the fit of this model, we use the model as a benchmark from which arise credible simplifying assumptions about the two-way interactions. Much of the simplification that can be achieved is as a result of constraining interactions to accord with the uniform association condition discussed in Chapter 5. This enables sets of parameters attributable to interacting polytomies to be replaced by a single uniform association parameter with, in some cases, no inordinate loss of fit considering the extra degrees of freedom made available.

Various comparisons of models described in Table 6.32 indicate the loss of fit brought about by imposing the uniform association constraint on the cross-lagged associations $V1P2$ and $P1V2$, giving ϕ^{V1P2} and ϕ^{P1V2} respectively, and on the across-time $P1P2$ interaction which simplifies to ϕ^{P1P2}. The remaining across-time interaction $V1V2$ only entails one parameter since it comprises two dichotomies and thus it cannot be simplified in this way. Comparing models 5 and 2 shows that replacing $V1P2$ by ϕ^{V1P2} only very marginally worsens the

Table 6.32. *The fit of models with various across-time interactions*

Model		df	Y^2
1	$P1V1/P2V2/P1P2/V1V2/V1P2/P1V2$	16	22.56
2	$P1V1/P2V2/P1P2/V1V2/V1P2$	18	25.24
3	$P1V1/P2V2/P1P2/V1V2/\phi^{V1P2}/P1V2$	17	22.95
4	$P1V1/P2V2/P1P2/V1V2/\phi^{V1P2}/\phi^{P1V2}$	18	24.64
5	$P1V1/P2V2/P1P2/V1V2/\phi^{V1P2}$	19	25.84
6	$P1V1/P2V2/P1P2/V1V2/\phi^{P1V2}$	19	49.12
7	$P1V1/P2V2/P1P2/V1V2/P1V2$	18	48.46
8	$P1V1/P2V2/\phi^{P1P2}/V1V2/\phi^{V1P2}/\phi^{P1V2}$	21	37.28
9	$P1V1/P2V2/\gamma^{P1P2}/V1V2/\phi^{V1P2}/\phi^{P1V2}$	21	26.47
10	$P1V1/P2V2/\alpha^{P1P2}/\beta^{P1P2}/V1V2/\phi^{V1P2}/\phi^{P1V2}$	20	26.47
11	$P1V1/P2V2/\alpha^{P1P2}/\beta^{P1P2}/V1V2/V1P2/P1V2$	18	23.81
12	$P1V1/P2V2/\gamma^{P1P2}/V1V2/V1P2/P1V2$	19	23.87
13	$P1V1/P2V2/\gamma^{P1P2}/V1V2/\phi^{V1P2}$	22	28.12
14	$P1V1/P2V2/\alpha^{P1P2}/\beta^{P1P2}/V1V2/\phi^{V1P2}$	21	28.07

note: data reproduced by listing 13 (Appendix).

fit of the model, since $25.84 - 25.24 = 0.6 < \chi^2_{1,0.05} = 3.84$. Observe that the two independent parameters of $V1P2$ are replaced by the solitary ϕ^{V1P2} and hence the two models differ by 1 df. An alternative comparison is of models 3 and 1, which produces a similar conclusion. Comparing models 6 and 7 or models 4 and 3 shows that the simplification entailed by ϕ^{P1V2} is also tenable. However, we refrain from replacing $P1P2$ by ϕ^{P1P2} since a comparison of the Y^2 of models 8 and 4 gives $37.28 - 24.64 = 12.64 > \chi^2_{3,0.05} = 7.82$. Observe, however, that $P1P2$ can be replaced by the single parameter γ^{P1P2} which represents (undifferentiated) bipolar loyalty, a concept mentioned earlier in connection with Table 6.1(a). In other words, the association between parties in 1956 and 1960 is summarised by γ^{P1P2} representing equal amounts of loyalty to the Democratic or Republican parties. Differentiated bipolar loyalty relaxes the equality constraint so that unequal amounts of loyalty $(\alpha^{P1P2}, \beta^{P1P2})$ are possible, but comparison of models 11 and 12 and 9 and 10 shows this to be an unnecessary refinement. Note that model 10 is equivalent to Duncan's (1981) model H_{35}.

Table 6.33 gives the estimates of the simplified across-time interactions and from the standardised values and the fit of other models there is a clear indication that ϕ^{P1V2} is nullifiable. For example, a comparison of models 9 and 13 in Table 6.32 shows that setting ϕ^{P1V2} to zero does not significantly increase Y^2 since $28.12 - 26.47 = 1.65 < \chi^2_{1,0.05} = 3.84$. Comparing models 13 and 14 suggests that the removal of ϕ^{P1V2} does not call for the reintroduction of differentiation bipolar loyalty. Table 6.34 contains the parameter estimates and standardised values of model 13.

Table 6.33. *Some parameter estimates of the model*
$P1V1/P2V2/\gamma^{P1P2}/V1V2/\phi^{V1P2}/\phi^{P1V2}$

Param.	γ^{P1P2}	$V1V2$	ϕ^{V1P2}	ϕ^{P1V2}
Est.	3.08	-2.12	1.38	0.31
sv	14.91	-7.50	4.82	1.29

Table 6.34. *Across-time parameter estimation of the model*
$P1V1/P2V2/\gamma^{P1P2}/V1V2/\phi^{V1P2}$

Param.	γ^{P1P2}	$V1V2$	ϕ^{V1P2}
Est.	3.13	-2.20	1.26
sv	15.46	-8.04	4.69

The interpretation of $\hat{\phi}^{V1P2}$ is aided by observing in Table 6.35 that the expected log-odds of an Independent, vis-à-vis a Democratic, identification in 1960 are increased by 1.26 by voting Republican in 1956, and the expected log-odds of a Republican, vis-à-vis an Independent, 1960 identification are similarly increased by 1.26 by voting Republican in 1956. Hence the expected odds of a Republican, as opposed to Democratic, identification in 1960 increase by a factor $(e^{\hat{\phi}^{V1P2}})^2 = 12.46$, given a Republican vote in 1956. Duncan (1981) gives graphic illustrations of this kind of relation for a collapsed version of Table 6.31. Note that these contrasts only hold for table cells in which the levels of $V2$ and $P1$ are constant. If these other variables are allowed to vary, the odds are also conditioned by either γ^{P1P2} or $V1V2$ or both. For example, $\log(51.04/3.34) - \log(2.78/132.28) = 1.26 + 2.2 + 3.13 = 6.59$.

Multiway tables with temporal and spatial autocorrelation
In this section consideration is given to observations that are sufficiently close in time (or space) to fail to satisfy the independence assumption required by multinomial sampling. The temporal observations encountered so far in this chapter have been independent in the sense that, though an individual's response is often conditioned by his or her previous response or responses, the response profile designates a table category independent of the category allotted to another individual. However, if the observations that total to the table cell counts are closely spaced measurements on the same individual(s), then the counts will fail to comprise independent observations if the categories occupied by close observations are interdependent. Such autocorrelated observations were discussed in Chapter 4 where the existence was reported of deflating factors

Table 6.35. *Expected frequencies of the model $P1V1/P2V2/\gamma^{P1P2}/V1V2/\phi^{V1P2}$*

			1960					
		Party: Vote:	Dem Dem	Dem Rep	Ind Dem	Ind Rep	Rep Dem	Rep Rep
	Party	Vote						
1956	Dem	Dem	132.28	28.93	10.34	2.78	0.20	0.48
	Dem	Rep	11.51	22.79	3.16	7.70	0.21	4.63
	Ind	Dem	8.04	1.73	14.39	3.87	0.27	0.66
	Ind	Rep	3.34	6.61	20.96	51.04	1.39	30.68
	Rep	Dem	0.98	0.21	1.75	0.47	0.75	1.84
	Rep	Rep	0.86	1.70	5.40	13.14	8.18	180.72

note: data reproduced in listing 13 (Appendix).

appropriate to the chi-squared statistic derived from the independence test and the two-way table. This application is now extended to the multiway table and to the various associated log–linear models. Thus we are here concerned with observations on more than two variables on each occasion. Table 6.36, for example, describes the three-way table arising from observing three dichotomous attributes of the mother and infant monkey pair discussed in Chapter 4. The data are compiled from lists of sequential observations published by Altham (1979) to illustrate the structure of the much larger data set that is the source of Table 4.5. As for the two-way table there is a direct analogy between the spatial and temporal autocorrelation problems, which enables the multiway application initially given in the context of spatial data (Fingleton (1983*b*)) to be carried over to the temporal observations which are of initial concern here. The discussion can again be brief, for the theory and rationale of the method were outlined earlier.

If one temporarily ignores the interdependence of close observations and assumes instead that the data are consistent with multinomial sampling, there is evidently a three-way interaction whereby the relation between mother's head position and whether or not she is looking at the infant varies according to the latter's upper body position. The model from which this interaction is absent, $AB/AC/BC$, fails to fit the data ($Y^2 = 9.60$, $X^2 = 8.04 > \chi^2_{1,\,0.05} = 3.84$). Since the previous two-way analysis of very similar data assumed that observations more than 25 units of time apart were approximately independent, we set $r = 25$ and thus the lower bound for X^2_t becomes $8.04/(2r - 1) = 0.16$, whereas the upper bound is $X^2 = 8.04$. This indicates that, depending on the (unknown) amount of interdependence of observations, the three-way interaction may be no more than an artifact of the sample design. Note that

Table 6.36. *Time-dependent observations on three dichotomous attributes of a mother and infant monkey pair*

	C_1				C_2	
	A_1	A_2			A_1	A_2
B_1	15	10		B_1	6	13
B_2	3	6		B_2	4	0

key: A_1 = mother's head lowered.
A_2 = mother's head raised.
B_1 = infant's torso lowered.
B_2 = infant's torso raised.
C_1 = mother looking at infant.
C_2 = mother not looking at infant.

models much simpler than even $AB/AC/BC$ become consistent with Table 6.36 once account is taken of this interdependence. For example, the model designated ECP (equal cell-probability) with expected frequency 7.13 in each of the eight cells and for which, nominally, $X^2 = 25.95$ and $Y^2 = 30.81$ ($\chi^2_{7,\,0.05} = 14.07$) now becomes feasible since the lower bound for X^2_t is 0.53. This apparent equiprobability of each of the eight possible response categories is despite evidence to the contrary in Table 6.36 in which, for example, the infant's torso is more often lowered than raised. Observe from the two-way analysis of the much larger data set (Table 4.5) that raised torso positions prevail and that B and C interact. This is not contradictory but merely a reflection of the greater information content of Table 4.5 and of the fact that a two-way, as opposed to a multiway, analysis is the source of the inference. Whilst Table 6.36 suggests that the ECP model and other simple models are potential candidates for adoption, more-definite claims require a more precisely specified autocorrelation process. Tavaré & Altham (1983) obtain some results by assuming that Markov chain models provide a good approximation to the dependence structure of categorical variables observed over time. Fingleton (1983a, b) gives some illustrative analysis of two-way and multiway tables with 'precisely' specified spatial autocorrelation, though, in general, accurate information on the nature of autocorrelation functions may not be easy to obtain. Observe also that the above 'conclusions' are conditional on an assumption of instantaneous interaction. In general, interaction may only occur after some time-lag k and, as suggested by Altham (1979), it may be more appropriate to cross-tabulate, say, mother's behaviour at time t against infant's behaviour at $t + k$.

We illustrate the spatial analogy with reference to Table 6.37 taken from Fingleton (1983b). An earlier source of the data presented in a different form is Diggle (1979). Assuming multinomial sampling, Aitkin's (1980) *STP* identifies OH/HM as a feasible model, but the simpler model $O/H/M$ is infeasible

Table 6.37. *The presence and absence of oaks, hickories and maples in 576 grid cells*

	M_1			M_2	
	O_1	O_2		O_1	O_2
H_1	84	32	H_1	177	61
H_2	91	30	H_2	86	15

key: O_1 = oaks present; H_1 = hickories present; M_1 = maples present.
O_2 = oaks absent; H_2 = hickories absent; M_2 = maples absent.

$(X^2 = 31.32, Y^2 = 32.89 > \chi^2_{4,\,0.34} = 4.53)$. Since the grid cells are contiguous, it seems appropriate to assume positive autocorrelation extending to $d = 2$ for reasons similar to those given in the earlier two-way analysis of grid cell data in Chapter 4. Invoking the deflating factor $[1 + 2d(d + 1)]$, both OH/HM and $O/H/M$ now become feasible since the lower bound of

$$X_t^2 = 31.32/[1 + 2d(d + 1)] = 2.41 < \chi^2_{4,\,0.34}(\alpha = 0.10).$$

Other models also become feasible once the deflating factor takes effect. Table 6.38 identifies the upper and lower bounds of X_t^2 for various models and d.

The 'benchmark' ECP model of Table 6.38 nullifies seven parameters, thus setting $\alpha = 0.05$ gives an acceptable overall type I error rate

$$\gamma = 1 - (0.95)^7 = 0.302.$$

Table 6.39 shows that assuming $d = 2$, setting all seven parameters to zero is not acceptable since $19.72 > \chi^2_{7,\,0.302} = 8.36$. Thus a model more complex than ECP is required. The result of introducing extra parameters in a specified order is also given in Table 6.39.

Table 6.38. *Upper and lower bounds of X_t^2 for various log–linear models*

| Model | df | Upper bound | | Lower bounds | | |
		(Y^2)	X^2	$d = 1$	$d = 2$	$d = 3$
ECP	7	245.79	256.39	51.28	19.72	10.26
O	6	81.57	87.86	17.57	6.76	3.51
H	6	215.27	214.08	42.82	16.47	8.56
M	6	227.63	218.82	43.76	16.83	8.75
O/H	5	51.05	49.12	9.82	3.78	1.96
O/M	5	63.41	59.59	11.92	4.58	2.38
H/M	5	197.11	189.09	37.82	14.55	7.56
O/H/M	4	32.89	31.32	6.26	2.41	1.25

Table 6.39. *STP analysis with autocorrelation*

Model	df	X_a^2	Source	df	X^2
ECP	7	19.72			
O	6	6.76	O	1	12.96
O/H	5	3.78	H	1	2.98
O/H/M	4	2.41	M	1	1.37
			3 three-way	4	2.41
			1 four-way		

note: a = lower bound, approximate Y^2 lower bound.

Since $2.98 + 1.37 + 2.41 = 6.76 < \chi^2_{7,\,0.302} = 8.36$, only parameter O needs to be introduced, H and M can be set to zero. Thus model O is the simplest that can be invoked without describing the autocorrelation process more precisely. This means that even with maximum possible autocorrelation, a parameter is still required to control for the greater than even odds of 'observing' oaks. On the other hand, once allowance is made for the effects of the autocorrelation, grid cells containing hickories and maples can, to some extent, be assumed to be as equally likely as grid cells from which they are absent.

The procedure outlined in this section and in Chapter 4 is a simple device that acknowledges the influence of autocorrelation in the inferential process. However, care should be taken not to wrongly attribute to autocorrelation what is in fact the influence of variables omitted from the analysis. The extension to multivariate models described above enables the analyst to explore this possibility more fully.

Appendix

This appendix contains selected 'listings' of GENSTAT directives that reproduce results given in the text. A number of alternative computer programs are available, some of which are mentioned on appropriate pages, and thus access to the GENSTAT system is not a prerequisite for practical application of the models under discussion. However, GENSTAT (which is a close relative of the GLIM system) is a highly acclaimed package which can be used generally throughout the book and which has been found particularly useful for fitting some of the more intricate models of Chapters 5 and 6.

In fact, GENSTAT is more a programming language than a conventional statistics package, and this gives it immense flexibility. The large number of directives available to perform a wide variety of functions in areas such as matrix algebra, time series analysis, optimisation and generalised linear modelling, calls for some guidance, in the form of the listings below, as to those appropriate to models of category counts. From these the analyst will be able to work out how to fit a range of models additional to those specifically discussed.

The compact nature of the programming language enables some otherwise tedious and lengthy procedures to be quickly implemented. This is readily evident from the listings below, though these can be developed and improved in elegance once some familiarity with the system has been gained, for the aim at this juncture is simply to provide the reader unfamiliar with GENSTAT with an entry point into practical modelling with the minimum of fuss. 'An introduction to GENSTAT' by Alvey *et al.* (1982) gives information about the application of GENSTAT to other types of data and gives an insight into changes that can be effected, and the GENSTAT manual provides the definitive statement on the system. Further details can be obtained from the publishers, the Numerical Algorithms Group (NAG), NAG Central Office, 7 Banbury Road, Oxford OX2 6NN, England, or from the Genstat Secretary, Statistics Department, Rothamsted Experimental Station, Harpenden, Hertfordshire, England.

GENSTAT LISTINGS (Release 4.04)

LISTING 1

```
'REFERENCE' HOLT(1)
'' THIS FITS THE INDEPENDENCE MODEL THEN THE SATURATED MODEL
TO THE 4 BY 4 TABLE (TABLE 1.16). EACH CELL IS ASSIGNED TO A
LEVEL OF EACH FACTOR. MORE CONCISE WAYS OF DOING THIS APPEAR
IN OTHER LISTINGS. THE COUNTS ARE SPECIFIED AS POISSON VARIABLES
AND THE APPENDAGES TO FIT AND ADD CONTROL THE INFORMATION OUTPUT
WITH EACH MODEL FITTED''
'UNIT' $16
'VARIATE' COUNT=
60,49,134,22,25,122,60,49,25,122,148,20,74,40,55,55
'FACTOR' ROW$4=2,2,2,2,3,3,3,3,4,4,4,4,1,1,1,1
'FACTOR' COL$4=2,3,4,1,2,3,4,1,2,3,4,1,2,3,4,1
'FACTOR' RC$16=2,3,4,1,5,6,7,8,9,10,11,12,13,14,15,16
'TERMS' COUNT,ROW,COL,RC
'Y/ERROR=POISSON' COUNT
'FIT/A' ROW,COL
'ADD/CAU' RC
'RUN'
'CLOSE'
'STOP'
```


LISTING 2

```
'REFERENCE' UAFM(1)
'' THIS FITS THE UNIFORM ASSOCIATION MODEL TO A 2 BY 3 TABLE
(TABLE 5.6) . NOTE THE USE OF FLOAT TO OBTAIN THE ASSOCIATION TERM
ASS FROM THE INTEGER VALUES OF THE ROW AND COLUMN FACTORS''
'UNIT' $6
'VARIATE' COUNT=
193,39,34,58,59,114
'FACTOR' F$2=3(1),3(2)
'FACTOR' M$3=(1,2,3)2
'CALC' ASS=FLOAT(F)*FLOAT(M)
'TERMS' COUNT,F,M,ASS
'Y/ERROR=POISSON' COUNT
'FIT/A' F,M
'ADD/CAU' ASS
'RUN'
'CLOSE'
'STOP'
```


LISTING 3

```
'REFERENCE' PLACK(1)
'' ONE OF THE FACTORS FROM WHICH THE ASSOCIATION TERM IS DERIVED
HAS REAL VARIATE VALUES CORRESPONDING TO ITS LEVEL NAMES, HENCE
THE USE OF VARFAC IN PLACE OF FLOAT. ALSO 1...6 MEANS 1,2,3,4,5,6.
DATA FROM TABLE 5.11 ."
'UNIT' $12
'VARIATE' COUNT=
15,24,26,24,29,29,
35,25,24,26,21,20
'FACTOR' R$2=6(1,2)
'VARIATE' Q=1.082,1.161,1.212,1.258,1.31,1.348
'FACTOR' COL$Q=(1...6)2
'CALC' ASS=VARFAC(COL)*FLOAT(R)
'TERMS' COUNT,R,COL,ASS
'Y/ERROR=POISSON' COUNT
```

```
'FIT/CAU' R,COL
'ADD/CAU' ASS
'RUN'
'CLOSE'
'STOP'
```

LISTING 4

```
'REFERENCE' BREATH(1)
'' THIS FITS MODELS TO A THREE-WAY TABLE (TABLE 5.14) INCLUDING
A UNIFORM THREE-WAY INTERACTION ASSAWB OBTAINED IN A SIMILAR
WAY TO UNIFORM TWO-WAY INTERACTION. ''
'UNIT' $36
'VARIATE' COUNT=
9,7,95,1841,
23,9,105,1654,
54,19,177,1863,
121,48,257,2357,169,54,273,1778,269,88,324,1712,404,117,245,1324,
406,152,225,967,372,106,132,526
'FACTOR' AGE$9=4(1...9)
'FACTOR' WH$2=(1,2,1,2)9
'FACTOR' BR$2=(1,1,2,2)9
'FACTOR' AW$18=(1,2)2,(3,4)2,(5,6)2,(7,8)2,(9,10)2,
(11,12)2,(13,14)2,(15,16)2,(17,18)2
'FACTOR' ABR$18=2(1,2),2(3,4),2(5,6),2(7,8),2(9,10),2(11,12),
2(13,14),2(15,16),2(17,18)
'FACTOR' WHBR$4=(1,2,3,4)9
'CALC' ASSAWB=FLOAT(AGE)*FLOAT(WH)*FLOAT(BR)
'TERMS' COUNT,AGE,WH,BR,AW,ABR,WHBR,ASSAWB
'Y/ERROR=POISSON' COUNT
'FIT/CAU' AGE,WH,BR,AW,ABR,WHBR
'ADD/CAU' ASSAWB
'RUN'
'CLOSE'
'STOP'
```

LISTING 5

```
'REFERENCE' DRUNKS(1)
'' THIS FITS A SEQUENCE OF MODELS TO THE THREE-WAY TABLE INCLUDING
VARIOUS UNIFORM PARTIAL ASSOCIATIONS, ASSAB,ASSAC, AND ASSBC.
DATA FROM TABLE 5.19 .''
'UNIT' $27
'VARIATE' COUNT=
25,21,20,21,18,19,26,23,21,
29,16,8,27,13,11,38,24,30,
44,18,6,19,9,8,9,4,3
'FACTOR' A$3=(3(1,2,3))3
'FACTOR' B$3=(1,2,3,1,2,3,1,2,3)3
'FACTOR' C$3=9(1),9(2),9(3)
'FACTOR' AB$9=(1,2,3,4,5,6,7,8,9)3
'FACTOR' AC$9=3(1...9)
'FACTOR' BC$9=(1,2,3)3,(4,5,6)3,(7,8,9)3
'CALC' ASSABC=FLOAT(A)*FLOAT(B)*FLOAT(C)
'CALC' ASSAB=FLOAT(A)*FLOAT(B)
'CALC' ASSAC=FLOAT(A)*FLOAT(C)
'CALC' ASSBC=FLOAT(B)*FLOAT(C)
'TERMS' COUNT,A,B,C,AB,AC,BC,ASSAB,ASSAC,ASSBC,ASSABC
'Y/ERROR=POISSON' COUNT
'FIT/CAU' A,B,C
'ADD/CAU' AB,AC,BC,ASSABC
'DROP' ASSABC
```

```
'FIT/CAU'  A,B,C,BC,AC,ASSAB
'FIT/CAU'  A,B,C,BC,ASSAC,ASSAB
'FIT/CAU'  A,B,C,BC,AC
'FIT/CAU'  A,B,C,BC,ASSAC
'RUN'
'CLOSE'
'STOP'
```

LISTING 6

```
'REFERENCE'SILK(1)
'' THE FACTOR ASS ILLUSTRATES HOW TO ASSIGN A SINGLE PARAMETER
TO A SINGLE CELL. HERE THIS HAPPENS TO BE A CORNER CELL OF
A TWO-WAY TABLE (TABLE 1.8) . THE FACTOR ASS2 CREATES, IN EFFECT,
A SINGLE PARAMETER FOR TWO CORNER CELLS, AND ASS3 ASSIGNS A
SEPARATE PARAMETER TO EACH OF THEM. GENERATE IS AN ALTERNATIVE
WAY OF ALLOCATING FACTOR LEVELS . ''
'UNIT' $15
'VARIATE' COUNT=
55,11,16,17,100,101,7,18,23,103,91,20;25,16,77
'FACTOR' CAR$3
'FACTOR' AG$5
'GENERATE' CAR,AG
'FACTOR' ASS$2=
2,1,1,1,1,
1,1,1,1,1,
1,1,1,1,1
'FACTOR' ASS2$2=
1,2,2,2,2,
2,2,2,2,2,
2,2,2,2,1
'FACTOR' ASS3$3=
1,2,2,2,2,
2,2,2,2,2,
2,2,2,2,3
'TERMS' COUNT,CAR,AG,ASS,ASS2,ASS3
'Y/ERROR=POISSON' COUNT
'FIT/A' CAR,AG
'ADD/CAU' ASS
'FIT/CAU' CAR,AG,ASS2
'FIT/CAU' CAR,AG,ASS3
'RUN'
'CLOSE'
'STOP'
```

LISTING 7

```
'REFERENCE' PCJO(1)
'' THIS LISTING REPRODUCES DUNCAN'S METHOD FOR POLYTOMIES.
THE TABLE (TABLE 5.42) IS 4 BY 2 BY 2 BUT IT IS MORE
CONVENIENT TO TREAT THE POLYTOMY AS THE DICHOTOMIES
P,C,J AND O . ''
'UNIT'$16
'VARIATE' COUNT=
104,42,165,142,
65,44,100,130,
4,3,5,6,
13,6,32,23
'FACTOR'AT$2=(1,2)8
'FACTOR'Y$2=(1,1,2,2)4
'FACTOR'P$2=4(1),12(2)
'FACTOR'C$2=4(1),4(2),8(1)
'FACTOR' PA$4=1,2,1,2,
```

```
3,4,3,4,
3,4,3,4,
3,4,3,4
'FACTOR' CA$4=1,2,1,2,
3,4,3,4,
1,2,1,2,
1,2,1,2
'FACTOR' JA$4=1,2,1,2,
1,2,1,2,
3,4,3,4,
1,2,1,2
'FACTOR' YOJCP$8=1,1,2,2,3,3,4,4,5,5,6,6,7,7,8,8
'FACTOR'J$2=8(1),4(2),4(1)
'FACTOR'O$2=12(1),4(2)
'FACTOR' OA$4=1,2,1,2,
1,2,1,2,
1,2,1,2,
3,4,3,4
'FACTOR' AY$4=1,2,3,4,
1,2,3,4,
1,2,3,4,
1,2,3,4
'TERMS' COUNT,AT,Y,P,C,J,O,PA,CA,YOJCP,AY,JA,OA
'Y/ERROR=POISSON' COUNT
'FIT/A' AT,Y
'ADD/CAU' P,C,J,O,AY,CA,YOJCP
'DROP' AY,CA
'ADD' JA,OA,CA
'FIT' AT,Y,P,C,J,O,AY,CA,YOJCP,PA,JA,CA
'RUN'
'CLOSE'
'STOP'


LISTING 8

'REFERENCE' UPSARL(1)
'' THIS SHOWS THE LAYOUT FOR THE 5 BY 5 TABLE (TABLE 6.8)
OF VARIOUS FACTORS COMMONLY REQUIRED IN MODELS OF COUNTS FROM
TEMPORAL OBSERVATIONS. INCLUDED ARE DIAGONAL (DIAG,DP,DP2),
MOVER-STAYER (MS), DISTANCE (LD1,LD2,LD3,LD4) AND
SYMMETRY (QS) COMPONENTS . ''
'UNIT' $25
'VARIATE' COUNT=
22,27,4,1,0,
16,861,57,30,8,
4,26,248,14,7,
8,20,61,201,11,
0,4,31,32,140
'FACTOR' ROW$5=5(1),5(2),5(3),5(4),5(5)
'FACTOR' COL$5=(1,2,3,4,5)5
'FACTOR' DIAG$2=1,4(2),2,1,3(2),2(2),1,2(2),3(2),1,2,4(2),1
'FACTOR' MS$6=
2,1,1,1,1,
1,3,1,1,1,
1,1,4,1,1,
1,1,1,5,1,
1,1,1,1,6
'FACTOR' DP$5=
1,2,3,4,5,
2,1,2,3,4,
3,2,1,2,3,
4,3,2,1,2,
5,4,3,2,1
'FACTOR' DP2$9=
1,2,3,4,5,
6,1,2,3,4,
```

```
7,6,1,2,3,
8,7,6,1,2,
9,8,7,6,1
'FACTOR' LD1$2=
1,2,2,2,2,
2,1,1,1,1,
2,1,1,1,1,
2,1,1,1,1,
2,1,1,1,1
'FACTOR' LD2$2=
1,1,2,2,2,
1,1,2,2,2,
2,2,1,1,1,
2,2,1,1,1,
2,2,1,1,1
'FACTOR' LD3$2=
1,1,1,2,2,
1,1,1,2,2,
1,1,1,2,2,
2,2,2,1,1,
2,2,2,1,1
'FACTOR' LD4$2=
1,1,1,1,2,
1,1,1,1,2,
1,1,1,1,2,
1,1,1,1,2,
2,2,2,2,1
'FACTOR' QS$15=
1,6,7,8,9,
6,2,10,11,12,
7,10,3,13,14,
8,11,13,4,15,
9,12,14,15,5
'TERMS' COUNT,ROW,COL,DIAG,LD1,LD2,LD3,LD4,MS,DP,DP2,QS
'Y/ERROR=POISSON' COUNT
'FIT/CAU' ROW,COL
'ADD/CAU' DIAG
'FIT/CAU' ROW,COL,MS
'FIT/CAU' ROW,COL,DP
'FIT/CAU' ROW,COL,DP2
'FIT/CAU' ROW,COL,LD1,LD2,LD3,LD4
'FIT/CAU' ROW,COL,DIAG,LD1,LD2,LD3,LD4
'FIT/CAU' ROW,COL,LD1,LD2,LD3,LD4,MS
'FIT' ROW,COL,QS
'RUN'
'CLOSE'
'STOP'
```

```
LISTING 9

'REFERENCE' MIGRANTS(1)
'' THE SYMMETRY THEN QUASI-SYMMETRY MODEL FOR THE 4 BY 4
TABLE (TABLE 6.12) . ''
'UNIT' $ 16
'VARIATE' COUNT =
```

```
118,12,7,23,
14,2127,86,130,
8,69,2548,107,
12,110,88,7712
'FACTOR' DEST,ORIG $4
'GENERATE' ORIG,DEST
'FACTOR' SYMM $10=
1,2,3,4,
2,8,5,6,
3,5,9,7,
4,6,7,10
'TERMS' COUNT,ORIG,DEST,SYMM
'Y/ERROR=POISSON' COUNT
'FIT/CAU' SYMM
'ADD/CAU' DEST,ORIG
'RUN'
'CLOSE'
'STOP'


LISTING 10

'REFERENCE'MIGS(1)
'' LISTING FOR WEAK SYMMETRY MODELS IN WHICH SYMMETRY IS
MODIFIED BY VARIOUS DIAGONAL PARAMETERS TO OBTAIN DIFFERENTIAL
ODDS FOR THE SUBSIDIARY DIAGONALS. DPS DISTINGUISHES BETWEEN
ALL THREE DIAGONALS, DPO SETS THE SECOND DIAGONAL PARAMETER TO
ZERO, DPEQ EQUATES THE FIRST TWO, AND CS EQUATES ALL THREE.
THE LAYOUT IS FOR THE 4 BY 4 TABLE (TABLE 6.12) AND EXTENDS
NATURALLY TO LARGER TABLES AND ALTERNATIVE CONSTRAINTS ON
THE DIAGONAL PARAMETERS . ''
'UNIT' $ 16
'VARIATE' COUNT =
118,12,7,23,
14,2127,86,130,
8,69,2548,107,
12,110,88,7712
'FACTOR' SYMM $10=
1,2,3,4,
2,8,5,6,
3,5,9,7,
4,6,7,10
'FACTOR' DPS$4=
1,2,3,4,
1,1,2,3,
1,1,1,2,
1,1,1,1
'FACTOR' DPO$3=
1,2,1,3,
1,1,2,1,
1,1,1,2,
1,1,1,1
'FACTOR' CS$2=
1,2,2,2,
1,1,2,2,
1,1,1,2,
1,1,1,1
'FACTOR' DPEQ$3=
1,2,2,3,
1,1,2,2,
1,1,1,2,
1,1,1,1
'TERMS' COUNT,SYMM,DPS,DPO,DPEQ,CS
'Y/ERROR=POISSON' COUNT
'FIT/CAU' SYMM,DPS
'FIT/CAU' SYMM,DPO
'FIT/CAU' SYMM,CS
```

```
'FIT/CAU' SYMM,DPEQ
'RUN'
'CLOSE'
'STOP'


LISTING 11

'REFERENCE' US3(1)
'' THE LOYALTY-DISTANCE AND RELATED MODELS FITTED TO THE
4 BY 4 BY 4 TABLE (TABLE 6.20) . NOTE THE VALUE WITH LARGE
TABLES OF GENSTAT'S HANDLING OF REPEATED PATTERNS IN THE
DISTRIBUTION OF FACTOR LEVELS. THE FACTOR R IS EQUIVALENT TO
THE TWO-WAY AB INTERACTION IN THE TEXT. ''
'UNIT' $64
'VARIATE' COUNT=
812,27,16,5,
5,20,6,0,
2,3,4,0,
3,3,4,2,
21,6,1,0,
3,216,6,2,
0,3,7,0,
0,9,0,4,
15,2,8,0,
1,37,8,0,
1,17,157,4,
0,2,12,6,
2,0,0,1,
0,13,1,4,
0,3,17,1,
0,12,11,126
'FACTOR' R$16=4(1...16)
'FACTOR' C$4=(1,2,3,4)16
'FACTOR' LOY1$2=
(2,4(1),2,4(1),2,4(1),2)4
'FACTOR' LOY2$2=
2,3(1),2,3(1),2,3(1),2,4(1),2,3(1),2,3(1),2,3(1),2,4(1),
2,3(1),2,3(1),2,3(1),2,4(1),2,3(1),2,3(1),2,3(1),2
'FACTOR' SYMM$7=
(1,2,3,4,
2,1,5,6,
3,5,1,7,
4,6,7,1)4
'FACTOR' LD1$2=
(1,2,2,2,
2,1,1,1,
2,1,1,1,
2,1,1,1)4
'FACTOR' LD2$2=
(1,1,2,2,
1,1,2,2,
2,2,1,1,
2,2,1,1)4
'FACTOR' LD3$2=
(1,1,1,2,
1,1,1,2,
1,1,1,2,
2,2,2,1)4
'TERMS' COUNT,R,C,LOY1,LOY2,LD1,LD2,LD3,SYMM
'Y/ERROR=POISSON' COUNT
'FIT/CAU' R,C,LOY1,LOY2,LD1,LD2,LD3
'DROP' LD2
'DROP' LD3
'FIT' R,C,LOY1,LOY2
'FIT' R,C,LD1,LD2,LD3
'FIT' R,C,SYMM,LOY1,LOY2
```

```
'RUN'
'CLOSE'
'STOP'




LISTING 12


'REFERENCE' VA(1)
''THIS LISTING FITS WEAK SYMMETRY MODELS WHERE SYMMETRY IS
MODIFIED BY ROW AND COLUMN EFFECTS APPROPRIATE TO MULTIVARIATE
PANELS. DATA FROM TABLE 6.24. NOTE THAT IN THE ORDER THEY ARE
ADDED, FACTORS C,D AND CD ARE ALREADY IMPLIED AND HAVE NO EFFECT''
'UNIT' $16
'VARIATE' COUNT=
0,9,0,1,
1,180,0,16,
3,20,59,120,
2,67,12,133
'FACTOR' A$2=(4(1,2))2
'FACTOR' B$2=8(1,2)
'FACTOR' C$2=(1,2)8
'FACTOR' D$2=(1,1,2,2)4
'FACTOR' AB$4=4(1...4)
'FACTOR' CD$4=(1...4)4
'FACTOR' TSYMM$10=
1,2,3,4,
2,8,5,6,
3,5,9,7,
4,6,7,10
'TERMS' COUNT,A,B,C,D,AB,CD,TSYMM
'Y/ERROR=POISSON' COUNT
'FIT' TSYMM
'ADD' A,C
'ADD' B,D
'ADD' AB,CD
'RUN'
'CLOSE'
'STOP'




LISTING 13


'REFERENCE' D80D(1)
'' VARIOUS PREVIOUSLY USED FACTOR LAYOUTS REAPPEAR HERE
IN MODELS TO SIMPLIFY POLYTOMOUS MULTIVARIATE PANEL DATA.
NOTE FROM FACTOR V1 THE FACILITY FOR THE COMPACT ASSIGNATION
OF LEVELS. THE DATA ARE FROM TABLE 6.31 . ''
'UNIT' $36
'VARIATE' COUNT=
127,29,17,2,0,0,
15,24,4,4,0,3,
11,3,9,5,0,1,
1,6,21,52,1,33,
1,0,3,0,1,1,
2,0,2,16,9,181
'FACTOR' P1$3=
12(1,2,3)
'FACTOR' P2$3=
(1,1,2,2,3,3)6
'FACTOR' V1$2=
(6(1,2))3
'FACTOR' V2$2=
(1,2)18
'FACTOR' P1V1$6=
6(1...6)
```

```
'FACTOR' P2V2$6=
(1...6)6
'FACTOR' P1P2$9=
(1,1,2,2,3,3)2,(4,4,5,5,6,6)2,(7,7,8,8,9,9)2
'FACTOR' V1V2$4=
(1,2,1,2,1,2,3,4,3,4,3,4)3
'CALC' ASSV1P2=FLOAT(V1)*FLOAT(P2)
'CALC' ASSP1V2=FLOAT(P1)*FLOAT(V2)
'FACTOR' ABP1P2$3=
2,2,1,1,1,1,
2,2,1,1,1,1,
1,1,1,1,1,1,
1,1,1,1,1,1,
1,1,1,1,3,3,
1,1,1,1,3,3
'FACTOR' AAP1P2$2=
2,2,1,1,1,1,
2,2,1,1,1,1,
1,1,1,1,1,1,
1,1,1,1,1,1,
1,1,1,1,2,2,
1,1,1,1,2,2
'FACTOR' V1P2$6=
(1,1,2,2,3,3,4,4,5,5,6,6)3
'FACTOR' P1V2$6=
(1,2)6,(3,4)6,(5,6)6
'CALC' ASSP=FLOAT(P1)*FLOAT(P2)
'TERMS' P1,P2,V1,V2,COUNT,P1V1,P2V2,P1P2,V1V2,ASSV1P2,ASSP1V2,
ABP1P2,AAP1P2,ASSP,V1P2,P1V2
'Y/ERROR=POISSON' COUNT
'FIT' P1,P2,V1,V2,P1V1,P2V2,P1P2,V1V2,V1P2
'ADD' P1V2
'DROP' V1P2
'ADD' ASSV1P2
'DROP' P1V2
'ADD' ASSP1V2
'DROP' ASSV1P2
'FIT' P1,P2,V1,V2,P1V1,P2V2,ABP1P2,V1V2,V1P2,P1V2
'FIT' P1,P2,V1,V2,P1V1,P2V2,AAP1P2,V1V2,V1P2,P1V2
'FIT/CAU' P1,V1,P2,V2,P1V1,P2V2,AAP1P2,V1V2,ASSV1P2
'FIT' P1,P2,V1,V2,P1V1,P2V2,ABP1P2,V1V2,ASSV1P2
'FIT' P1,P2,V1,V2,P1V1,P2V2,ASSP,V1V2,ASSV1P2,ASSP1V2
'FIT' P1,P2,V1,V2,P1V1,P2V2,ABP1P2,V1V2,ASSV1P2,ASSP1V2
'FIT' P1,P2,V1,V2,P1V1,P2V2,AAP1P2,V1V2,ASSV1P2,ASSP1V2
'RUN'
'CLOSE'
'STOP'
```

References

Agresti, A. (1983). 'A survey of strategies for modeling cross-classifications having ordinal variables', *Journal of the American Statistical Association*, 78, 184–98.

Aitkin, M. (1978). 'The analysis of unbalanced cross-classifications' (with discussion), *Journal of the Royal Statistical Society, A*, 141, 195–223.

Aitkin, M. (1979). 'A simultaneous test procedure for contingency table models', *Applied Statistics*, 28, 233–42.

Aitkin, M. (1980). 'A note on the selection of log–linear models', *Biometrics*, 36, 173–8.

Altham, P. M. E. (1975). 'Quasi-independent triangular contingency tables', *Biometrics*, 31, 233–8.

Altham, P. M. E. (1976). 'Discrete variable analyses for individuals grouped into families', *Biometrika*, 63, 263–9.

Altham, P. M. E. (1979). 'Detecting relationships between categorical variables over time: a problem of deflating a chi-squared statistic', *Applied Statistics*, 28, 115–25.

Alvey, N., Galwey, N. & Lane, P. (1982). *An Introduction to GENSTAT* (London). Academic Press.

Andersen, E. B. (1980). *Discrete Statistical Models with Social Science Applications* (Amsterdam). North-Holland.

Andrich, D. (1979). 'A model for contingency tables having an ordered response classification', *Biometrics*, 35, 403–15.

Anscombe, F. J. (1953). 'Contribution to discussion of paper by H. Hotelling. New light on the correlation coefficient and its transform,' *Journal of the Royal Statistical Society, B*, 15, 229–30.

Ashford, J. R. & Sowden, R. R. (1970). 'Multivariate probit analysis', *Biometrics*, 26, 535–46.

Bahr, H. M. (1969). 'Institutional life, drinking and disaffiliation', *Social Problems*, 16, 365–75.

Baker, R. J. & Nelder, J. A. (1978). *The GLIM System, Release 3*, printed and distributed by the Numerical Algorithms Group, Oxford.

Benedetti, J. K. & Brown, M. B. (1978). 'Strategies for the selection of log–linear models', *Biometrics*, 34, 680–6.

Berkson, J. (1944). 'Application of the logistic function to bio-assay', *Journal of the American Statistical Association*, 39, 357–65.

Berkson, J. (1953). 'A statistically precise and relatively simple method of estimating the bio-assay with quantal response based on the logistic function', *Journal of the American Statistical Association*, 48, 565–99.

Berkson, J. (1955). 'Maximum likelihood and minimum X^2 estimates of the logistic function', *Journal of the American Statistical Association*, 50, 130–62.

Berkson, J. (1980). 'Minimum chi-square, not maximum likelihood!' (with discussion), *Annals of Statistics*, 8 (3), 457–87.

Bhapkar, V. P. (1979). 'On tests of marginal symmetry and quasi-symmetry in two and three dimensional contingency tables', *Biometrics*, 35, 417-26.

Bibby, J. (1977). 'The general linear model: a cautionary tale', pp. 35-76. In: *The Analysis of Survey Data*, vol. 2, *Model fitting* (eds. O'Muircheartaigh, C. A. & Payne, C.) (London). Wiley.

Birch, M. W. (1963). 'Maximum likelihood in three-way contingency tables', *Journal of the Royal Statistical Society, B*, 25, 220-33.

Birch, M. W. (1964). 'The detection of partial association, I: the 2 × 2 case', *Journal of the Royal Statistical Society, B*, 26, 313-24.

Birch, M. W. (1965). 'The detection of partial association, II: the general case', *Journal of the Royal Statistical Society, B*, 27, 111-24.

Birnbaum, I. (1982). 'The causal analysis of contingency tables: a return to first principles', *Quality and Quantity*, 16, 217-41.

Bishop, Y. M. M. & Fienberg, S. E. (1969). 'Incomplete two-dimensional contingency tables', *Biometrics*, 25, 119-28.

Bishop, Y. M. M., Fienberg, S. E. & Holland, P. W. (1975). *Discrete Multivariate Analysis: Theory and Practice* (Cambridge, Massachusetts). MIT Press.

Blumen, I., Kogan, M. & McCarthy, P. J. (1955). *The Industrial Mobility of Labor as a Probability Process*, Cornell Studies of Industrial and Labor Relations, no. 6 (Ithaca, New York).

Blyth, C. R. (1972). 'On Simpson's paradox and the sure-thing principle', *Journal of the American Statistical Association*, 67, 364-6.

Bowlby, S. & Silk, J. (1982). 'Analysis of qualitative data using GLIM: two examples based on shopping survey data', *Professional Geographer*, 34, 80-90.

Brier, S. S. (1980). 'Analysis of contingency tables under cluster sampling', *Biometrika*, 67, 591-6.

Brown, M. B. (1976). 'Screening effects in multidimensional contingency tables', *Applied Statistics*, 25, 37-46.

Brown, M. B. & Benedetti, J. K. (1977). *Programs P1F, P2F and P3F, BMDP (Biomedical Computer Programs)*, University of California Press (available from Department of Biomathematics, School of Medicine, University of California, Los Angeles).

Caussinus, H. (1965). 'Contribution à l'analyse statistique des tableaux de corrélation', *Annales de la Faculté des Sciences de l'Université de Toulouse*, 29, 77-182.

Clogg, C. C. (1982a). 'Using association models in sociological research: some examples', *American Journal of Sociology*, 88 (1), 114-34.

Clogg, C. C. (1982b). 'Some models for the analysis of association in multiway cross-classifications having ordered categories', *Journal of the American Statistical Association*, 77, 803-15.

Cochran, W. G. (1977). *Sampling Techniques* (New York). Wiley.

Cohen, J. E. (1976). 'The distribution of the chi-squared statistic under clustered sampling from contingency tables', *Journal of the American Statistical Association*, 71, 665-70.

Cox, D. R. (1970). *The Analysis of Binary data* (London). Methuen.

Cox, M. A. A. & Plackett, R. L. (1980). 'Small samples in contingency tables', *Biometrika*, 67, 1-13.

Darroch, J. N. & Ratcliff, D. (1972). 'Generalized iterative scaling for log-linear models', *Annals of Mathematical Statistics*, 43, 1470-80.

Deming, W. E. & Stephan, F. F. (1940). 'On a least-squares adjustment of a sampled frequency table when the expected marginal totals are known', *Annals of Mathematical Statistics*, 41, 907-17.

Dickinson, G. E. (1977). 'An application of general linear modelling to the analysis of contingency tables', *New Zealand Statistician*, 12, 22-5.

Diggle, P. J. (1979). 'Statistical methods for spatial point patterns in ecology', pp. 95–150. In: *Spatial and Temporal Analysis in Ecology* (eds. Cormack, R. M., & Ord, J. K.) (Fairland, Maryland). International Co-operative Publishing House.

Draper, N. R. & Smith, H. (1981). *Applied Regression Analysis* (New York). Wiley.

Duncan, O. D. (1975). 'Partitioning polytomous variables in multiway contingency analysis', *Social Science Research*, 4, 167–82.

Duncan, O. D. (1979). 'How destination depends on origin in the occupational mobility table', *American Journal of Sociology*, 84, 793–803.

Duncan, O. D. (1980). 'Testing key hypotheses in panel analysis', pp. 279–89. In: *Sociological Methodology* (ed. Schuessler, K. F.) (San Francisco). Jossey-Bass.

Duncan, O. D. (1981). 'Two faces of panel analysis: parallels with comparative cross-sectional analysis and time-lagged association', pp. 281–318. In: *Sociological Methodology* (ed. Leinhardt, S.) (San Francisco). Jossey-Bass.

Duncan, O. D. & McRae, J. A., Jr (1979). 'Multiway contingency analysis with a scaled response or factor', pp. 68–85. In: *Sociological Methodology* (ed. Schuessler, K. F.) (San Francisco). Jossey-Bass.

Fay, R. E. & Goodman, L. A. (1975). *The ECTA Program: Description for Users* (available from Department of Statistics, University of Chicago, Illinois).

Fellegi, P. (1980). 'Approximate tests of independence and goodness-of-fit based on stratified multistage samples', *Journal of the American Statistical Association*, 75, 261–75.

Fienberg, S. E. (1979). 'The use of chi-squared statistics for categorical data problems', *Journal of the Royal Statistical Society, B*, 41, 54–64.

Fienberg, S. E. (1980). *The Analysis of Cross-classified Categorical Data* (Cambridge, Massachusetts). MIT Press.

Fienberg, S. E. & Mason, W. M. (1979). 'Identification and estimation of age-period-cohort models in the analysis of discrete archival data', pp. 1–67. In: *Sociological Methodology* (ed. Schuessler, K. F.) (San Francisco). Jossey-Bass.

Fingleton, B. (1983a). 'Independence, stationarity, categorical spatial data and the chi-squared test', *Environment and Planning, A*, 15, 483–99.

Fingleton, B. (1983b). 'Log–linear models with dependent spatial data', *Environment and Planning, A*, 15, 801–13.

Goodman, L. A. (1965). 'On the statistical analysis of mobility tables', *American Journal of Sociology*, 70, 564–85.

Goodman, L. A. (1968). 'The analysis of cross-classified data, independence, quasi-independence, and interactions in contingency tables with or without missing values', *Journal of the American Statistical Association*, 63, 1091–131.

Goodman, L. A. (1970). 'The multivariate analysis of qualitative data: interactions among multiple classifications', *Journal of the American Statistical Association*, 65, 226–56.

Goodman, L. A. (1971). 'The analysis of multi-dimensional contingency tables, stepwise procedures and direct estimation methods for building models for multiple classifications', *Technometrics*, 13, 33–61.

Goodman, L. A. (1972a). 'A modified multiple regression approach to the analysis of dichotomous variables', *American Sociological Review*, 37, 28–46.

Goodman, L. A. (1972b). 'A general model for the analysis of surveys', *American Journal of Sociology*, 77, 1035–86.

Goodman, L. A. (1972c). 'Some multiplicative models for the analysis of cross-classified data', pp. 649–96. In: *Proceedings of the Sixth Berkeley Symposium on Mathematical Statistics and Probability*, vol. 1 (eds Le Carn, L. *et al.*) (Berkeley, California). University of California Press.

Goodman, L. A. (1973a). 'Causal analysis of data from panel studies and other kinds of surveys', *American Journal of Sociology*, 78, 1135–91.

Goodman, L. A. (1973b). 'The analysis of multidimensional contingency tables when some variables are posterior to others: a modified path analysis approach', *Biometrika*, 60, 179–92.

Goodman, L. A. (1973c). 'Guided and unguided methods for the selection of models for a set of T multidimensional contingency tables', *Journal of the American Statistical Association*, 6, 165–75.

Goodman, L. A. (1978). *Analysing Qualitative/Categorical Data* (Cambridge, Massachusetts). Abt Books.

Goodman, L. A. (1979a). 'Simple models for the analysis of association in cross-classifications having ordered categories', *Journal of the American Statistical Association*, 74, 537–52.

Goodman, L. A. (1979b). 'Multiplicative models for the analysis of occupational mobility tables and other kinds of cross-classification tables', *American Journal of Sociology*, 84, 804–19.

Goodman, L. A. (1979c). 'Multiplicative models for square contingency tables with ordered categories', *Biometrika*, 66, 413–18.

Goodman, L. A. (1979d). 'A brief guide to the causal analysis of data from surveys', *American Journal of Sociology*, 84, 1078–95.

Goodman, L. A. (1979e). 'On quasi-independence in triangular contingency tables', *Biometrics*, 35, 651–5.

Goodman, L. A. (1981a). 'Three elementary views of log–linear models for the analysis of cross-classifications having ordered categories', pp. 193–239. In: *Sociological Methodology* (ed. Leinhardt, S.) (San Francisco). Jossey-Bass.

Goodman, L. A. (1981b). 'Criteria for determining whether certain categories in a cross-classification table should be combined, with special reference to occupational categories in an occupational mobility table', *American Journal of Sociology*, 87, 612–51.

Goodman, L. A. (1981c). 'Association models and the bivariate normal for contingency tables with ordered categories', *Biometrika*, 68, 347–55.

Goodman, L. A. (1981d). 'Association models and canonical correlation in the analysis of cross-classifications having ordered categories', *Journal of the American Statistical Association*, 76, 320–40.

Goodman, L. A. (1983). 'The analysis of dependence in cross-classifications having ordered categories, using log–linear models for frequencies and log–linear models for odds', *Biometrics*, 39, 149–60.

Goodman, L. A. & Fay, R. (1973). *Everyman's Contingency Table Analysis: Program Documentation* (available from Department of Statistics, University of Chicago, Illinois).

Grizzle, J. E., Starmer, C. F. & Koch, G. G. (1969). 'Analysis of categorical data by linear models', *Biometrics*, 25, 489–504.

Haberman, S. J. (1973a). 'Log–linear models for frequency data: sufficient statistics and likelihood equations', *Annals of Statistics*, 1, 617–32.

Haberman, S. J. (1973b). 'The analysis of residuals in cross-classified tables', *Biometrics*, 29, 205–20.

Haberman, S. J. (1974). *The Analysis of Frequency Data* (Chicago). University of Chicago Press.

Haberman, S. J. (1977). 'Log–linear models and frequency tables with small expected cell counts', *Annals of Statistics*, 5, 1148–69.

Haberman, S. J. (1978). *Analysis of Qualitative Data, Introductory Topics* (New York). Academic Press.

Hewlett, P. S. & Plackett, R. L. (1950). 'Statistical aspects of the independent joint action of poisons, particularly insecticides: II, Examination of data for agreement with the hypothesis', *Annals of Applied Biology*, 37, 527–52.

Hildebrand, D. K., Laing, J. D. & Rosenthal, H. (1977). *Prediction Analysis of Cross-classifications* (New York). Wiley.

Holt, D. (1979). 'Log–linear models for contingency table analysis: on the interpretation of parameters', *Sociological Methods and Research*, 7, 330–6.

Holt, D., Scott, A. J. & Ewings, P. D. (1980). 'Chi-squared tests with survey data', *Journal of the Royal Statistical Society, A*, 143, 303–20.

Holt, D., Smith, T. M. F. & Winter, P. D. (1980). 'Regression analysis of data from complex surveys', *Journal of the Royal Statistical Society, A*, 143, 474–87.

Hutchinson, T. P. (1979). 'The validity of the chi-square test when the expected frequencies are small: a list of recent research references', *Communications in Statistics, A*, 8, 327–35.

Ireland, C. T., Ku, H. H. & Kullback, S. (1969). 'Symmetry and marginal homogeneity of an $r \times r$ contingency table', *Journal of the American Statistical Association*, 64, 1323–41.

Kish, L. (1965). *Survey Sampling* (New York). Wiley.

Kish, L. & Frankel, M. R. (1974). 'Inferences from complex samples', *Journal of the Royal Statistical Society, B*, 36, 1–37.

Knoke, D. (1976). *Change and Continuity in American Politics* (Baltimore). Johns Hopkins University Press.

Kotze, T. J. V. W. (1982). 'The log–linear model and its application to multi-way contingency tables', pp. 142–82. In: *Topics in Applied Multivariate Analysis* (ed. Hawkins, D. M.) (Cambridge). Cambridge University Press.

Kotze, T. J. V. W. & Gokhale, D. V. (1980). 'A comparison of the Pearson X^2 and log-likelihood ratio statistics for small samples by means of probability ordering', *Journal of Statistical Computation and Simulation*, 12, 1–13.

Landis, J. R., Stanish, W. M., Freeman, J. L. & Koch, G. G. (1976). 'A computer program for the generalized chi-square analysis of categorical data using weighted least squares (GENCAT)', *Computer Programs in Biomedicine*, 6, 196–231.

Larntz, K. (1978). 'Small sample comparisons of exact levels for chi-square goodness-of-fit statistics', *Journal of the American Statistical Association*, 73, 253–63.

Lawal, H. B. & Upton, G. J. G. (1980). 'An approximation to the distribution of the X^2 goodness-of-fit statistic for use with small expectations', *Biometrika*, 67, 447–53.

Logan, J. A. (1981). 'A structural model of the higher-order Markov process incorporating reversion effects', *Journal of Mathematical Sociology*, 8, 75–89.

Mantel, N. & Brown, C. (1973). 'A logistic reanalysis of Ashford and Sowden's data on respiratory symptoms in British coal miners', *Biometrics*, 29, 649–65.

Markus, G. B. (1979). *Analyzing Panel Data* (Beverly Hills, California). Sage Publications.

McCullagh, P. (1980). 'Regression models for ordinal data', *Journal of the Royal Statistical Society, B*, 42, 109–42.

Mosteller, F. (1968). 'Association and estimation in contingency tables', *Journal of the American Statistical Association*, 63, 1–28.

Namboodiri, N. K. (ed.) (1978). *Survey Sampling and Measurement* (New York). Academic Press.

Nathan, G. & Holt, D. (1980). 'The effect of survey design on regression analysis', *Journal of the Royal Statistical Society, B*, **43**, 377–86.

Nelder, J. A. (1974). 'Log–linear models for contingency tables', *Applied Statistics*, **23**, 323–9.

Nelder, J. A. & Wedderburn, R. W. M. (1972). 'Generalized linear models', *Journal of the Royal Statistical Society, A*, **135**, 370–84.

Neyman, J. (1949). 'Contributions to the theory of the X^2 test', pp. 230–73. In: *Proceedings of the First Berkeley Symposium on Mathematical Statistics and Probability* (ed. Neyman, J.) (Berkeley, California). University of California Press.

Penick, B. K. E. & Owens, M. W. B. (eds.) (1976). *Surveying Crime* (Report of Panel for the evaluation of crime surveys), National Academy of Science, (Washington DC).

Plaskett, R. L. (1962). 'A note on interactions in contingency tables', *Journal of the Royal Statistical Society, B*, **24**, 162–6.

Plaskett, R. L. (1981). *The Analysis of Categorical Data* (London). Griffin.

Pontinen, S. (1982). 'Models and social mobility research: a comparison of some log–linear models of a social mobility matrix', *Quality and Quantity*, **16**, 91–107.

Rao, J. N. K. & Scott, A. J. (1979). 'Chi-squared tests for analysis of categorical data from complex surveys', *Proceedings of the American Statistical Association, Section on Survey Research and Methods*, pp. 58–66.

Rao, J. N. K. & Scott, A. J. (1981). 'The analysis of categorical data from complex sample surveys: chi-squared tests for goodness-of-fit and independence in two-way tables', *Journal of the American Statistical Association*, **76**, 221–30.

Reynolds, H. T. (1978). 'Some comments on the causal analysis of surveys with log–linear models', *American Journal of Sociology*, **83**, 127–43.

Seddon, B. (1971). *Introduction to Biogeography* (London). Gerald Duckworth.

Silk, J. (1979). *Statistical Concepts in Geography* (London). George Allen and Unwin.

Simpson, E. H. (1951). 'The interpretation of interaction in contingency tables', *Journal of the Royal Statistical Society, B*, **13**, 238–41.

Smith, J. E. K. (1976). 'Analysis of qualitative data', *Annual Review of Psychology*, pp. 487–99.

Snedecor, G. W. & Cochran, W. G. (1974). *Statistical Methods* (Ames, Iowa). Iowa State University Press.

Tavaré, S. & Altham, P. M. E. (1983). 'Serial dependence of observations leading to contingency tables, and corrections to chi-squared statistics', *Biometrika*, **70**, 139–44.

Theil, H. (1970). 'On the estimation of relationships involving qualitative variables', *American Journal of Sociology*, **76**, 103–54.

Upton, G. J. G. (1978*a*). *The Analysis of Cross-tabulated Data* (Chichester). Wiley.

Upton, G. J. G. (1978*b*). 'Factors and responses in multidimensional contingency tables', *Statistician*, **27**, 43–8.

Upton, G. J. G. (1980). 'Contingency table analysis: log–linear models', *Quality and Quantity*, **14**, 155–80.

Upton, G. J. G. (1981*a*). 'Log–linear models, screening and regional industrial surveys', *Regional Studies*, **15**, 33–45.

Upton, G. J. G. (1981*b*). Personal communication.

Upton, G. J. G. & Fingleton, B. (1979). 'Log–linear models in geography', *Transactions of the Institute of British Geographers*, **4**, 103–15.

Upton, G. J. G. & Sarlvik, B. H. (1981). 'A loyalty–distance model for voting change', *Journal of the Royal Statistical Society, A*, **144**, 247-59.

Wermuth, N. (1976). 'Model search among multiplicative models', *Biometrics*, **32**, 253–64.

Whittemore, A. S. (1978). 'Collapsibility of multidimensional contingency tables', *Journal of the Royal Statistical Society, B*, **40**, 328–40.

Williams, K. (1976). 'Analysis of multidimensional contingency tables', *Statistician*, **25**, 51–8.

Williams, N. J. (1979). 'The definition of shopper types as an aid in the analysis of spatial consumer behaviour', *Tidjdschrift voor Economische en Sociale Geografie*, **70**, 157–63.

Williams, O. D. & Grizzle, J. E. (1972). 'Analysis of contingency tables having ordered response categories', *Journal of the American Statistical Association*, **67**, 55–63.

Wrigley, N. (1980). 'Categorical data, repeated measurement research designs, and regional industrial surveys', *Regional Studies*, **14**, 455–71.

Yarnold, J. K. (1970). 'The minimum expectation in X^2 goodness-of-fit tests and the accuracy of approximation for the null distribution', *Journal of the American Statistical Association*, **65**, 864–86.

Yates, F. (1934). 'Contingency tables involving small numbers and the chi-squared test', *Journal of the Royal Statistical Society*, supplement **1**, 217–35.

Author index

Subject Index